For Reference

Not to be taken from this room

Modern Collectible Dolls

IDENTIFICATION & VALUE GUIDE
VOLUME V

PATSY MOYER

COLLECTOR BOOKS
A Division of Schroeder Publishing Co., Inc.

The values in this book are to be used only as a guide. They are not intended to set prices, which vary from one section of the country to another. Auction prices as well as dealer prices vary greatly and are affected by condition as well as demand. Neither the author nor the publisher assumes responsibility for any losses that might be incurred as a result of consulting this guide.

On the cover info:

Top left: 11½" vinyl Mattel "#4 Ponytail Barbie" dressed in Solo in the Spotlight, brunette hair, red lips, nostril paint, eyeshadow, faint cheek blush, finger/toe paint, straight legs, wearing gold hoop earrings, black sequin dress with tulle, flower accents, black nylon gloves, #1 light navy blue open toe shoes, bead choker, pink scarf, white rimmed glasses with booklet in cellophane bag, microphone on stand, black pedestal stand, near mint in box, circa 1960, $4,100.00, courtesy McMasters Doll Auctions.

Bottom left: 8" hard plastic Vogue "America's Sweetheart" Ginny, from the Ginny's Signature Series, marked "TM//1988//The Vogue Doll Company//Made in China," brown rooted hair, blue plastic sleep eyes, jointed hard plastic body, red dress, matching ribbon in hair, black leatherette shoes with a real snap on the strap, available to Ginny Doll Club Charter Members only, circa 1996, $40.00, courtesy Vogue Doll Company.

Top center: 17½" composition Madame Alexander "Wendy Ann" Bride, blue plastic sleep eyes, heavy eyeshadow above eyes, real lashes, painted lashes below, closed mouth, pretty color in cheeks, blonde mohair wig, long veil, all original in satin wedding dress with sweetheart neckline with wrist tag, mint with box, circa 1940s, $650.00, courtesy Harlene Soucy.

Bottom center: 15½" vinyl Ashton-Drake Galleries "Gene," designed by Mel Odom, marked "Gene TM//© 1995 Mel Odom" on head, painted eyes, brown rooted synthetic wig, earrings, jointed fashion type body, bendable knees, wearing St. Moritz ski outfit, white pants, matching short jacket with red and green embroidery trim, buttons, red turtleneck sweater, red gloves, red ski boots, skis, and poles, limited to 5,000, circa 2000, costume only, $49.95, photo courtesy Ashton-Drake Galleries.

Top right: 21" composition Arranbee "Nancy Lee," blue plastic sleep eyes, heavy eyeshadow above eyes, real lashes, painted lashes below, closed mouth, mohair wig, original red skating costume, mint condition, round R&B tag on outfit, faintly marked "R&B" on neck, boxed, circa 1949, $700.00, courtesy Harlene Soucy.

Bottom right: 18" composition Ideal Shirley Temple, green sleep eyes, open mouth with teeth, dimples in cheeks, mohair wig, Stand Up and Cheer outfit of white organdy with red dots, trimmed in red, circa 1934+, $1,050.00. Courtesy Iva Mae Jones.

Searching For A Publisher?

We are always looking for people knowledgeable within their fields. If you feel that there is a real need for a book on your collectible subject and have a large comprehensive collection, contact Collector Books.

Cover design: Beth Summers
Book design: Sherry Kraus
Book layout: Mary Ann Hudson

COLLECTOR BOOKS
P.O. Box 3009
Paducah, Kentucky 42002–3009
www.collectorbooks.com

Contents

Dedication

With thanks for the constant help and ongoing support of this dedicated group of collectors, The Southern Oregon Antique & Collectibles Club of Medford, Oregon.

Credits

Alexander Doll Co.
Allen, Richard
Allgeier, June
Antonick, Taras
Ashton-Drake Galleries
Auza-Smith, Susana
Baron, Cynthia
Bartell, Judie
Beaumont, Lee Ann
Bedenkop, Connie
Bets van Boxel, Atelier
Bohlin, Dorothy
Bolejack, Anna
Bollenbach, Cheryl
Booth, Lilian
Boyd, Myrna
Brown, Judy
Brown, Ruth
Burnside, Flo
Burror, Dickee
Busch, Millie
Cadwallader, Georgine
Cervantez, Ana-Lisa
Chase, Susan L.
Christlieb, Patricia
Conroy, Judie
Cote, DeAnn
Cotta, Martha
Crawford, Joy
Crosby, Betty
Crume, Debbie
Darin, Jane

DeSmet, Sally
Domm, Judy
Dubow, Susan
Dunn, Judy
Fabian, Fran
Fielding, Elizabeth
Ferguson, Lee
Flesher, Pauline
Ford, Cornelia
Freitas, Shari
Fronefield, Betty
Gervais, Cherie
Chrestman, Phyllis
Gilmore, Charlene
Gonzales, Angie
Graves, Diane
Hadley, Donna
Hagey, Adrienne
Hanrahan, Eileen
Hardy, Robert V.
Harrington, Sharon
Hash, Amanda
Haynes, Carolyn
Henke, Marilyn
Hill, Janet
Horst, Janet
Hull, Barbara
Hunker, Patrice
Hunt, Derra
Huston, Marilynn
Jeffrey, Sidney
Jeschien, Chan

Jesurin, Dolores
Johnson, Ashlyn
Jones, Iva Mae
Kimmel, Beverly
Klenke, Rae
Kline, Sandra
Kolibaba, Sharon
Lazenby, Nancy
Lizut, Sandra
Lundquist, Kris
Mata, Olivina
McMasters Doll Auctions
McPherson, Marlys
Melendez, Bertha
Millhouse, Peggy
Morris, Tom
Moulton, Pat
Munsey, Sarah
Nance, Donna
Newby, Michele
Ortlieb, Jeanette
Pardee, Elaine
Parker, Terri
Patterson, Joyce
Penn, Pamela
Perzyk, W. Harry
Poole, Daryl
Portias, Jodie
Prince, Suzanne
Quigley, Rachel
Ramsey, Marilyn
Reid, Ginger

Ritchey, Nancy
Robertson, Sue
Sakraida, Mary
Sanders, Jill
Scott, Jennifer
Shelton, Nelda
Sickler, Joan
Simonds, Sandy
Smedes, Gay
Smith, Kathy
Soucy, Harlene
Strong, Betty
Sumner, Sandy
Surber, Elizabeth
Sutton, Linda Lee
Sweeney, Martha
Tannenbaum, Leslie
Teeter, Geri
Tonner, Robert Doll Co.
Traver, Maria
Treber, Kate
Vogue Doll Company
Vought, Lisa
Walimaa, Kay
Warder, Betty
Ware, Susan
Whiteman, Lessa
Williams, Thelma
Woodside, Oleta
Ybarra, Richard
Zumwalt, Chlois

Introduction

We start the new millennium with more collectors participating in our hobby of doll collecting than ever before. One of the biggest reasons that this hobby is available to collectors worldwide is the influence of the Internet. It has leveled the playing field, tossed aside old considerations, and brought a whole new outlook to today's collectors. It has made objects that were unavailable to many in their lifetime actually obtainable and has brought with it also a horde of new and novice collectors and sellers who have little knowledge of what they have or are seeking. While the new influx of collectors brings new items to the market place, it also skews the market as unsophisticated collectors pay astronomical prices for some things that previously had modest values.

To help seasoned collectors keep up with all of that and to help new collectors more realistically look at collecting, this book brings you examples of what is available or has been recently sold. Doll collecting ranks in the top ten of collectibles, with Barbie finishing the millennium as the most popular doll today. As with any collectible, as an experienced or novice collector you want to get the most for your money. In all cases, knowledge is power.

You need that knowledge to get the best for your money. Unless you have won the lottery or made your million in software or the stock market, you probably have a limited budget. Those of us who are not independently wealthy need to know that we are spending our money wisely — perhaps so that when the time comes for us to part with our collection, it will have increased in value. Thus your next doll might be considered a portable asset.

The novice collector needs to learn as much about doll collecting and your chosen niche as possible. This means you need to see a large number of dolls so that you can tell the good from the bad. You need to find out as much about your next doll as possible — perhaps to ease your conscience when you want one so badly, it is nice to know that you got a good buy. This book provides some of those answers in that it is a showcase of dolls that collectors have acquired. It can help you when you need to find an example of a certain costume, and it gives examples of how some dolls that were new many years ago may look now.

Perhaps "modern" is a misnomer for dolls over 70 years old but still considered by doll collectors to be modern. One factor influencing this, however, is that some doll companies that made dolls at the turn of the century are still operating and producing dolls. For this book, I am grouping dolls made of composition, cloth, rubber, hard plastic, porcelain, vinyl, and wood as modern as opposed to dolls of bisque, wax, wood, and china that were made before World War I or earlier. There are no easy cut-off dates, and some spill over from one category to the next. This book will give you examples of dolls for you to compare for identification.

Collectors wanting to know more about the dolls they have or wanting to start collecting have several ways to gain knowledge. One way to do this is to research and arm yourself with books, periodicals, and magazines that deal with the subject and also seek other informed collectors. Beginning collectors should begin to list their dolls, with the prices paid, the size, marks, note of what material they are made of, and other pertinent facts, such as originality and condition. Collectors need to be able to identify their dolls, and one way to do this is by noting the material of which they made.

One very basic thing beginning doll collectors need to understand is that experienced doll collectors refer to a doll by whatever material is used for making the doll's head.

Introduction

So a composition doll has a composition head but may have a cloth, composition or wood body. A doll with a vinyl head and a hard plastic body is a vinyl doll. The head commands the order of reference to the doll in relation to materials used to produce it. A doll made entirely of vinyl is referred to as all-vinyl.

It is also helpful when exact measurements are given to describe the height of the doll. The doll's height is important because it immediately confirms the identity of certain dolls and the height of the doll influences its value. Usually larger dolls are more valuable than smaller doll's, but sometimes smaller dolls or a certain size doll have unique characteristics that make them more sought-after.

When collectors find a doll they wish to identify without any packaging or box, they first need to examine the back of the head, then the torso, the usual places the manufacturers place marks, and then the rest of the body. Some dolls may have only a mold number or no mark at all. Nursing students are often given the task of writing a physical description of their patient, starting at the top of their head, down to the bottoms of their feet. This is also a good method for describing dolls and their attire.

Collectors like to meet and network with other collectors that share their interests. For this reason we have included a Collectors' Network section in the back of this book. There are many that have special interest groups that focus on one area of doll collecting. These are experienced collectors in a certain area who will network with others. It is considered proper form to send a SASE when contacting others if you wish to receive a reply. If you would like to be included in this section, please send your area of expertise and references.

In addition, a national organization, the United Federation of Doll Clubs, has information for doll collectors who are seeking or wish to form a doll club. The goals of this nonprofit organization focus on education, research, preservation, and enjoyment of dolls. They also sponsor a Junior Membership for young doll collectors. They will put you in contact with one of 16 Regional Directors who can assess your needs and advise you if a doll club in your area is accepting members. You may write for more information to UFDC, 10920 North Ambassador Drive, Suite 130, Kansas City, MO 64153, or FAX 816 891 – 8360 or on the Net, www.UFDC.org.

Beginning collectors need to do their homework and gain power (knowledge) about dolls before spending their money. Most collectors have to budget and do not have unlimited funds. It seems prudent to investigate thoroughly all avenues regarding an addition to one's collection before actually making a purchase. What should the buyer consider?

Novice collectors may wonder where they can find dolls to buy. There are many different ways to locate the doll of your dreams, including finding dealers or shops that specialize in locating a particular doll for you. There are numerous focus groups that list special sales and where they are being held. Collector groups usually post doll shows and sales in their newsletters.

Auctions may also prove to be an aid in finding additions for your collection. Some offer absentee bidding which is most helpful if you do not live near where the auction is being held. Some also offer over-the-phone bidding if you want to be able to be in on the actual bidding. Auction houses usually send out catalogs and are most helpful to answer questions over the phone or fax if you need more information. See Collectors' Network at the back of this book for more information.

One of the latest and greatest shopping malls is the Internet. And this is where it does get scary. Not only is the novice collector unsure of what she actually wants to buy, but also she may be dealing with an unknown person at the other end of her computer. And there is this great place called eBay that has thousands of dolls on auction every day, 24 hours a day, seven days a week, year in and year out — barring electrical disturbances and Internet traffic jams. More and more, eBay is becoming the acceptable spot for collectors to shop and sell. The site also features a query section that will allow you to look at prices realized in closed auctions.

Again, novice collectors need to arm themselves with as much information as they can find as they begin to build their collections. Not only are books, magazines, and videos available for collectors, but also simple observance of dolls at museums, doll shows, and displays provides a wonderful way to see dolls. To help the novice collector, we have added simple tips on what to look for in dolls under consideration for addition to their collection.

Just as the three most valuable qualities that make real estate desirable are location, location, and location, a doll collector must consider condition, condition, and condition. This is by far the most important thing to consider when buying a doll. You need to be able to recognize what a desirable condition is and how that relates to the age, originality, and desirability of the doll. Dolls with good color, original clothing, tags, brochures, and boxes will always be desirable.

The trick is to find those dolls that also have rarity, beauty or some other unique quality that makes them appealing to the collector. It could be that only a few dolls were made. It could be that a collector recalls his/her childhood dolls with nostalgia. Or it could be that a doll's production, presentation or identity makes a historical statement.

Other factors can also contribute to the desirability and popularity of a doll. Cleanliness, good color, and good condition are always desirable qualities. We have included "What to look for" tips with each category.

Keep in mind if your collecting is an investment you need good records. Even though you think you will never forget what you paid for a single doll, after a few years and many dolls later, that memory becomes hazy. A simple, easy way to keep track of the money spent on doll collections is to utilize the Quicken money program on your computer. Using a number and description to keep track of each doll, enter the amount you spend when purchasing it. If you sell the doll or dispose of it, the doll can be checked during the reconciling procedure and thus will not be seen when you wish to see a list of your current inventory. This is a very simple way to utilize something you also may use to keep your checkbook in order to help you with your doll inventory.

With time, collectors' interests vary, but playthings seem to remain a consistent, enjoyable hobby. This book does not mean to set prices and should only be used as one of many tools to guide the collector. It is the collector's decision alone on which doll to purchase. It is the responsibility of the collector to choose his own area of collecting and how to pursue it. This book is meant to help you enjoy and learn about dolls of our past and present and to share indications with the thoughtful collector on the trends of the future. If you would like to suggest other categories or wish to share your own collection, please write to the address in Collectors' Network in the back of the book.

Happy collecting!

Advertising Dolls

Manufacturing companies often use dolls as a means of advertising their products, either as a premium or in the form of a trademark of their company. Sometimes dolls were given as a reward for subscriptions to a magazine. This entrepreneurial spirit has given us some delightful examples and can bring a whole new realm of discovery for the collector. Primarily not meant as a collectible but as a means to promote products or services, the advertising doll has been around since the late 1800s and continues to be a viable form of advertising. Advertising dolls now can be made just as a collectible item — look at the Christmas ornaments that advertise Barbie or space adventurers, and the McDonald's premiums in their "Happy Meal" boxes. All these dolls or figurines that promote a product or service are called advertising dolls. Early companies that used dolls to promote their products were Amberg with "Vanta Baby," American Cereal Co. with "Cereta," American Character with the "Campbell Kids," Buster Brown Shoes with "Buster Brown," Ideal with "Cracker Jack Boy" and "ZuZu Kid", Kellogg Company with a variety of characters, and many others.

What to look for:

This is a wonderful field for collectors. Dolls can be of any material, but those mint-in-box or with original advertising will remain the most desirable. Cloth should have bright colors, no tears, little soil, and retain printed identifying marks. On dolls of materials such as composition, hard plastic, and vinyl, look for rosy cheeks, little wear, clean, original tags, labels, boxes or brochures. Retain dates and purchasing information for your purchases when you obtain current products. This information will add to the value of your collectibles.

Left, 10½"; center, 17"; right, 11" cloth, commercially made Kiwis advertising Kiwi fruit, Kiwi cloth forms mouth, felt leaves on top, brown plush body with felt eyes, bought in Australia, circa 1985 – 1990, 10½" – $30.00, 17" – $45.00, 11" – $30.00. *Courtesy Ginger Reid.*

17" vinyl, Green Giant corn, blue sleep eyes, closed mouth, rooted hair, stuffed magic skin, yellow dress with green checked shirt, green rickrack, matching bonnet and purse, all original, circa 1950s, $35.00. *Courtesy Betty Strong.*

7½" hard plastic, Austrian Knorr Dolls, for Knorr Soup, a Best Foods product, blue sleep eyes, European look faces with full lips, jointed, will stand alone; the dolls came in pairs, a boy and a girl, dressed in costumes representing several countries, circa 1963 – 1964, $15.00/pair. *Courtesy Betty Strong.*

7½" hard plastic, Swedish Knorr Dolls, for Knorr Soup, a Best Foods product, blue sleep eyes, European look faces with full lips, jointed, will stand alone; the dolls came in pairs, a boy and a girl, dressed in costumes representing several countries, circa 1963 – 1964, $15.00/pair. *Courtesy Betty Strong.*

7½" hard plastic, Italian Knorr Dolls, for Knorr Soup, a Best Foods product, blue sleep eyes, European look faces with full lips, jointed, will stand alone; the dolls came in pairs, a boy and a girl, dressed in costumes representing several countries, circa 1963 – 1964, $15.00/pair. *Courtesy Betty Strong.*

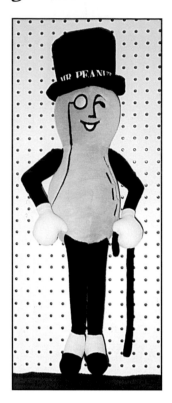

26" cloth, Mr. Peanut, commercially made, advertising Planter's Peanuts, circa 1970s, $45.00. *Courtesy Ginger Reid.*

15" vinyl, Northern Advertising Doll for Northern toilet tissue, marked "Northern Doll//™//James Riner Corp.," vinyl head and hands, painted features, blue eyes, smiling mouth with painted teeth, blonde hair in braids, cloth body including feet, legs, and arms, dressed in long white nightgown with blue trim, circa 1980s, $20.00. *Courtesy Betty Strong.*

7" all-vinyl, Pillsbury Doughboy, marked "1971//Pillsbury Company//Minneapolis, Minn.," molded features with a big smile, blue dots for eyes and a blue dot on hat, with molded chef hat and neckerchief, circa 1971, $10.00. *Courtesy Betty Strong.*

Buddy Lee

Buddy Lee is a display doll made for the H. L. Lee Company to promote Lee uniforms and was first offered to dealers circa 1922. The Lee Company's most popular dolls were the Cowboy and Engineer, reflecting their production of denim jeans and overalls. The early 12½" dolls were made in composition and then later 13" dolls in hard plastic circa 1949. This is one doll that really appeals to men, especially men who wore uniforms in their work on the railroad, at gas stations, and in Coca-Cola plants. Buddy Lee was discontinued in 1962. Collectors can look for outfits including Coca-Cola, Phillips 66, Sinclair, MM, Standard, John Deere, TWA, Cowboy, and Engineer in striped and plain denim and also two versions (farmers) dressed in plaid shirt and jeans.

13" hard plastic, tag on cap and overalls reads "Lee//Union Made," painted side-glancing eyes, molded painted hair, closed smiling mouth, wearing original engineer overalls and cap, long sleeve shirt, painted on black boots, circa 1948+, $400.00. *Courtesy Betty Strong.*

12" hard plastic, marked Buddy Lee on back, "Union Made//Lee" on label on pants, "Ride 'em in Lee Rider Cowboy Pants" on paper hat band, stiff neck, large painted eyes to side, painted upper lashes, closed smiling mouth, molded painted hair, hard plastic body jointed at shoulders only, molded painted black boots, original plaid flannel shirt, yellow kerchief, denim dungarees with Lee label, black belt, black felt cowboy hat, circa 1950s, $400.00. *Courtesy McMasters Doll Auctions.*

13" very heavy composition, Glassmasters Coca-Cola Buddy Lee, second edition limited to 2,000, marked "1998//The Coca Cola Company//All rights reserved" on foot, tagged "Glassmasters//of the Stained Glass Guild// Richmond, VA.," painted side-glancing white uniform with green stripes, solid green jacket and matching cap, red "Drink//Coca-Cola" embroidered badges on jacket and cap, circa 1997 – 1998, $350.00. *Private collection.*

Alexander Doll Co.

Alexander Doll Company has made news on the financial pages as reorganization from their 1995 Chapter 11 bankruptcy has led new management to use the Japanese "kaizen" flow type manufacturing. Located in the Harlem section of the borough of Manhattan, New York, the company is owned by TBM Consulting Group. The new management has redesigned the production flow in the turn of the century Studebaker plant, to allow groups of workers to oversee the manufacturing process from start to finish on selected items. Instead of each person doing one particular job all day, the group works together to finish dolls within their group, thus increasing productivity and cutting costs.

The financial and production changes seem not to have slowed the interest in Alexander dolls which have increased in popularity under the guidance of the Alexander Doll Collectors Club, a company sponsored marketing tool that has been used successfully by Effanbee during the 1930s and more recently by Vogue with their Ginny club.

Beatrice and Rose Alexander started the Alexander Doll Co. around 1912, and were known for their doll costumes. They began using the Madame Alexander trademark in 1928. Beatrice A. Behrman became a legend in the doll world with her long reign as head of the Alexander Doll Company. The company produced cloth, composition, and wood dolls, making the transition to hard plastic after World War II and later into vinyl.

The doll world was shocked these past few years with skyrocketing prices paid for some wonderful collectible Alexander dolls at auction, including $56,000.00 for an 8" hard plastic doll redressed as the Infante of Prague. Alexander's rare and beautiful mint dolls continue to attract young collectors. Alexander dolls continue to increase in value as shown by one-of-a-kind extraordinary, fully documented special dolls as they appear on the market. These gains should continue with the support of avid Alexander fans. And there seems to be no lack of them as premier Madame Alexander Doll Club events are held around the country. For information, write: Madame Alexander Doll Club, PO Box 330, Mundelein, IL 60060. Telephone: 847-949-9200; Fax 847-949-9201.

One of the Alexander Company's luckiest breaks was obtaining the exclusive license to produce the Dionne Quintuplets dolls after the children's birth in 1934. The Alexander Dionne Quintuples were introduced in 1935, made in both cloth and composition as babies and toddlers. Some of the rarer groups are the bathtub set and sets with playground accessories like the carousel or Ferris wheel. Other companies tried to fill out their lines with matching sets of five identical dolls even though this brought copyright suits from Madame Alexander. Quintuplet collectors collect not only dolls, but also clothing, photographs, and a large assortment of other related memorabilia.

Quint News is published quarterly by Jimmy and Fay Rodolfos, founders of the nonprofit, Dionne Quint Collectors, $10.00 a year, PO Box 2527, Woburn MA 01888.

For photos of the Alexander and other quintuplets, see the Quintuplet section.

What to look for:

Alexander cloth dolls should be clean, all original, and with bright colors. Newer Alexander dolls require mint, all original dolls with brochures, tags, boxes, and accessories to bring top prices.

Composition Alexander dolls may have minute crazing, but must have good color, original clothes, labels, tags, and brochures to bring highest prices. Buy dolls with severe cracking, peeling or other damage *only* if they are all original, tagged or mint.

Painted hard plastics are transitional dolls and may be mistaken for composition. Hard plastic dolls should have good color, tagged outfits, and be all-original. The newer the doll, the closer to mint it should be. Alexander dolls were produced in the 1970s and 1980s with few changes, and collectors can find many of these dolls at reasonable prices. The dolls from the 1950s and early 1960s, as well as the limited edition special event dolls, are eagerly sought after.

Composition

13" all composition, Fairy Princess, (Wendy-Ann face), eyeshadow over glassine eyes, closed mouth, dark brown mohair wig, tagged Fairy Princess dress, all original, circa 1939 – 1942, $325.00. *Courtesy Sally DeSmet.*

24" cloth, Alice in Wonderland, formed mask face, blue painted eyes with real lashes, painted features, yarn hair, red and white checked dress with white apron, circa 1933, $475.00.
Courtesy Elizabeth Fielding.

Left: 13" composition, Kate Greenaway, "x" in circle on head, tagged "Kate Greenaway//Madame Alexander//New York" on dress, brown sleep eyes, open mouth, four upper teeth, gold mohair wig, 5-piece compo body, peach and flower print dress, matching bonnet and purse, circa 1938 – 1943, $550.00; right: 10" cloth, Little Shaver, painted features, yellow yarn hair, stockinet body, wire armature, original clothing, circa 1940 – 1944, $325.00.
Courtesy McMasters Doll Auctions.

11" composition, McGuffey Ana, brown sleep eyes, blonde wig, closed mouth, tagged red dress with matching hat, missing apron, circa 1937 – 1939, $650.00. *Courtesy Iva Mae Jones.*

15" composition, Little Colonel, (Betty), green sleep eyes, closed mouth, mohair wig, Civil War outfit with pantaloons, tagged with Madame Alexander logo, circa 1935, $700.00. *Courtesy Iva Mae Jones.*

13" composition, McGuffey Ana, brown sleep eyes, open mouth with teeth, blonde human hair braided wig, in shipping box, circa 1938, $700.00+; with four extra tagged outfits, $1,100.00. *Courtesy Rae Klenke.*

22" composition, McGuffey Ana, marked "Princess Elizabeth//Alexander Doll Co." on back of head, brown sleep eyes, open mouth with four upper teeth, original blonde human hair wig in braids, 5-piece composition body, original pink polka dot dress, white pinafore, underclothing, replaced socks, original snap shoes, circa 1937 – 1942, $500.00. *Courtesy McMasters Doll Auctions.*

14" composition, Scarlett, blue sleep eyes, eyeshadow, real lashes above, painted lashes below, closed mouth, black wig, green velvet dress with matching feathered hat, with wrist tag that reads, "Scarlett O'Hara//From//Gone With//The Wind//by//Madame Alexander//By Special Permission of//The Copyright Owners//all Rights Reserved" with box, circa 1941 – 1943, $650.00. *Courtesy Harlene Soucy.*

18" composition, Wendy Ann, blue sleep eyes, eyeshadow, closed mouth, red mohair wig, straw hat, tagged silk dress, circa 1938 – 1944, $600.00. *Courtesy Oleta Woodside.*

17½" composition, Wendy Ann Bride, blue plastic sleep eyes, heavy eyeshadow above eyes, real lashes, painted lashes below, closed mouth, pretty color in cheeks, blonde mohair wig, long veil, all original in satin wedding dress with sweetheart neckline with wrist tag, mint with box, circa 1940s, $650.00. *Courtesy Harlene Soucy.*

21" composition, Wendy Ann Bride, dark blonde wig, blue sleep eyes, real lashes, painted lower lashes, eyeshadow, closed mouth, jointed compo body, white bridal gown, replaced veil, circa 1942 – 1943, $285.00. *Courtesy Jeanette Ortlieb.*

14" composition, Wendy Ann Bride, marked "Mme. Alexander" on back of head, blue sleep eyes, real lashes, closed mouth, auburn mohair wig in original set, 5-piece composition body, original bride dress and veil, socks, shoes, original bouquet, near mint, circa 1944 – 1945, $375.00. *Courtesy McMasters Doll Auctions.*

Hard Plastic and Vinyl

Two 8" hard plastic, "Alexander-kins" marked "Alexander-kins//Madame Alexander//Re. U.S. Pat. Off. N.Y.//U.S.A." on original tagged dresses, bent knee walkers, blue sleep eyes. Left: Bridesmaid in pink flowered organdy dress, pink snap shoes, pink picture hat, with original box, circa 1956+, $750.00; right: #580 Wendy, blue taffeta dress, orange coat and hat with blue lining matching dress, black side snap shoes, circa 1956 – 1965, $575.00. *Courtesy McMasters Doll Auctions.*

17" hard plastic, Cinderella, with beautiful color hair, satin long gown with star trim, tag and box, circa 1950 – 1951, $1,500.00. *Courtesy Elaine Pardee.*

9" hard plastic, Cissette, blue sleep eyes with molded lashes, single stroke brows, painted lower lashes, closed mouth, original wig in original set, body jointed at shoulders, hips, and knees, high heel feet, dressed in original tagged lace teddy, nylon stockings, silver high heels with elastic straps. Marked "Mme Alexander" on back. Comes with extra boxed outfit with pink/navy blue taffeta dress and accessories, circa 1957 – 1963, $1,000.00. *Courtesy McMasters Doll Auctions*

21" hard plastic, Cissy, blue sleep eyes, real lashes, feathered brows, painted lower lashes, closed mouth, original wig in original set, fashion-type body jointed at knees, vinyl arms jointed at elbows, high heel feet. Dressed in original turquoise taffeta dress, black suede jacket, pink taffeta panties and matching half slip, stockings, black high heels with elastic straps, black flower hat and veil, circa 1955 – 1959, $850.00. *Courtesy McMasters Doll Auctions.*

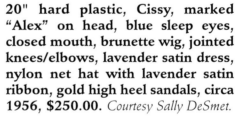

20" hard plastic, Cissy, marked "Alex" on head, blue sleep eyes, closed mouth, brunette wig, jointed knees/elbows, lavender satin dress, nylon net hat with lavender satin ribbon, gold high heel sandals, circa 1956, $250.00. *Courtesy Sally DeSmet.*

20" hard plastic, Cissy, eyeshadow over blue sleep eyes, closed mouth, auburn synthetic wig, blue street dress, fur collar with pink rose, straw hat with flowers, nylons, high heels, circa 1955 – 1959, $295.00. *Courtesy Mary Sakraida.*

14" hard plastic, Easter Doll, left, $275.00; and 14" Renoir Child, #1474, right, $135.00; used Mary Ann doll for both, blue sleep eyes, closed mouths, vinyl arms and legs, circa 1968 only. *Courtesy McMasters Doll Auctions.*

16" hard plastic, Elise Bridesmaid, sleep eyes, closed mouth, blonde wig, hard plastic body, vinyl arms, jointed ankles and knees, pleated nylon dress with flowers on the bodice and flared, pleated sleeves, large straw hat, all original, circa 1959, $425.00. *Courtesy Flo Burnside.*

21" hard plastic, Jenny Lind Portrait, vinyl arms, #2191, ca. 1969, $575.00; 14" Jenny Lind, #1491, (Mary Ann), ca. 1970, $250.00; 10" Jenny Lind Portrette, #1184, ca. 1970, $275.00; all in pink/lace. *Courtesy McMasters Doll Auctions.*

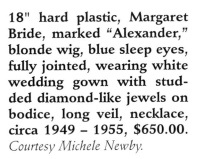

18" hard plastic, Margaret Bride, marked "Alexander," blonde wig, blue sleep eyes, fully jointed, wearing white wedding gown with studded diamond-like jewels on bodice, long veil, necklace, circa 1949 – 1955, $650.00. *Courtesy Michele Newby.*

14" hard plastic, Nat (Little Men), Maggie face, blue sleep eyes, real lashes, painted lower lashes, closed mouth, original synthetic wig, 5-piece hard plastic body, original white piqué shirt with red ribbon tie, blue pants, gold felt jacket and cap, dark socks, brown suede snap shoes, marked "Nat//© Madame Alexander//New York//U.S.A." on clothing tag, circa 1952, $600.00. *Courtesy McMasters Doll Auctions.*

8" hard plastic, Parlour Maid (Wendy Ann), #579, blue sleep eyes, closed mouth, black maid dress with white apron and feather duster, circa 1956, $550.00. *Courtesy McMasters Doll Auctions.*

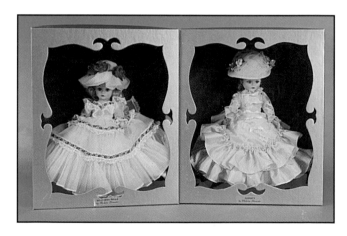

10" hard plastic, Portrette Iceland (Cissette), sleep eyes, closed mouth, synthetic wig, pierced ears, seven-piece adult body, jointed elbows and knees, circa 1962 – 1963, $215.00. *Courtesy McMasters Doll Auctions.*

10" hard plastic, Southern Belle, left, white gown, green ribbon, three rows of lace (Cissette), $325.00; 10" hard plastic, Godey, all pink/ecru lace/bows down front (Cissette), $255.00; both boxed, circa 1968. *Courtesy McMasters Doll Auctions.*

12" hard plastic, Southern Belle (Lissy), blonde hair, blue sleep eyes, closed mouth, jointed knees and elbows, pale blue dress with lace and pink ribbon, pink feather on white hat, circa 1963, $400.00. *Courtesy McMasters Doll Auctions.*

8" hard plastic, Wendy Goes on Train Journey, #468, marked "Alex" on body, blue sleep eyes, molded lashes, closed mouth, blonde saran wig in original set, hard plastic walker body with unjointed knees, sleeveless dress with pleated skirt, white felt jacket with star trim, matching tam with red pompon, red snap shoes, original box, circa 1955, $400.00. *Ccourtesy McMasters Doll Auctions.*

18" hard plastic, Winnie Walker, head marked "Alexander," blonde synthetic wig, blue sleep eyes, fully jointed, standard walking mechanism, navy coat/hat, red taffeta dress, hat box, hang tag, circa 1954, $475.00, Peggy Millhouse photo. *Courtesy Sidney Jeffery collection.*

21" viny, Jacqueline Ice Capades doll, sleep eyes, closed mouth, eyeshadow, black beaded headpiece, elaborate handmade costume with beadwork; these dolls were used and dressed by the Ice Capades staff to help in set design, lighting, and production, circa 1961 – 1962, $2,500.00. *Courtesy Sandra Kline.*

10" vinyl, Hyacinth, large painted blue eyes, multi-stroke brows, molded and painted hair, non-jointed "latex" baby body. Dressed in original pink organdy dress, matching bonnet and under clothing, rayon socks, and pink side snap shoes. Marked "Alexander" on head, boxed, round foil tags on wrists. Circa 1953, $475.00. *Courtesy McMasters Doll Auctions.*

17" black vinyl, Leslie Ballerina, brown synthetic rooted wig, brown sleep eyes, closed mouth, painted and real lashes, in original blue Ballerina costume, marked "© Alexander Doll//1965" circa 1966 – 1971, $350.00. *Courtesy June Allgeier.*

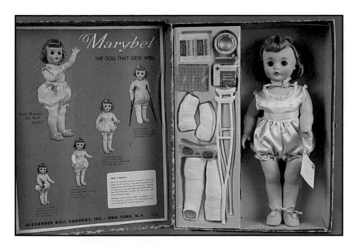

15" vinyl, Marybel, The Doll That Gets Well, marked "Alexander" (in circle) on back, brown sleep eyes, real lashes, closed mouth, blonde hair in original set, child body jointed at shoulders, waist, and hips, dressed in tagged pink satin romper, pink velvet slippers with pompons, unplayed-with in case with Band-Aids, adhesive tape, gauze bandage, measles and chicken pox spots, yellow sunglasses, arm and leg casts, and crutches, circa 1959 – 1956, $275.00. *Courtesy McMasters Doll Auctions.*

12" vinyl, Pamela, blue sleep eyes, molded lashes, feathered brows, painted lower lashes, closed mouth, original wig attached with Velcro, 5-piece hard plastic body, marked "Alexander//19©63" on back of head, dressed in tagged pink tutu, wardrobe case with two extra dresses and accessories, circa 1963, $650.00. *Courtesy McMasters Doll Auctions.*

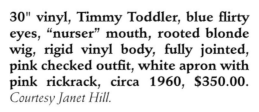

30" vinyl, Timmy Toddler, blue flirty eyes, "nurser" mouth, rooted blonde wig, rigid vinyl body, fully jointed, pink checked outfit, white apron with pink rickrack, circa 1960, $350.00. *Courtesy Janet Hill.*

22" vinyl, Sweetie Baby, blue sleep eyes, open/closed mouth, blonde rooted hair, original pink tagged Madame Alexander dress, new leatherette shoes, circa 1962, $125.00. *Courtesy Nelda Shelton.*

16" vinyl, Alexandra Fairchild Ford, wears Timothy J. Alberts' design, with keyhole neckline and wrap skirt with a matching pearl closure handbag and translucent Lucite shoes, 2000 line, $79.95 retail, and "Lunch at 2" also by Timothy J. Alberts, boatneck dress in metallic diamond fabric, with silver chained purse, style #27290, $69.95 retail, 2000 line. *Courtesy Alexander Doll Co.*

16" vinyl, Alexandra Fairchild Ford, "Editor-in-Chief, born in a Boston suburb, now in New York City, with the new fashion magazine, *Elan*," wears coat, skirt, sweater, scarf, and boots, 2000 line $89.95 retail. *Courtesy Alexander Doll Co.*

16", vinyl, new fashion doll, Alexandra Fairchild Ford, "Millennium Ball Alex" in long gown with tie around neck, sparkles on the full skirt, feather boa, style #25580, 2000, $124.95 retail. *Courtesy Alexander Doll Co.*

16", fashion doll Alexandra Fairchild Ford, "Runway Review Alex," "Museum Gala Alex," and "Magazine Launch," retailing for $84.95, $109.95, and $79.95, **2000 line.** *Courtesy Alexander Doll Co.*

27015
MISTY MAGIC
Includes mirror, brush, teddy, stockings, camisole and panties.

Misty Magic Accessory Pack for their 16" vinyl fashion doll, Alex, includes mirror, brush, teddy, stockings, camisole, and panties, **2000 line,** $29.95, **retail.** *Courtesy Alexander Doll Co.*

27075
PASHMINA ACCESSORY PACK
Includes pashmina shawl, crochet purse and sunglasses.

Pashmina Accessory Pack for their 16" vinyl fashion doll, Alex, includes pashmina shawl, crochet purse, and sunglasses, **2000 line,** $29.95 **retail.** *Courtesy Alexander Doll Co.*

Sensual Essentials Accessory Pack for their 16" vinyl fashion doll, Alex, includes camisole, panties, teddy, stockings, slip, robe, and mule slippers, **2000 line,** $39.95 **retail.** *Courtesy Alexander Doll Co.*

27295
SENSUAL ESSENTIALS
ACCESSORY PACK
Includes camisole, panties, teddy, stockings, slip, robe and mule slippers.

Alexander Doll Co.

"Cape Cod" (outfit only), to fit their 16" vinyl fashion doll Alex, includes double breasted jacket, long pants, scarf, and boots, style #25575, 2000 line, $39.95 retail. *Courtesy Alexander Doll Co.*

"Dinner and a Movie" (outfit only), to fit their 16" vinyl fashion doll Alex, includes long pants with floral embroidery, knit top and "leather" jacket, style #27270, retail $39.95. *Courtesy Alexander Doll Co.*

10" vinyl, "Spring Promenade," and 10" "Out for a Stroll," each $119.95 retail, and 8" vinyl, "Victorian Marigold," retail $79.95, 2000 line. *Courtesy Alexander Doll Co.*

he
ard
of Oz™

...your little dog, too!"

...very special limited edition
...n rich brocade with a soft
...ch of the West peers
...her spell on Dorothy...

27760
NEW
LIMITED EDITION
WICKED WITCH OF THE WEST
(Mini Dorothy Globe Included)
21"
EDITION SIZE 500

A different version of this doll was part of the
Wizard of Oz™ auction piece for the Walt
Disneyworld™ Teddy Bear and Doll Convention.

21" vinyl, "Wicked Witch of the West," Limited Edition of 500, dressed in rich brocade with soft velvet cape, included mini Dorothy Water Globe, 2000 line, $449.95 retail. *Courtesy Alexander Doll Co.*

27335
NEW
1920's HONEYMOON
TRUNK SET
12"

Set Includes:
One porcelain doll
1920's wedding ensemble
Cotton day dress
Brocade nightgown and robe
Undergarments and shoes
Trunk

12" porcelain, "1920s Honeymoon Trunk Set," with 1920s wedding dress ensemble, cotton day dress, brocade nightgown and robe, undergarments, shoes, and trunk, 2000 line, $239.95 retail. *Courtesy Alexander Doll Co.*

Sweet
Sentiments

Begin each day with one of our seven darlings from this traditional rhyme. Each doll comes with an embroidered panel that can be buttoned together. Collect all seven dolls to complete the days of the week quilt.

Assembled Quilt

27775
NEW
TUESDAY'S CHILD
8"

27780
NEW
WEDNESDAY'S CHILD
8"

27770
NEW
MONDAY'S CHILD
8"

27785
NEW
THURSDAY'S CHILD
8"

27790
NEW
FRIDAY'S CHILD
8"

27800
NEW
SUNDAY'S CHILD
8"

27795
NEW
SATURDAY'S CHILD
8"

Monday's child is fair of face,
Tuesday's child is full of grace,
Wednesday's child is full of woe,
Thursday's child has far to go,
Friday's child is loving and giving,
Saturday's child works hard for a living,
But the child that's born on the Sabbath day
Is bonny and blithe, and good and gay.

8" vinyl, "Seven Days of the Week," set includes seven dolls from the children's rhyme, each with an embroidered panel that can be buttoned together to make a quilt. Each $89.95; set $629.95, 2000 line. *Courtesy Alexander Doll Co.*

Alexander Doll Co.

The Little Women Collection, one of the timeless classics, will be available for a limited time only through the end of this year. Complete your collection with Laurie while there is still time...and cherish them for a lifetime.

28160 BETH 8"

27765 NEW LIMITED EDITION LAURIE 8"

28150 MEG 8"

8" vinyl, "Laurie," a Limited Edition of the Little Women Collection, wears plaid pants, jacket, shirt, cap, and shoes, $74.95 retail; shown with 8" Beth in plaid long dress, and 8" Meg in checked long dress, $79.95 each retail, 2000 line. *Courtesy Alexander Doll Co.*

8" vinyl, Little Women Collection, Jo in long floral print with checked apron, Marmee in dark floral print dress with cameo at neck, and Amy with checked dress with white apron. Jo and Amy, $79.95 each, Marmee $94.95 retail, 2000 line. *Courtesy Alexander Doll Co.*

28180 MARMEE 8"

28140 JO 8"

28170 AMY 8"

5" porcelain, Rumpelstiltskin and 8" vinyl, The Miller's Daughter included in this set, with Miller's Daughter wearing long embroidered gown, with matching hat, $199.95 retail; 8" vinyl Princess and the Pea, includes mattress and pea, $109.95 retail; and 8" The Frog Princess, includes the frog, $89.95 retail, 2000 line. *Courtesy Alexander Doll Co.*

8" vinyl, "Millennium Bouquet" doll, a Limited Edition to start the new millennium, in long dress with new overskirt, floral headpiece, 2000 line, $99.95. *Courtesy Alexander Doll Co.*

Alexander Doll Co.

8" vinyl, "'Twas the Night Before Christmas," in long white gown with eyelet trim and robe, $84.95 retail, 6½" fireplace stocking holder with replaceable battery included, $59.95, 2000 line. *Courtesy Alexander Doll Co.*

16" vinyl, fashion doll, Alexandra Fairfield Ford, in "Crimson Christmas Alex," red beaded charmeuse and chiffon gown with matching stole, 2000 line, $159.95. *Courtesy Alexander Doll Co.*

8" vinyl, "Season's Greetings Wendy," with flower wreath in hair; "Chanukah Celebration" has ribbons in hair, and "Season's Greetings Maggie" has freckles, flower wreath in hair, 2000 line, $94.95 retail each. *Courtesy Alexander Doll Co.*

Season's Greetings

Bring in the holiday cheer! Celebrate Chanukah and Christmas with our darlings, dressed in festive silk smocks with hand-stitched details. They are sure to fill your home with joy. Decked in their holiday finest, our babies also capture the tradition of the holiday season. They're dressed in exquisitely embroidered soft knit sweaters with cranberry-colored outfits.

14" vinyl, "Berry Berry Christmas Victoria," wears cranberry colored outfits with embroidered soft knit sweater and matching hairband, $104.95, and 12" vinyl, "Berry Berry Christmas Huggums," in cranberry outfit with embroidered soft knit hooded jacket, $59.95, 2000 line. *Courtesy Alexander Doll Co.*

8" vinyl, Special Occasions Collection, includes, "Happy Birthday" in blonde, brunette, or African-American, holding balloons, has Happy Birthday on hat, $69.95 retail; "Emerald Lass" has short green dress with short puffed sleeves, $79.95 retail; and "Valentine Kisses" in red and white with a red hat trimmed with lace, $69.95 retail, 2000 line. *Courtesy Alexander Co.*

8" vinyl, "Pumpkin Patch Treats," includes three outfits, one doll dressed in leopard costume, one witch outfit that reverses to a little devil costume, and one pumpkin costume that converts to a carry pouch to hold all the outfits, 2000 line, $189.95. *Courtesy Alexander Doll Co.*

10" vinyl, Jenny Lind, in long gown with rosette trim on skirt and bodice, Hall of Fame Collection, 2000 line, $119.95; 8" vinyl, Scarlett O'Hara, in green drapery dress with gold tassel belt, matching hat, 2000 line, $84.95. *Courtesy Alexander Doll Co.*

21" hard plastic, "Yardley Cissy," Limited Edition of 500, includes English Lavender soap and reproduction of 1952 Yardley ad, 2000 line, $349.95. *Courtesy Alexander Doll Co.*

Louis Amberg & Sons

Louis Amberg & Sons operated in Cincinnati, Ohio, from about 1878 until moving to New York City in 1898; before 1907, the company also used other names. An importer of dolls made by other firms, Amberg was one of the first manufacturers to produce American-made dolls in quantities and used a cold press composition as early as 1911. These early dolls had cold press composition with straw stuffed bodies and composition lower arms. In 1915 they introduced a character doll, Charlie Chaplin, which was a big hit for them. In 1918 Otto Denivelle joined the firm and introduced a hot press baking process for composition dolls. "Mibs," a soulful composition child with painted eyes and molded hair, was introduced in 1921, and the company soon was making Mama-dolls and "Baby Peggy." In 1927, they introduced the Vanta baby that promoted Vanta baby clothing. Amberg patented in 1928 a waist joint and used several different heads on this body twist torso, one of which was called the "It" doll. In 1930, Amberg was sold to Horsman who continued to make some of the more popular lines.

What to look for:

Amberg produced some very interesting composition characters and being able to recognize these early dolls will be a plus for you. Labeled clothing, good color, and minimal crazing are points to keep in mind when searching flea markets, estate or garage sales for these dolls.

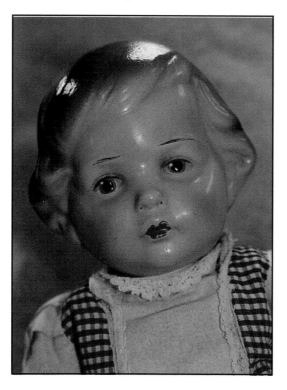 

14" composition, Edwina, marked "Amberg//Pat. Pend.//LA&S © 1928," painted molded hair with side part and swirl bangs across forehead, painted brown eyes, swivel waist, red and white checked skirt and vest over white top, circa 1928, $450.00. *Courtesy Sharon Kolibaba.*

American Character

The American Character Doll Co. (1919+, New York City) made composition dolls; in 1923 the company began using "Petite" as a tradename for mama and character dolls, and later made cloth, hard plastic, and vinyl dolls. Sweet Sue, Tressy, Mary Make-up, and other dolls with high heels and fashion-type figures reflect the focus on women as objects of beauty that remains an ongoing theme in dolls.

What to look for:

Composition American Character dolls should have good color, little crazing, and tagged original outfits or be appropriately dressed in copies of original costumes using natural or period fabrics.

Hard plastic and vinyl dolls should have great color, be clean, and should be dressed in original costumes, with tags, labels, and brochures intact. Again, the newer the doll, the more complete and mint it must be to command higher prices. Reject soiled or nude dolls unless they have wonderful color and you have original clothes you can use to redress the doll.

Composition

19" composition, Petite Sally, marked "Petite Sally," wig, blue sleep eyes, closed mouth, compo arms and legs, cloth body, original orange coat and hat, circa 1931 – 1934, $350.00. *Courtesy Janet Hill.*

12½" composition, Sally, marked "Sally//A Petite Doll," brown painted side-glancing eyes, closed rosebud mouth, painted brown hair, original tagged yellow dress reads "A Loveable Petite Doll//Sally," circa 1930+, $200.00. *Courtesy Janet Hill.*

15" composition, Puggy, has molded painted hair, side-glancing brown painted eyes, painted lashes above eyes, closed mouth, frowning expression, with original Bronco Billy red shirt, leather vest, and chaps, tan cowboy hat, marked on neck "A Petite Doll," circa 1929+, $500.00. *Courtesy Joy Crawford.*

Hard Plastic and Vinyl

14" hard plastic, Sweet Sue, dressed as "Annie Oakley", blonde saran wig in original set, sleep eyes, closed mouth, jointed hard plastic walker body, original clothing, green vest and skirt with gold fringe, name embroidered on skirt, yellow blouse, circa 1954, $325.00+. *Courtesy McMasters Doll Auctions.*

18" hard plastic, Sweet Sue, skater, sleep eyes, real lashes, painted lower lashes, closed mouth, blonde wig, dressed in blue trimmed with pink crocheted skating outfit, matching hat, white skates, circa 1953, $250.00. *Courtesy Kris Lundquist.*

17" hard plastic, Sweet Sue, marked "Amer. Char. Doll" on back of head, long blonde braided wig, blue sleep eyes, closed mouth, green and white checked dress trimmed in white rickrack, white shoes, circa 1953, $200.00. *Courtesy Donna Hadley.*

17" hard plastic, walker, marked "Amer. Char. Doll" on back of head, auburn rooted skullcap, sleep eyes, closed mouth, vinyl arms jointed at elbows, pink satin evening gown, circa 1950s, $125.00. *Courtesy Donna Hadley.*

15" hard plastic, Sweet Sue, marked "A.C." on neck, green plastic sleep eyes, real lashes, painted lashes below, eyeshadow, closed mouth, dark blonde saran wig, flat feet, original "Tea Dance" rayon dress with pink skirt and aqua blue top, circa 1952, $225.00. *Private collection.*

17½" hard plastic, Sweet Sue walker, long red wig, blue sleep eyes, closed mouth, pearl necklace, peach colored satin and lace dress, pink shoes, circa 1950s, $375.00. *Courtesy Michele Newby.*

24" hard plastic, Sweet Sue, glued-on auburn wig, blue sleep eyes, closed mouth, long pink dress with lace, blue ribbon, white shoes, marked "Amer. Char.," circa 1953, $210.00. *Courtesy Judie Conroy.*

18" hard plastic, Sweet Sue Bride, inserted skull cap, blue sleep eyes, real lashes, closed mouth, vinyl arms jointed at elbows, jointed at knees, wedding gown and veil, marked "American Character Doll" on head, box marked "#1118//American Char. Doll," MIB, circa 1950s, $350.00. *Courtesy Sharon Harrington.*

17½" hard plastic, Sweet Sue, glued-on brown wig, blue sleep eyes, closed mouth, long pink gown with lace, long sleeves, pink shoes, circa 1950s, $165.00. *Courtesy Judie Conroy.*

15" hard plastic, Sweet Sue-type, blue sleep eyes, closed mouth, reddish-blonde wig, composition body, jointed arms and legs, original blue dress trimmed with flowers and lace, blue shoes, straw hat, circa 1953, $225.00. *Courtesy Nelda Shelton.*

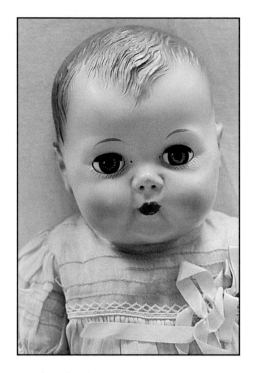

15" hard plastic, Tiny Tears, sleep eyes with tear ducts, drinks and wets, nurser mouth, molded painted hair, rubber body, old costume, circa 1950 – 1962, $175.00. *Courtesy Judie Bartell.*

16" hard plastic, Tiny Tears, hair rooted into skullcap, blue sleep eyes, lashes above, tear ducts at inner eye, open mouth to accept bottle, marked "American Character Doll," vinyl bent leg baby body, original outfit, circa 1950 – 1962, $165.00. *Courtesy Debbie Crume.*

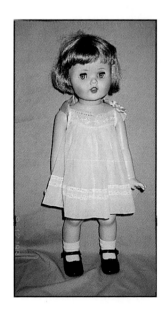

24" vinyl, Toodles, marked "American Doll & Toy Corp.//19© 60," blue sleep eyes, open/closed mouth, painted teeth, blonde hair, white dress, hard plastic body, circa 1960, $85.00. *Courtesy Kate Treber.*

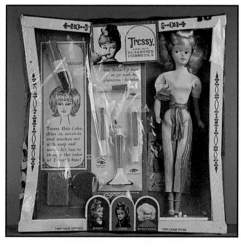

11" vinyl, Tressy and her Hi-Fashion Cosmetics, grow-hair, blonde hair with hair pins, high heel doll, wearing white shirt, orange/tan/yellow/white striped pants with matching belt, one white shoe, booklet, white plastic and metal stand, cosmetics include Hair Coloring Applicator, Romantic Red Lipstick, Eyebrow Pencil, Royal Red Nail Polish, Eye Shadow, two Cosmetic Sponges, in box with partial cellophane, NRFB, circa 1963 – 1966, $130.00. *Courtesy McMasters Doll Auctions.*

Arranbee Dolls

Arranbee Doll Co., operating from 1922 until 1958 in New York, was sold to Vogue Doll Co. who continued to use the Arranbee molds until 1961. Armand Marseille and Simon & Halbig made some of their bisque dolls. Arranbee also produced composition baby, child, and mama-dolls; their early dolls have an eight-sided tag. They went on to make hard plastic and vinyl dolls, many carrying the R & B trademark. Some hard plastic and vinyl dolls (Littlest Angel and Li'l Imp) were made for Vogue by the Arranbee division and may be marked by either.

What to look for:

Composition dolls should have good color, only very fine crazing (preferably none), and original clothes or appropriate copies. Always look for mint-in-box and tagged dolls in excellent to mint condition.

Hard plastic and vinyl dolls should be clean with bright rosy cheek color, and tagged or labeled clothes, preferably with brochures and/or boxes to command higher prices in the future.

Composition

16½" composition, Nancy, a Patsy look-alike, marked "Nancy" on back of head, molded painted hair, blue tin sleep eyes, open mouth with teeth, green coat and matching hat, dress, shoes, socks, trunk with wardrobe, circa 1930, $300.00. *Courtesy Donna Hadley.*

16" composition, Nancy, marked "Arranbee//Nancy" on head, sleep eyes, open mouth with teeth, auburn wig, original blue dress with matching hat and blue ribbons, replaced shoes, circa 1930+, $375.00. *Courtesy Donna Nance.*

12" composition, Nancy-type, marked "Arranbee" on back, molded painted hair, blue tin eyes, closed mouth, pink romper, red coat and matching tam, white shoes, socks; trunk and wardrobe, circa 1930, $250.00. *Courtesy Donna Hadley.*

15" composition, Nancy Lee, blue plastic sleep eyes, eyeshadow, real lashes, painted lashes below, closed mouth, brown mohair wig, original black dot on white long dress with pink flower and feather trim, gold and blue foil round hangtag reads "Nancy Lee//R&B//Quality Doll," no other marks noted, boxed, circa 1940s, $650.00. *Courtesy Kay Walimaa.*

21" composition, Ice Skater, unmarked, short blonde wig, blue sleep eyes, eyeshadow, painted lower lashes, closed mouth, red and white skirt with matching jacket and hat, skirt trimmed in white fur, white ice skates, all original, circa 1945, $275.00. *Courtesy Donna Hadley.*

21" composition, Nancy Lee, blue plastic sleep eyes, heavy eyeshadow above eyes, real lashes, painted lashes below, closed mouth, mohair wig, original red skating costume, mint condition, round R&B tag on outfit, faintly marked "R&B" on neck, boxed, circa 1949, $700.00. *Courtesy Harlene Soucy.*

18" composition, Nannette, brown plastic sleep eyes, eyeshadow, real lashes, painted lashes below, closed mouth, blonde mohair wig, yellow and gold short dress, matching bloomers, straw hat, tagged "Nannette//Re. U.S. Pat. Off. //Walking//and//Talking//doll//An R&B Quality Product" and also "The Wig on This Doll is Made of 100% Virgin Mohair//Arranbee Doll Co.," boxed, circa 1940s, $500.00. *Courtesy Geri Teeter.*

26" composition, Nannette, brown glassine sleep eyes, eyeshadow, real lashes, painted lashes, open mouth, two upper teeth, blonde human hair wig, original tagged aqua cotton dress and matching hat, red white and blue tag reads, "Nannette//Walking//and//Talking//doll//An R&B Quality Product," no marks noted on body, circa 1940s, $650.00. *Courtesy Harlene Soucy.*

14" composition, Debu' Teen, sleep eyes, closed mouth, dark blonde human hair wig, 1940s blue print dress not original, circa 1940, $225.00. *Courtesy Peggy Millhouse.*

18" composition, Debu' Teen, brown mohair wig, heavy eyeshadow over brown sleep eyes, real lashes and painted lashes, closed mouth, pink organdy-over-net formal, pink rayon slip, circa 1940s, $250.00. *Courtesy June Allgeier.*

14" hard plastic, Arranbee girl, marked "R&B" on back of head, blonde synthetic hair, blue sleep eyes, closed mouth, brown and gold dress, gold socks, brown shoes, circa 1950+, $225.00. *Courtesy Donna Hadley.*

Artist Dolls

While a hot debate goes on in some doll making and collecting circles as to the exact definition of an artist doll, we use this definition: original, one-of-a-kind, limited edition or limited production dolls of any medium (cloth, porcelain, wax, wood, vinyl or other material) made for public sale. Dolls may be considered works of art, and some collectors may wish to have just that in their collection. Other collectors define a doll as a play object and choose to collect them as such. You, as a collector, are free to make your own decision to suit yourself, and we can all appreciate the creativity that these talented artists exhibit.

What to look for:
One should remember with all collectibles, a well-made object of beauty will always be appealing. Well-made dolls by artists should appeal to you. Some, not all, will increase in value. Study the range of dolls to find what you like. Some may only be popular fads.

A doll that is artistically done and is in proper proportion stands a greater chance of increasing in value over time. You can enjoy such a doll as part of your collection, rather than acquiring it solely as an investment. With artist dolls, one may need six examples or more of the artist's work to show the range of his or her talents. The artist doll category offers something for everyone.

Alphabetically by Maker

16" cloth boy, by Christine Adams, tagged "Christine Adams//Tiny Tots//Hand Made Dolls," mask face, features are hand painted in oils, brown eyes, brown human hair wig, stitched fingers, all hand knitted clothes, circa 1980, $1,000.00. *Private collection.*

16" cloth girl, by Christine Adams, tagged "Christine Adams//Tiny Tots//Hand Made Dolls," mask face, features are hand painted in oils, blue eyes, curly blonde human hair wig, stitched fingers, jointed at hips and shoulders, circa 1980, $1,000.00. *Private collection.*

8" porcelain, Esmeralda, by Atelier Bets van Boxel, child in basket, glass eyes, open mouth, turquoise and tan outfit, matching cap, circa 1999, $1,900.00. *Courtesy Atelier Bets van Boxel.*

8" porcelain, Pearl, by Atelier Bets van Boxel, oriental child in basket, glass eyes, pouty mouth, red outfit, black hat with red pompon, circa 1999, $1,900.00. *Courtesy Atelier Bets van Boxel.*

14" polymer clay, Cynthia Baron Designs, "and the Dish ran away with the Spoon" artist doll, with painted eyes, wig, peaked black hat, striped long dress with wine bodice, holds crook in one hand, dish taking spoon from basket on base, 1998, $1,600.00. *Courtesy Cynthia Baron.*

6½" resin, Cynthia Baron Designs, limited edition of 100, original "Father Christmas" #104 artist doll, fully articulated on wired body, jointed neck and waist, painted features, $195.00, circa 1999. *Courtesy Cynthia Baron.*

14" polymer clay, one-of-a-kind Cynthia Baron Designs artist doll, "Monkies," holding marionettes, with well-sculpted white face, painted eyes, closed smiling mouth, red painted nose, in clown costume, circa 1998, $1,600.00. *Courtesy Cynthia Baron.*

14" Sculpey, Cynthia Baron Designs one-of-a-kind, "Tutti Punchinelli" artist doll, 19th century masked figure, with painted features, smiling mouth, holds marionette in one hand, a stack of masks and dolls in the other, circa 1997, $2,200.00. *Courtesy Cynthia Baron.*

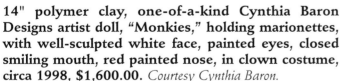

21" cernit, Cheryl D. Bollenbach "Man-Dan Warrior," finely sculpted features, black wig, feather headdress, colorful bead, feathers, fur, and leather costume, 1999, $1,000.00. *Courtesy Cheryl Bollenbach.*

24" hard vinyl, by Sabine Esche of Sigikid Co., "Leroy," limited edition, painted eyes, closed mouth, dark blonde human hair wig, nicely made clothes, cloth body, circa 1980s, $1,500.00. *Private collection.*

13" cloth figure, "I Dream of the Sky," by Jane Darin, hand needle sculptured/painted face from 100% Swiss pima cotton knit, figure made from silk, wool, and cotton, the artist felted her chrysalis, which drapes on the human-sized hand and through her hands, and contains fibers from her fabrics, hand-dyed wools, and iridescent netting, fully jointed for ease of posing, the human hand turns and is also wired, circa 1999, $1,800.00. *Courtesy Jane Darin.*

Two 13" cloth figures, "At Aunt Eleanor's Farm – After Chagall," by Jane Darin, hand needle sculptured/painted faces from 100% Swiss pima cotton knit, created in the manner of painter Marc Chagall but using Darin's own childhood experiences, choosing a rooster, chair, washtub, wash board, milk pail, broom, and kimono silk as symbols, made from wire, batting, nylons, and paint, horse's head is pima cotton knit, rooster is Styrofoam and wood, circa 1995, $5,940.00. *Courtesy Jane Darin.*

28" polymer clay, black "Santa and Sumayah," by Marilyn Henke. Santa holds 10" Sumayah, one-of-a-kind, mohair wigs and beard, glass eyes, open mouths with teeth, foam rubber over wire armature, Santa is wearing velvet outfit with mink trim, gold lamé shirt, leather boots; Sumayah is wearing a cotton jumper and suede shoes, both holding Christmas lights, circa 2000, $895.00. *Courtesy Marilyn Henke.*

28" polymer clay, "Mistletoe Mischief," by Marilyn Henke Santa is 28" and Mrs. Santa is 24", one-of-a-kind, Santa has gray mohair wig and beard, Mrs. Santa has gray acrylic wig, both with glass eyes, bodies are rubber over wire armature, Santa is dressed in cream polar fleece, mink trim; leather boots with fur trim; Mrs. Santa dressed in white crushed velvet, rabbit and braid trim, gold and white blouse, leather shoes, circa 2000, $495.00 each, $990.00 set. *Courtesy Marilyn Henke.*

Left, 14½" polymer clay "Hark, It's Harold," and 15½" polymer clay, "Joy to the World," by Marilyn Henke, both with foam rubber over wire armature bodies, acrylic wigs, glass eyes, open singing mouths, polymer clay hands, dressed in satin robes, velvet capes with mink trim, vinyl boots with mink, circa 2000, $395.00 each, $790.00 set. *Courtesy Marilyn Henke.*

25" hard vinyl, Annette Himstedt Barefoot Children "Fiene," glass eyes, blonde wig, marked "Fiene//Annette Himstedt//©" on neck, vinyl shoulder plate, cloth body, vinyl arms and legs, bare feet, original dress, pink ribbon trim, circa 1990, $650.00. *Courtesy Elizabeth Surber.*

14" Super Sculpey, "A Rag Coat for Annabelle," by Marilynn Huston with signature on doll, green glass eyes, freckles, closed mouth, red braided synthetic hair, multicolored coat, crocheted hat, holding a rag doll, circa 1998, $495.00. *Courtesy Marilynn Huston.*

23" Super Sculpey, "Katlyn," by Pat Moulton, auburn wig, green eyes, closed mouth, wire armature, cloth body, sculpted shoes, limited edition of 20, circa 2000, $1,200.00. *Courtesy Pat Moulton.*

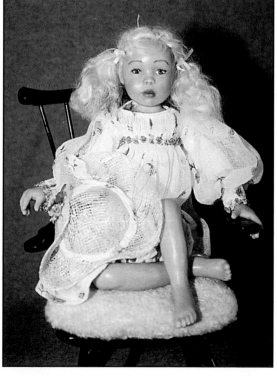

10" Super Sculpey, "Savanna," by Pat Moulton, painted brown eyes, closed mouth, blonde mohair wig, seated in chair with one knee up and other leg folded beneath, one-of-a-kind, circa 2000, $500.00. *Courtesy Pat Moulton.*

17½" Super Sculpey, "Black Tankia," by Pat Moulton, painted brown eyes, white outfit with matching turban, one-of-a-kind, mounted on base, circa 2000, $500.00. *Courtesy Pat Moulton.*

17" cloth, "Carmen Miranda," by Joyce Patterson of FabricImages, one-of-a-kind cloth character, hand-painted face, smiling mouth with painted teeth, fruit head covering, red painted fingernails, lots of jewelry, hoop earrings, red sequin skirt, silver shoes, on stand, circa 1999, $300.00. *Courtesy Joyce Patterson.*

18" cloth, "Let's Do the Cotton-Eyed Joe," by Joyce Patterson of FabricImages, one-of-a-kind, four figures with hand-painted faces, cowboy hats, Western outfits, boots, on wooden stand, created for the 2000 Santa Fe Doll Art Show in Albuquerque, awarded a third place ribbon in the Professional Tableau Category, circa 2000, $600.00. *Courtesy Joyce Patterson.*

18" cloth, "Widow Johnson's Wares," by Joyce Patterson of FabricImages, one-of-a-kind, cloth character with hand-painted features, wire-rimmed glasses, crocheted shawl, straw hat, white dress, accompanied by miniature wares in a wooden cart, and a purchased resin dog, circa 2000, $400.00. *Courtesy Joyce Patterson*

24" porcelain, "Murasaki," by W. Harry Perzyk, Japanese Geisha, handmade glass eyes, silk hair fastened to the head by individual hairs, handmade clothes, one-of-a-kind, circa 1999, $1,000.00. *Courtesy W. Harry Perzyk.*

40" carved porcelain, "Honda Tadakatsu," by W. Harry Perzyk, Japanese warrior of the 16th century, handmade glass eyes, silk hair fastened to the head by individual hairs, handmade clothes, one-of-a-kind, circa 1999, $6,500.00. *Courtesy W. Harry Perzyk.*

24" carved porcelain, "Yuki," by W. Harry Perzyk, Japanese woman of the 18th century, handmade glass eyes, silk hair fastened to the head by individual hairs, soft body, handmade clothes, one-of-a-kind, circa 1999, $900.00. *Courtesy W. Harry Perzyk.*

24" solid wood carved, "Plain Indian," by W. Harry Perzyk, handmade glass eyes, silk hair fastened to the head by individual hairs, handmade clothes, one-of-a-kind, circa 1999, $4,500.00. *Courtesy W. Harry Perzyk.*

24" porcelain, "Joseph in Egypt," by W. Harry Perzyk, fully sculpted, anatomically correct, handmade glass eyes, silk hair fastened to the head by individual hairs, handmade clothes, one-of-a-kind, circa 1999, $1,500.00. *Courtesy W. Harry Perzyk.*

18" Premo Sculpey, "Don Diablo," by Daryl Poole, one-of-a-kind, signed original, head, hands, and feet are of Premo Sculpey; doll has a soft-sculpted body over wire armature, chair is hand crafted white pine with a music box inside that plays "Speak Softly, Love" (the "Godfather" theme), this is the first doll the artist made, finished in 1997, not for sale. *Courtesy Daryl Poole.*

24" porcelain, "Kochina Indian," by W. Harry Perzyk, fully sculpted, anatomically correct, handmade glass eyes, silk hair fastened to the head by individual hairs, handmade clothes, one-of-a-kind, circa 1999, $1,500.00. *Courtesy W. Harry Perzyk.*

16" Premo Sculpey, "Ziggy Ripstitch the Obscene Jester," by Daryl Poole, one-of-a-kind, signed original, head, hands, and feet are of Premo Sculpey, soft sculpted body over wire armature, circa 1997, not for sale. *Courtesy Daryl Poole.*

14" Premo Sculpey, "Vincent," by Daryl Poole, one-of-a-kind, signed original, head, hands, and feet are of Premo Sculpey, soft sculpted body over wire armature, circa 1999, $895.00. *Courtesy Daryl Poole.*

13" Creall-therm, "Kate," by Sandy Simonds, one-of-a-kind, molded painted features, auburn synthetic wig, black velvet top, brown and black skirt, wool hat, black stockings, black leather high-top boots, seated on a wooden crate with a wicker basket of silk flowers between her feet, circa 1998, $1,350.00. *Courtesy Sandy Simonds.*

15" vinyl, "Marjorie Doll" made for Marjorie Spangler Doll Club, blue sleep eyes, closed mouth, blonde synthetic wig, with Marjorie Spangler pin, marked "Marjorie Spangler Dolls Inc., © 1979," $150.00. *Courtesy Dickee Burror.*

16" Creall-therm, "Murray," by Sandy Simonds, one-of-a-kind, molded painted features, canvas body stuffed with polyfill, wire armature, old bent man with a wooden cane and paper cigar, black checked pants, white mohair sweater, black leather shoes, circa 1999, $1,050.00. *Courtesy Sandy Simonds.*

10½" porcelain, Linda Lee Sutton's "Bee-Lieve," curly blonde tendrils frame her face and feelers crown her head, dark brown paperweight eyes, closed smiling mouth, full porcelain body, black knit fabric with yellow gold velveteen costume, "A Little Honey" sits on her Bible of Wisdom, limited edition of 41, circa 2000, $395.00. *Courtesy Linda Lee Sutton Originals.*

11½" porcelain, Linda Lee Sutton's "Millennium Quints," four girls and one boy, Misty, Star Bright, Twinkle Toes, Sunny, and Twilight, individually sculpted porcelain heads, arms, and legs on armature cloth bodies blue paperweight eyes, faces framed with blonde hair, costumed in coordinated pink, blue, purple Deponi silk and flower accented chenille fabrics, wooden seated high chairs hand crafted by Cliff Craft, limited to 11 sets, circa 2000, $1,495.00. *Courtesy Linda Lee Sutton.*

18" porcelain, Linda Lee Sutton's "Peek-A-Boo," marked "Linda Lee Sutton Originals//©1999" on back of head, brown paperweight eyes, closed mouth, light brown hair with blue ribbon, dressed in a 1920s design made of powder blue Crystalline, all porcelain chubby body, playing peek-a-boo with limited edition puppy designed and made by California plush animal artist Katherine Millingar, limited edition of 20, circa 1999, $825.00. *Courtesy Linda Lee Sutton.*

25" bisque, Linda Lee Sutton's "Miss Sadie," #9 of 30, blue paperweight eyes, curly mohair wig, composition body, bisque lower arms/legs, choice of pink costume or apricot Swiss batiste, white cotton pinafore, circa 1993, $1,150.00. *Courtesy Linda Lee Sutton.*

21" porcelain, Linda Lee Sutton's "Mary Christmas," marked "Linda Lee Sutton Originals//©1987" on back of head, blue-gray paperweight eyes, dark brown human hair French wig, porcelain lower arms and hands on a composition body, Holly Berry Christmas dress, cream colored wool coat and leggings, white rabbit collar and hat, muff with her face, limited edition of 75, circa 1987, $825.00. *Courtesy Linda Lee Sutton.*

9½" bisque, Linda Lee Sutton's "Travel Angel," #1 of an open series Sept., 1998, painted features, wire armature upper arms, bisque lower arms/bare feet, cloth body, white mohair wig, cloth wings, antique fabrics, $175.00. *Courtesy Linda Lee Sutton.*

18" porcelain, Linda Lee Sutton's "Wounded Bear," long dark braided hair, large brown paper-weight eyes, closed mouth, cloth body, sitting on a handmade drum, holding his hand-painted animal rock, medicine pouch in leather suede, arrowhead, royal purple and red Indian costume, limited edition of 10, circa 2000, $625.00. *Courtesy Linda Lee Sutton.*

12" polymer clay, "Annabelle – Kickin' Back," by Susan Ware, hand sculpted, one-of-a-kind, lovely old Grandma, hair is hand implanted into the clay strand by strand, a process that took 35 hours alone, handmade clothing includes a hand crocheted shawl, old-fashioned cotton stockings that wrinkle around her ankles, sitting in a wooden chair with a wicker basket filled with flowers beside her, circa 2000, $600.00. *Courtesy Susan Ware.*

10" polymer clay "Nicki," by Susan Ware, hand sculpted, one-of-a-kind, Eskimo toddler, brown hair, genuine muskrat and black mink fur parka, ultra suede pants and boots with otter fur trim, on white base, circa 2000, $299.00. *Courtesy Susan Ware.*

28" polymer clay, "Mikasi," by Susan Ware, hand sculpted, one-of-a-kind, old, weathered Eskimo man, gray hair, genuine muskrat and black mink fur parka, otter fur boots, on white base, circa 2000, $450.00. *Courtesy Susan Ware.*

11" cloth, R.J. Wright's "Christopher Robin and Pocket Pooh Characters," Christopher Robin has pressed felt swivel head, painted brown eyes, mohair wig, felt body, blue smock, brown shorts, suspenders, white hat, brown leather sandals; animal characters are 5" Pooh bear, 6" Eeyore, 4½" Tigger, with swivel heads, jointed shoulders/hips, and 3" Piglet, jointed shoulders, labels, RJW gold buttons, all are mint-in-box, circa 1980s, $1,300.00. *Courtesy McMasters Doll Auctions.*

Barbie Dolls

First produced by Mattel, Inc. in Hawthorne, California, Barbie doll remains the top collectible doll at the dawn of the new century and is becoming stronger and stronger as twentieth century children grow up and become avid collectors of their childhood dolls. Of interest to collectors, too, is the reflection of fashion trends as they view Barbie doll's seemingly endless wardrobe.

Marks:
1959-62: BARBIE ™/PATS. PEND.// ©MCMLVIII//by//Mattel, Inc.
1963-68: Midge ™/©1962//BARBIE®/ ©1958//BY//Mattel, Inc.
1964-66: ©1958//Mattel, Inc. //U.S. Patented//U.S. Pat. Pend.
1966-69: ©1966//Mattel, Inc.//U.S. Patented//U.S. Pat. Pend//Made in Japan

Description of the first five Barbie dolls:
Number One Barbie™ 1959
11½" heavy vinyl solid body, faded white skin color, white irises, pointed eyebrows, soft ponytail, brunette or blonde only, black and white striped bathing suit, holes with metal cylinders in balls of feet to fit round-pronged stand, gold hoop earrings.

Number Two Barbie™ 1959 – 1960
11½" heavy vinyl solid body, faded white skin color, white irises, pointed eyebrows, but no holes in feet, some with pearl earrings, soft ponytail, brunette or blonde only.

Number Three Barbie™ 1960
11½" heavy vinyl solid body, some fading in skin color, blue irises, curved eyebrows, no holes in feet, soft ponytail, brunette or blonde only.

Number Four Barbie™ 1960
11½", same as #3, but solid body of skin-toned vinyl, soft ponytail, brunette or blonde only.

Number Five Barbie™ 1961
11½", vinyl head, now less heavy doll, has hard plastic hollow body, with firmer texture Saran ponytail, and now can be redhead, has arm tag.

What to look for:
It is still possible to assemble outfits from loose wardrobe pieces and sell or trade your extras. The under 2,000 production limited edition dolls are the ones that will go up in price — or the fad doll that hits the collector's fancy, such as the Harley Davidson Barbie. Check out *Miller's Price Guide,* PO Box 8722, Spokane, WA 99203, 1-800-874-5201 (orders only), a must-have if you are a hard-core Barbie fan. This is one category that is so broad you are sure to find a niche that will keep you happy.

11½", vinyl No. One Ponytail Barbie, #850, white irises, dark eyeliner, red lips, arched eyebrows, brunette soft hair with ringlet bangs, holes in feet, heavy solid body, circa 1959, $7,100.00. *Courtesy McMasters Doll Auctions.*

11½" vinyl, No. Two Barbie, #850, brunette, soft hair, ringlet bangs, white irises, dark eyeliner, red lips, arched eyebrows, same as No. 1 but no holes in feet, MIB, circa 1959, $6,350.00. *Courtesy McMasters Doll Auctions.*

11½" vinyl, No. 3 Ponytail Barbie brunette, blue irises, red lips, gently curved eyebrows, brown eyeliner, heavy solid body, black and white swimsuit, "Barbie ™ //Pats. Pend.//© MCMLVIII//by Mattel Inc.," #850, circa 1960, $950.00. *Courtesy McMasters Doll Auctions.*

11½" vinyl, No. 4 Ponytail Barbie, brunette, blue irises, red lips, gently curved eyebrows, blue eyeliner only, black and white swimsuit, vinyl retains tan tone, marked "Barbie ™ //Pats. Pend.//© MCMLVIII//by Mattel//Inc.," circa 1960, $800.00. *Courtesy McMasters Doll Auctions.*

11½" vinyl, No. 5 Barbie Ponytail, straight leg, blue painted eyes, blue eyeshadow, nostril paint, red lips, brunette hair in original set, black and white striped one-piece strapless swimsuit, black open toe shoes, white rimmed glasses with blue lenses, pedestal stand marked T.M., circa 1961, $265.00. *Courtesy McMasters Doll Auctions.*

11½" vinyl No. 6 Ponytail Barbie, #850, brunette hair in original set with bottom curl, coral lips, nostril paint, finger paint, toe paint, straight legs, wearing red nylon one-piece swimsuit, pearl earrings, white cover Barbie/Ken/Midge booklet in cellophane bag, near mint, circa 1962, $265.00. *Courtesy McMasters Doll Auctions.*

11½" vinyl, Bubble Cut Barbie, blue irises, red lips, gently curved eyebrows, dressed in red one-piece swimsuit, circ 1962 – 1967, $225.00. *Courtesy McMasters Doll Auctions.*

11½" vinyl, Swirl Ponytail Barbie, blue irises, gently curved eyebrows, blue dress, boxed, marked "Midge ™ //© 1958//by Mattel Inc.//Patented," circa 1964 – 1965, $400.00. *Courtesy McMasters Doll Auctions.*

11½" vinyl, Bubble Cut Barbie, with blue irises, gently curved eyebrows, red head, dressed in black/white striped swimsuit, boxed #850, circa 1961, $325.00. *Courtesy McMasters Doll Auctions.*

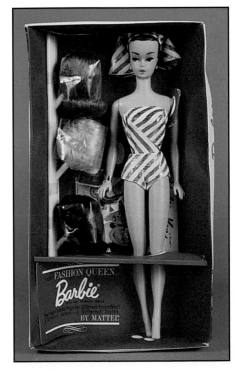

11½" vinyl, Fashion Queen Barbie, #870, molded, painted dark brown hair with a blue vinyl headband, blue irises, light pink lips, eyeshadow, wearing original gold lamé and white striped swimsuit with matching turban, pearl earrings, wrist tag, three interchangeable wigs and a white wig stand, white cover booklet, white open toe shoes in cellophane bag, black wire stand, NRFB, circa 1963, $370.00. *Courtesy McMasters Doll Auctions.*

11½" vinyl, American Girl Barbie, #1070, brunette hair, coral lips outlined in gold, finger paint, bendable legs, wearing original one-piece swimsuit, near mint, circa 1965 – 1966, $330.00. *Courtesy McMasters Doll Auctions.*

11½" vinyl, Talking Busy Barbie, blonde hair, pink lips, rooted eyelashes, wearing red shirt and matching headband, blue satin jumper with green belt, green knee-high boots, wrist tag, in stand with accessories, clear plastic stand, NRFB, circa 1972, $325.00. *Courtesy McMasters Doll Auctions.*

11½" vinyl, Quick Curl Miss America, blonde hair with plastic band and attached sliver crown, painted eyelashes, pink lips, cheek blush, bendable legs, wearing silver/white gown with attached white Miss America ribbon, red cape with fur trim, plastic scepter (one point is missing from top), white plastic hair curler, NM, circa 1973, $75.00. *Courtesy McMasters Doll Auctions.*

11½" vinyl, Sun Valley Barbie, The Sports Set, #7806, blonde hair, wearing original ski outfit with accessories, wrist tag, NRFB, circa 1973, $175.00. *Courtesy McMasters Doll Auctions.*

11½" vinyl, Living Barbie, #1116, light blonde hair with plastic covering, pink lips, cheek blush, rooted eyelashes, bendable arms, bendable legs, wearing original one-piece silver/gold swimsuit, orange net cover-up, NM, circa 1970, $185.00. *Courtesy McMasters Doll Auctions.*

11½" vinyl, Barbie Festival 1994 Banquet Set, blonde and red hair dolls with curly bangs in a replica of the #1 Barbie, wearing black/white striped swimsuits with accessories, wrist tag, Festival banner, in boxes with pink Festival sticker on back, circa 1994, $260.00. *Courtesy McMasters Doll Auctions.*

11½" vinyl, Pink Splendor Barbie, Limited Edition #16091, #00915 out of 10,000 produced, bendable legs, NRFB with cardboard shipping box, circa 1996, $265.00. *Courtesy McMasters Doll Auctions.*

11½" vinyl, Twist 'n Turn Stacey, light blonde hair, pink lips with painted teeth, rooted eyelashes, finger paint, bendable legs, wearing 1970 T'nT Stacey pink/blue floral nylon swimsuit, clear plastic stand, very good condition, circa 1970, $110.00. *Courtesy McMasters Doll Auctions.*

11½" vinyl, Snow Princess Barbie, Enchanted Seasons Collection Limited Edition #11875, bendable legs, brunette hair doll, one of 285 created for Mattel's 35th Anniversary Barbie Festival, with certificate of authenticity, festival label on upper left front box corner, NRFB, with cardboard shipping box, includes Festival Brochure, circa 1994, $265.00. *Courtesy McMasters Doll Auctions.*

11½" vinyl, Haute Couture Barbie, Red Velvet Delight, one of 480 created for Mattel's 35th Anniversary Barbie Festival, with certificate of authenticity, accessories, silver box with Festival logo on front, NRFB, circa 1994, $180.00. *Courtesy McMasters Doll Auctions.*

11½" vinyl, Midge, boxed with brochure, blonde rooted wig, blue painted eyes, freckles, closed mouth, turquoise and blue two-piece sunsuit, circa 1963, $130.00. *Courtesy Sarah Munsey.*

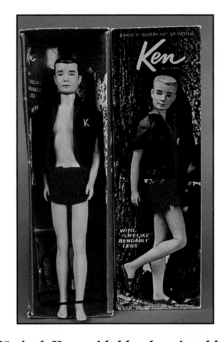

12" vinyl, Ken, with blonde painted hair, painted eyes, blue beach jacket and red cotton trunks, marked "© 1960//by//Mattel, Inc.//Hawthorn//Calif. USA." #1020, boxed, circa 1962, $75.00. *Courtesy McMasters Doll Auctions.*

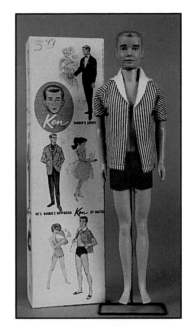

11¾" vinyl, Ken, #750, molded painted blonde hair, pink lips, straight legs, wearing red swim trunks, striped jacket, black wire stand, NMIB, circa 1963, $65.00. *Courtesy McMasters Doll Auctions.*

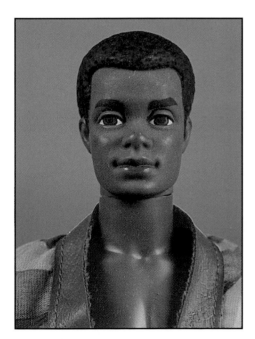

11¾" vinyl, Black Talking Brad, #1114, dark brown eyes, painted black hair, brown lips, bendable legs, dark brown skin, wearing original shirt and orange vinyl shorts, wrist tag, NM, non working, circa 1970, $70.00. *Courtesy McMasters Doll Auctions.*

12" vinyl, Allan, boxed, painted eyes, straight legs, with blue swimsuit, beach sandals, striped beach jacket, molded reddish brown hair, with brochure, #1000, circa 1964, $65.00. *Courtesy McMasters Doll Auctions.*

11½" vinyl, Yellowstone Kelley, from the Sports Set, #7808, titian hair, suntan skin, long straight red hair, bendable legs, twist waist, original outfit of red and white dotted blouse, white shoes, white knee length socks, blue and white striped shorts, matching slacks included, sleeping bag and camping gear, wrist tag, NRFB, circa 1974, $300.00. *Courtesy McMasters Doll Auctions.*

11¼" vinyl, black Francie, dark hair with red tint, pink lips, rooted eyelashes, bendable legs, wearing original swimsuit, booklet, clear plastic stand, NMIB, circa 1966, $900.00. *Courtesy McMasters Doll Auctions.*

9¼" vinyl, Skipper, blonde hair with metal headband and plastic cover, beige lips, bendable legs, wearing original one-piece swimsuit, Exclusive Fashion Book 1 booklet in cellophane bag with white plastic brush and comb, NMIB, circa 1965, $245.00. *Courtesy McMasters Doll Auctions.*

6¼" vinyl, Tutti, "Walkin' My Dolly," blonde hair in original set, pink lips, cheek blush, bendable arms and legs, wearing red and white outfit, white socks, straw hat with ribbon band, flower accents, pink and white plastic baby buggy, plastic baby with painted features, red painted hair, attached flannel blanket, lace trim, booklet, NMIB with plastic window lid, circa 1966, $215.00. *Courtesy McMasters Doll Auctions.*

King-Seeley Thermos Company, black vinyl Barbie and Francie Lunchbox, includes Barbie/Midge/Skipper thermos on black background, red cap, and attached cup with handle, beige thermos cap, dated 1965, $175.00. *Courtesy McMasters Doll Auctions.*

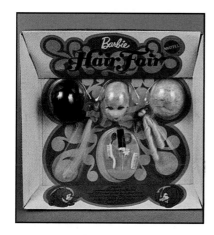

Vinyl Barbie Record Tote, blue vinyl, black plastic handles, and ten paper record holders, dated 1961, $45.00. *Courtesy McMasters Doll Auctions.*

Whitman Publishing Company, Barbie Paper Dolls, with 61 costumes and accessories, package says "no scissors necessary, clothes ready to punch out," NRFB, package date 1963, $95.00. *Courtesy McMasters Doll Auctions.*

Hair Fair Barbie Set, blonde hair doll head with pink lips, cheek blush, rooted eyelashes, brunette wig, blonde wiglet with bow accent, blonde switch with bow accent and curly swirls with blue metal barrette, fashion accessories include white plastic brush and comb, flowers, two rubber bands, metal barrettes, metal hair pins, NRFB, boxed date 1970, $105.00. *Courtesy McMasters Doll Auctions.*

Betsy McCall Dolls

Betsy McCall was a paper doll published in *McCall's* magazine for many years. About 1952 – 53, Ideal had Bernard Lipfert fashion a doll after this paper doll. This 14" Betsy McCall doll had a vinyl head, used a "P" marked Toni Body, and had a glued-on saran wig. She was marked "McCall Corp." on the head, and "Ideal Doll//P-90" on her back. She came with a McCall pattern for an apron. In 1958, American Character made an 8" hard plastic Betsy McCall, and in 1959 a 35" Betsy McCall with vinyl head and limbs and plastic body. Today Robert Tonner has new releases of this childhood favorite.

What to look for:
Vinyl Betsys should be clean, retaining color in their cheeks, and having original clothes. The large size can still be found in good condition. If you can't find an old one, try the new ones from Robert Tonner.

Ideal

14" vinyl, marked "McCall Corp®" on head, "Ideal Doll//P-90" on body, designed by Bernard Lipfert, black rooted hair, brown sleep eyes, watermelon smile, strung hard plastic Toni body, original pink dress with black flowered top, replaced shoes, circa 1952 – 1953, $160.00. *Courtesy Judie Conroy.*

14" vinyl, marked "McCall Corp®" on head, "Ideal Doll//P-90" on body, designed by Bernard Lipfert, black rooted hair, brown sleep eyes, watermelon smile, strung hard plastic Toni body, original red dress/white trim, replaced shoes, circa 1952 – 1953, $175.00. *Courtesy Judie Conroy.*

American Character

8" hard plastic, with blue sleep eyes, molded lashes, single stroke brows, painted lower lashes, closed mouth, original wig, hard plastic body with jointed knees, wears original nylon teddy, socks, and black shoes, with box, booklets, and two original boxed outfits, "On the Ice" and "Sunday Best," circa 1957, $1,050.00. *Courtesy McMasters Doll Auctions.*

8" hard plastic, marked "McCall© Corp." on mid back, glass sleep eyes, closed mouth, seven-piece body with jointed knees and rigid vinyl arms, auburn rooted Saran wig, original riding habit with brown pants, green vest, and red checked shirt, white scarf in hair, circa 1957, $200.00. *Courtesy Nelda Shelton.*

19" vinyl, marked "McCall 19©58 Corp." in a circle, with closed mouth, green sleep/flirty eyes, reddish rooted hair, wears original red and green dotted Swiss street dress, circa 1958 – 1962, $325.00. *Courtesy Cornelia Ford.*

29" vinyl, brown eyes, red rooted hair, closed mouth, all original in pink velveteen jumper, made for one year 1962, $350.00. *Courtesy Sally DeSmet.*

29" vinyl, marked "McCall 19©61 Corp." in a circle, closed mouth, brown sleep eyes, brown long straight rooted hair, wears original pink and mauve striped dress with heart button and watch pin, missing black waist ribbon, circa 1961 – 1962, $425.00. *Courtesy Cornelia Ford.*

Robert Tonner

14" vinyl, rooted brown hair, brown plastic eyes, closed smiling mouth, style #20552, "Swiss Miss," black coat with fur trimmed sleeves and hood, embroidery trim, matching black boots with fur trim, white stockings, open edition, circa 2000, $39.99 outfit only. *Courtesy Robert Tonner Doll Company.*

14" vinyl, rooted brown hair, brown plastic eyes, closed smiling mouth, style #20553, "Simply Spring," pink and yellow plaid pleated skirt, pink jacket with embroidered flowers, white shirt with buttons and lace, pink shoes, white stockings, pink ribbon in hair, open edition, circa 2000, $39.99 outfit only. *Courtesy Robert Tonner Doll Company.*

14" vinyl, "Betsy for President," two-piece red suit, short reddish brown wig, brown acrylic eyes, closed mouth, with podium, flags, and accessories, centerpiece for 2nd Betsy McCall convention, Dallas, TX, May, 2000, limited edition of 25, $200.00. *Courtesy Marilyn Ramsey.*

14" vinyl, in "Back to the Future," short brunette wig, brown acrylic eyes, souvenir doll in white vinyl and silver lamé dress, boots, matching helmet, from the 2nd Betsy McCall convention, Dallas, TX, May, 2000, limited edition of 225, tagged, $200.00. *Courtesy Marilyn Ramsey.*

14" vinyl, "Jimmy Weeks visits Roy Rogers Ranch," Betsy McCall's friend, wearing red embroidered shirt, black pants, holster and gun, leopard print underwear, a companion doll for the "Back to the Future" 2nd Betsy McCall convention, Dallas, TX, May 2000, limited edition of 225, tagged Sandy McCall, $200.00. *Courtesy Marilyn Ramsey.*

Betsy McCall Dolls

14" vinyl, rooted hair, brown plastic eyes, closed smiling mouth, style #20550, "Sweet Dreams," pink print long sleeve nightgown with lace and ruffles, rag doll with yellow yarn hair wearing matching pink print nightgown, open edition, circa 2000, $39.99 outfit only. *Courtesy Robert Tonner Doll Company.*

14" vinyl, rooted long blonde hair, brown plastic eyes, closed smiling mouth, style #20551, "Perfect 10," blue skating outfit with net ruffles, blue tights, white skates, white headband, open edition, circa 2000, $39.99 outfit only. *Courtesy Robert Tonner Doll Company.*

14" vinyl, rooted long auburn hair, brown plastic eyes, closed smiling mouth, style #20503, "Irish Dancing," long sleeved rose colored dress with lilac pleats, heavy embroidery, lace collar, white socks, black shoes, marked "Betsy McCall//by//Robert Tonner//©Gruner & Jahr USA PUB," open edition, circa 2000, $89.99. *Courtesy Robert Tonner Doll Company.*

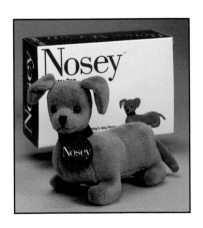

14" vinyl, rooted brown hair, brown plastic eyes, closed smiling mouth, style #20504, "Red Riding Hood," red cape with embroidery and red and white plaid on inside, multi-colored plaid skirt, yellow vest with embroidery, white shirt, lace petticoat, white stockings, black shoes, carrying basket, marked "Betsy McCall//by//Robert Tonner//©Gruner & Jahr USA PUB," limited to 1000, circa 2000, $99.99. *Courtesy Robert Tonner Doll Company.*

6" cloth, "Nosey," Betsy's plush stuffed dachshund dog, circa 1998, $18.00. *Courtesy Robert Tonner Doll Company.*

14" vinyl, rooted brown braided hair, brown plastic eyes, closed smiling mouth, style #20501, Indian dress with beads and belt, fringe, matching moccasins with beads, marked "Betsy McCall//by//Robert Tonner//©Gruner & Jahr USA PUB," limited to 1,000, circa 2000, $99.99. *Courtesy Robert Tonner Doll Company.*

14" vinyl, rooted brown hair, brown plastic eyes, closed smiling mouth, style #20502, "Travel Time Betsy," gray pleated skirt, navy jacket, white shirt, matching tam, white stockings, black shoes, carrying scrap book, marked "Betsy McCall//by//Robert Tonner//©Gruner & Jahr USA PUB," open edition, circa 2000, $89.99. *Courtesy Robert Tonner Doll Company.*

14" vinyl, rooted brown hair, brown plastic eyes, closed smiling mouth, style #20500, blue denim jumper with name in red embroidery, red and white striped shirt, white socks and shoes, marked "Betsy McCall//by//Robert Tonner//©Gruner & Jahr USA PUB," open edition, circa 2000, $79.99. *Courtesy Robert Tonner Doll Company.*

10" vinyl, "Linda McCall," little cousin to Betsy McCall, rooted blonde hair, blue plastic eyes, closed smiling mouth, style #20573, "Party Dress Linda," pink flowered dress, puff sleeves, ruffle, dark pink sash, ring of roses in hair, dark pink one-strap shoes, white stockings, circa 2000, $35.00 costume only. *Courtesy Robert Tonner Doll Company.*

14" vinyl, rooted brown hair, brown plastic eyes, closed smiling mouth, wearing "Bee Charmer," style #20506, limited to 500, carrying beehive, straw hat with netting, blue dress with multi-colored print pinafore, brown one-strap shoes, white socks, circa 2000, $99.99. *Courtesy Robert Tonner Doll Company.*

14" vinyl, "Betsy, Sandy & Nosey Travel Time Gift Set," rooted brown hair, brown plastic eyes, closed smiling mouths, style #20507, Betsy McCall has gray pleated skirt, navy jacket, white shirt, matching tam, white stockings, black shoes; Sandy wears matching clothes, but with gray short pants; Nosey in matching navy blue outfit and tam, marked "Betsy McCall//by//Robert Tonner//©Gruner & Jahr USA PUB," open edition, circa 2000, $189.99 set. *Courtesy Robert Tonner Doll Company.*

14" vinyl, "Barbara McCall," rooted long curly blonde hair, blue plastic eyes, closed smiling mouth, style #20511, blue dotted Swiss dress with puffed sleeves, white pinafore with flower embroidery, white stockings and shoes, limited edition of 1000, circa 2000, $89.99. *Courtesy Robert Tonner Doll Company.*

14" vinyl, "Barbara McCall," rooted long blonde hair, blue plastic eyes, closed smiling mouth, style #20515, blue jacket, red and white shorts, white T-shirt with "Barbara" in red, white socks and shoes, open edition, circa 2000, $74.99. *Courtesy Robert Tonner Doll Company.*

14" vinyl, "Drew," Betsy McCall's school chum, rooted dark brown curly hair, brown plastic eyes, closed smiling mouth, style #20526, blue denim skirt, white T-shirt with name on front, red and white plaid shirt, red ribbon in hair, white shoes and socks, circa 2000, $69.99. *Courtesy Robert Tonner Doll Company.*

10" vinyl, "Linda McCall," advertised as little cousin to Betsy McCall, rooted blonde hair, blue plastic eyes, closed smiling mouth, style #20574, "Raincoat Linda," red plastic raincoat with black cuffs and collar, matching hat and boots, black plaid skirt, white shirt, open edition, circa 2000, $35.00 costume only. *Courtesy Robert Tonner Doll Company.*

10" vinyl, "Linda McCall," little cousin to Betsy McCall, rooted blonde hair, blue plastic eyes, closed smiling mouth, style #20572, "Bunny Slippers Linda," pink print pajamas, pink terry cloth robe with belt, fluffy bunny slippers, pink ribbon in hair, open edition, circa 2000, $35.00 costume only. *Courtesy Robert Tonner Doll Company.*

8" vinyl, souvenir from Chicago's UFDC dinner "Betsy Travels to Windy City," rooted hair, plastic sleep eyes, real lashes, painted lashes below, closed smiling mouth, rigid vinyl body, red jacket, dress with red and black plaid skirt, black top with red apple appliquéd on front, white collar, limited edition of 500, circa 2000, $225.00. *Private collection.*

10" vinyl, "Linda McCall," little cousin to Betsy McCall, rooted blonde hair, blue plastic eyes, closed smiling mouth, red and white striped dress with pockets and buttons, navy blue ribbon in hair, white socks and shoes, open edition, circa 2000, $69.99. *Courtesy Robert Tonner Doll Company.*

10" vinyl, "Linda McCall," little cousin to Betsy McCall, rooted blonde hair, blue plastic eyes, closed smiling mouth, style #20516, "Travel Time Linda," red plaid dress with white collar, blue beret with red plaid bow, black shoes, white stockings, open edition, circa 2000, $79.99. *Courtesy Robert Tonner Doll Company.*

14" vinyl, "Sandy McCall," rooted brown hair, blue plastic eyes, closed smiling mouth, style #20525, blue T-shirt with red collar and cuffs, "Sandy" embroidered in red on shirt, blue jeans, white shoes, circa 2000, $69.99. *Courtesy Robert Tonner Doll Company.*

8" vinyl, "Merry & Kerry McCall," twin baby sister and brother to Betsy McCall; Merry has blue plastic eyes and blonde hair, Kerry has brown plastic eyes and strawberry blonde hair, both dressed in red and white striped shirts, Merry in blue denim jumper and Kerry in matching denim overall shorts, white socks and shoes, circa 2000, $39.99 each. *Courtesy Robert Tonner Doll Company.*

Black Dolls

A great collectible category is black dolls. Because fewer were made, black dolls almost always place over white dolls in competition. Fewer of these survived their owners' childhoods and finding one in mint condition is difficult. These come in many different mediums, offering a wide range of collecting possibilities in cloth, composition, hard plastic, porcelain, rubber, and vinyl.

What to look for:

Condition is still the number one factor in great collectible dolls. From a Leo Moss papier-mache/composition to a modern vinyl one, black dolls can be an intriguing part of your collection. Almost any out-of-production black doll mint in the box will remain a good collectible and may also increase in value. Check for marks to find those Shindana dolls — these included the infamous O.J. Simpson as well as other celebrities. Do not overlook black dolls at garage sales, flea markets, and other sales.

Golliwogs, circa early 1900s to present

Florence Kate Upton, born 1873 in Flushing, New York, to English immigrant parents, was a struggling young artist who tried illustrating to finance her art studies. Her first book, *The Adventures of Two Dutch Dolls and a Golliwogg,* was first published in England. Florence did the simple illustrations and her mother Bertha Upton created a poem to tell the story of the illustrations. The characters were two "Dutch" German (Deutsch) wooden dolls named Peg and Sarah Jane who live in a toyshop. During the night when the shop is closed, the dolls come alive and make themselves a dress out of an American flag, Peg in red and white stripes and Sarah Jane in blue with white stars. During the evening they meet a congenial black character with fuzzy hair wearing a blue jacket and red trousers who announces that he is "The Golliwogg," spelled with two "g's." Florence wrote 12 books about these characters, but retained no copyright and like the teddy bear, they soon were widely copied.

The story and Golliwog character became a staple in England, but did not receive the same warm reception in the U.S. as it may have been perceived as a desecration of the American flag. With the passage of time and perhaps to avoid copyright infringements, the Golliwog spelling dropped the last "g." Even later in the 1960s, when "wog" was used as a racial slur in Europe, the name was shortened to Golli or Golly. With racial tension in the U. S. during this period, a black doll with fuzzy hair was not politically correct. After 100 years have passed since the introduction of the Golliwog character, interest has been revived with collectors — even if it is no longer the staple with English children.

Deans, Hermman, Merrythought, and Steiff are just some of the well-known companies that made Gollies during the early 1900s. In addition, home sewers could create their own rendition from commercial patterns. Robertson's, who produced jam in England, took the Golly image as their logo and has used it continually, producing a series of pins and other memorabilia. The pins, or brooches as they are also called, can be a collecting field in itself. Gollies remain a charming collectible and can be found at several sites on the Internet including the International Golliwog Collector's Club and Golliwogs.com — just type "Golliwog" into your search engine.

Black Dolls

Shindana, 1968 – 1983, Los Angeles, California

After the Watts riots in Los Angeles, Shindana Toys was formed in 1968, the first major manufacturer of black dolls with ethnically correct features, of high quality, covering a wide selection of babies, children, and adults. Shindana was a division of Bootstrap Inc., a non-profit black community organization founded by Lou Smith and Robert Hall. Its motto was "Learn Baby, Learn!" and the company presented positive images of black children. It ceased production in 1983 and because of the short 15-year span of operation, only a few of these dolls are still available. Dolls may be marked "Div. Of//Operation Bootstrap, Inc, USA//©1968 Shindana" or have other Shindana marks.

Golliwog

13" cloth, Dean's Rag, tagged "Dean's Gwentoy Group//Rye-Pontejpool" in mid back seam, sewn-on black synthetic hair, red pants, yellow vest, black shoes with white spats form the body of the doll, removable blue felt jacket, with Robertson's Premium Golly Jar marked "50 GOLDEN YEARS//1930 – 1980//Robertson's Golly," jam jar marked "Golliberry Bramble Seedless," and Golly tokens, circa 1978, jar and Golly, $60.00, tokens, $6.00 each. *Courtesy Ginger Reid.*

14" cloth, Australian sheepskin, made in Ballarat, Australia, button eyes, plush body, felt mouth and nose, circa 1999, $150.00. *Courtesy Ginger Reid.*

20½" plush cloth, English, plastic disk googly eyes, red felt mouth, straw stuffed, circa 1950s, $60.00. *Courtesy Ginger Reid.*

10" cloth, knitted, felt features, arms knitted into jacket, made by Mrs. Thomas in 1940, $75.00. *Courtesy Ginger Reid.*

33½" plush cloth, possibly Robertson's, tagged "Made in Korea," felt features, all plush, red plush pants, blue jacket, yellow vest, and white shirt all make up body, circa 1950s, $125.00. *Courtesy Ginger Reid.*

21" felt, button eyes, glued-on felt features, yarn hair, navy blue cloth jacket, short cloth red and white striped pants, hand crafted, circa 1980s, $70.00. *Courtesy Ginger Reid.*

15½" cloth, knitted, hand crafted in Christie's Beach, Australia, button eyes, stitched on features, stuffed knitted nose, knitted body, circa 1999, $65.00. *Courtesy Ginger Reid.*

20½" cloth, glued-on felt features, cotton clothes, velvet jacket, home crafted, circa 1950s, $70.00. *Courtesy Ginger Reid.*

32" cloth, tagged "Made in Australia," glued-on felt features, green corduroy sewn-on trousers, red jacket, circa 1950s, $150.00. *Courtesy Ginger Reid.*

19" plush cloth, purchased in Australia, glued-on felt features, all plush, red plush pants, blue jacket, white vest all make up body, circa 1950s, $75.00. *Courtesy Ginger Reid.*

7½" cloth, made in China for Teddy & Friends, button eyes, felt mouth, removable cloth clothes, circa 1999, $15.00. *Courtesy Ginger Reid.*

12" cloth, knitted, glued-on felt features, legs in one piece stitched down center to form legs, all home crafted, circa 1980, $35.00. *Courtesy Ginger Reid.*

20" plush cloth, commercially made in England, no tag, button eyes, felt mouth, plush face, body, feet, blue and white striped cloth pants, circa 1970s, $50.00. *Courtesy Ginger Reid.*

27" cloth, hand-crafted, boy and girl, plastic eyes, felt mouths, removable clothes, girl in red print dress with white lace trim, boy in red jacket and red and black plaid pants, very well made, circa late 1990s, $95.00 each. *Courtesy Ginger Reid.*

16" cloth, Dean's Rag, tagged "Made in GB," button eyes, felt mouth, navy blue jacket, red pants, yellow vest, white hands, black and white feet, circa 1950s, $150.00. *Courtesy Ginger Reid.*

9" cloth, by Maggie Booth from Australia, button eyes, felt features, red felt jacket, blue felt pants, limited edition of 4, certificate, circa 1998, $60.00. *Courtesy Ginger Reid.*

Shindana

15" vinyl, "Kim Jeans 'n things," with painted eyes, closed mouth, long black hair, jointed vinyl body, wears blue jumpsuit, red striped knit dickey and cap, "©1969//Shindan Toys//Division of Operation Bootstrap USA," circa 1975, $75.00. *Courtesy Cornelia Ford.*

13" cloth black lady, embroidered features, short legs, excelsior stuffed body, old green dress and matching turban, lots of beads, large torso compared to lower body, made to sit, from head to end of dress is 24", circa 1960s – 1970s, $285.00. *Courtesy Fran Fabian.*

14" cloth, primitive black lady, body is a clear glass milk bottle, white button eyes, red dress and turban, circa 1930s, $65.00. *Courtesy Olivina Mata.*

16" Armand Marseille composition toddler, mold 518 with open mouth, sleep eyes, molded ears, one-stroke painted eyebrows, molded and lightly painted hair, in red sweater with white trim around neck, circa 1938, $195.00. *Courtesy McMasters Doll Auctions.*

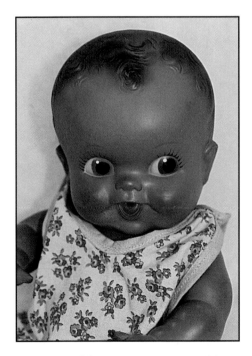

10" rubber, Sun Rubber "Amosandra," designed by Ruth E. Newton, for Columbia Broadcasting Systems, painted side-glancing brown eyes, open mouth for bottle, bent limb baby body, circa 1949 – 1950, $50.00. *Courtesy Charlene Gilmore.*

20" vinyl, Beatrice Wright black child, marked "9//B. Wright" on neck, black rooted hair, brown sleep eyes, closed mouth, jointed rigid vinyl body, green shirt trimmed with stripes, matching striped pants, circa 1967, $30.00. *Courtesy Judi Domm.*

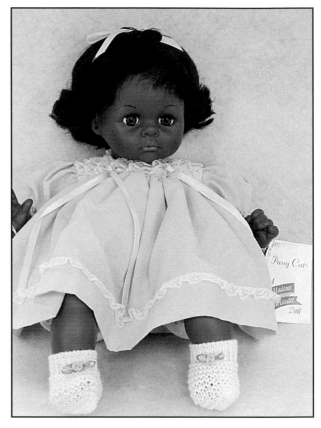

11" vinyl, Vogue "Black Li'l Imp," marked "1964 ©//Vogue//Dolls," black synthetic hair, brown sleep eyes, closed mouth, white dress with green polka dots and ribbon, matching green ribbon in hair, tagged, with box, circa 1964, $100.00. *Courtesy Ana-Lisa Cervantez.*

20" vinyl, Madame Alexander "Pussy Cat," brown sleep eyes, rooted hair, closed pouty mouth, tagged "Alexander 19©77," made circa 1977 – 1983, all original with box, $175.00. *Courtesy Janet Hill.*

Cameo Dolls

Joseph L. Kallus's company operated from 1922 to 1930 in New York City and Port Allegheny, Pensylvania. They made composition dolls with segmented wood or cloth bodies as well as all composition ones.

What to look for:

Seek out composition with little crazing, no cracks, no peeling paint, good cheek color, original costumes that are tagged; costumes should not be faded or soiled. When looking for vinyl, look for clean dolls with good color, and costumes that are clean and bright. Wood segmented dolls are a great collectible and are sometimes overlooked by collectors focusing on better-known dolls.

12" composition, "Giggles," with molded loop for ribbon on back of molded hair, side-glancing painted eyes, closed smiling mouth, no marks, redressed, circa 1946, $200.00. *Courtesy Elizabeth Surber.*

Celebrity Dolls

Celebrity dolls must represent real people, someone who lived — they cannot be a literary, comic or cartoon character. A celebrity doll may also be a person who plays a fictional character on television, in the movies or in a play.

Dorothy of the Wizard of Oz fame could not be a celebrity doll, but Judy Garland portraying the Dorothy character is regarded as a celebrity doll.

This is an exciting, fun, and interesting category of collecting. Shirley Temple dolls are so collectible and so famous, they usually have their own category. The same is true for the Dionne Quints. Avid Quint and Shirley fans usually collect all sorts of accessories, ephemera, and related memorabilia as well as the dolls. You might collect just television or movie celebrities, athletes, African Americans, or whoever catches your fancy.

What to look for:

Condition and originality greatly influence the collecting status of these dolls as well as associated boxes, labels, brochures, and other paper products. Look for clean dolls with original tagged or labeled costumes, good color, and related items that enhance the collector's knowledge of the doll.

Alphabetically by Celebrity

7" ceramic, Car Mascots, Inc., "Beatles," box marked "The Bobb'n Head Beatles," molded painted features, in blue suits with instruments, signatures on base, circa 1964, a similar set did not make reserve of $1,100.00 at a recent auction. *Private collection.*

19" hard plastic, International Doll Co. "Betty Grable," sleep eyes, closed mouth, blonde Dynel hair, musical, tagged dress by Mollye's, circa 1940s, $400.00+. *Courtesy Martha Sweeney.*

14" vinyl, Christy Lane, country-Western gospel singer, marked "Christy Lane" on back, painted features, smiling mouth with painted teeth, auburn wig, white ruffled blouse, long red skirt, 1965 – 1970s, $25.00. *Courtesy Betty Strong.*

14" cloth, Dorothy Lamour, marked "Autographed Movie Star Dolls//Dorothy Lamour//Popular Paramount//Motion Picture Star//Made in California by//Film Star Creations Inc.//of Hollywood" on hang tag, printed blue eyes, nose, open/closed smiling mouth, shading on face, mohair wig with pink flower on side, cloth body jointed at hips only, mitten hands, original pale blue bathing suit with red/white flowers, plastic flower at waist, circa 1940s – 1950s, $135.00. *Courtesy McMasters Doll Auctions.*

20" vinyl, World Doll, Ginger Rogers, blonde rooted hair, blue painted eyes, eyeshadow, painted lashes, open/closed smiling mouth with painted teeth, jointed vinyl body, in pink evening dress, box reads "World//Doll/Presents//Ginger Rogers//from the// Barkley's of Broadway//Sixth Edition In the Celebrity Collection//Edition Limit 17,500//Features Poseable Head//Beveled Swivel Waist//Designed and Produced in America by World Doll," MIB, circa 1976, $100.00. *Courtesy Tom Morris.*

11½" vinyl, Mattel, Twist 'n Turn Julia, red tinted hair, pink lips, cheek blush, rooted eyelashes, bendable legs, wearing white nurse's uniform with attached metal pin and button accents, white panties, white cap with black trim attached to head, white high top shoes, wrist tag, from the T.V. show "Julia," as portrayed by actress Diahann Carroll, NM, circa 1969, $105.00. *Courtesy McMasters Doll Auctions.*

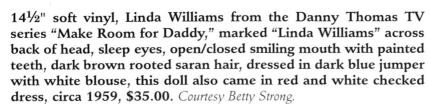

14½" soft vinyl, Linda Williams from the Danny Thomas TV series "Make Room for Daddy," marked "Linda Williams" across back of head, sleep eyes, open/closed smiling mouth with painted teeth, dark brown rooted saran hair, dressed in dark blue jumper with white blouse, this doll also came in red and white checked dress, circa 1959, $35.00. *Courtesy Betty Strong.*

30" vinyl, Mattel, Marie Osmond, a "Modeling Doll" marked "Osbro Productions//1976//USA" on head and neck, brown painted eyes with eyeshadow, smiling mouth with painted teeth, dark brown rooted hair, fully-jointed rigid vinyl body, bra and panties are molded into the body construction, pink formal and feather boa, fashion-type body, No. 9826, circa 1976, $35.00. *Courtesy Betty Strong.*

14" papier-mache over cloth, Dean's Rag Book, "Princess Margaret," marked "Made in England by Dean's Rag Book Co. Ltd.//London" on label on bottom of right shoe, swivel head, painted brown eyes, painted upper lashes, closed mouth, original mohair wig, cloth body jointed at shoulders and hips, stitched fingers, white lace-edged socks as part of lower legs, original green felt coat, matching hat, shoes, white dress or slip, unplayed-with condition, circa 1920s, $340.00. *Courtesy McMasters Doll Auctions.*

11¼" vinyl, Mattel, Twiggy, blonde hair with plastic band, rooted eyelashes, pink lips, painted teeth, bendable legs, twist waist, wearing original striped knit dress, yellow boots, wrist tag, copied from the well-known English model Twiggy, NMIB with cellophane, circa 1967, $325.00. *Courtesy McMasters Doll Auctions.*

Five 11" – 12" composition, Schoen & Yondorf dolls representing "Our Gang," the Hal Roach juvenile movie stars from the 1920s Our Gang features include Mary, Farina, Fatty, Freckles, and Jackie, five in a box distributed by Borgfeldt and Charles William, painted eyes and features, Mary and Jackie have mohair wigs, Farina has molded painted hair, others have painted hair, cloth bodies, compo hands, wind-up metal mechanism in torso

to make them dance, circa 1925 – 1930, $580.00. *Courtesy McMasters Doll Auctions.*

Chalkware Dolls

Carnival chalkware production started in the early 1900s in the United States and really isn't chalk at all, but plaster of Paris. Chalk is a soft limestone while plaster of Paris is calcined gypsum or burned limestone that sets up hard with the addition of water. Carnival dolls emerged after the big Columbia Exposition in Chicago in 1893. There may be a link between chalkware and Pennsylvania chalkware, a gaudy pottery made almost 100 years earlier. The Pennsylvania Dutch word for lime is "kalk." With the popularity of Rose O'Neill's Kewpie figures, carnival dolls were frequent give-aways and production costs were cut with the advent of the use of the airbrush for painting.

Carnival dolls are not dolls at all as we normally think of children's jointed play dolls, but correctly called figurines with only a few having jointed arms. Early chalkware dolls had a pink tint until the mid 1920s, and some have mohair wigs and crepe paper dresses. At first glance, collectors may find these figures too garish to suit their taste, but after looking at a number of them, this interesting part of Americana of the twentieth century can be quite intriguing.

Because they are easily broken and not highly valued, many of them have been discarded. Some have been copywritten by J.Y. Jenkins (June Yates Jenkins of Venice, California) 1923 – 1950, William Rainwater (Seattle, Washington) 1925+, and J. T. Gittins.

Carnival dolls were usually given as prizes for games, and many have added glitter and feathers. Thomas G. Morris of Medford, Oregon has published two volumes on *The Carnival Chalk Prize* with photos identifying many of the dolls.

What to look for and where:

Many chalkware dolls are politically incorrect, so figures such as Ku Klux Klan and black characters may be quite rare. Early dolls with wigs or clothing are desirable. The quality of these objects really has a huge range — some are well done and some are quite garish. The challenge is to find those items which are well painted with an appealing overall quality. You can run the gamut and find something to suit everyone's taste, from Shirley Temple look-alikes to the early vamps. Look for them at garage sales and flea markets, junk shops, and on the Internet. On an average day, your online search can find 10 chalkware dolls out of over 1,000 chalkware items on eBay. These make a fun collectible and are a fascinating category.

9" chalkware seated girl, auburn mohair wig, dark painted eyes, painted lashes, rosy cheeks, in green outfit with yellow polka dots, circa 1920s, $95.00. *Courtesy Tom Morris.*

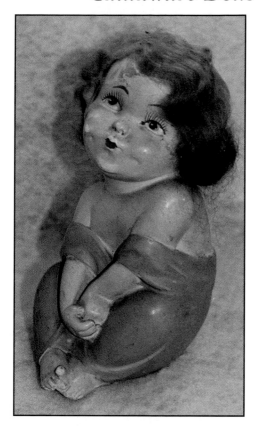

9" seated girl with hands under chin, dark mohair wig with hair net, dark painted eyes, in orange outfit with black dots, seated on dark orange pillow, circa 1920s, $95.00. *Courtesy Tom Morris.*

13" vamp, Sheba, mohair tufts, painted side-glancing eyes, painted upper lashes, rosy cheeks, green off-the-shoulder dress with blue flowers and matching hat, on black base, circa 1920s, $145.00. *Courtesy Tom Morris.*

6½" seated girl, mohair wig, molded painted blue eyes looking up, pursed lips, dimples, molded painted gray dress falling off shoulders, hands clenched and bare feet crossed, circa 1917, $175.00. *Courtesy Tom Morris.*

10½" carnival doll seated in yellow flower, dark wig, large painted dark eyes, painted lashes, hair net, red outfit trimmed in silver, and red strap shoes, circa 1920s, $195.00. *Courtesy Tom Morris.*

Chalkware Dolls

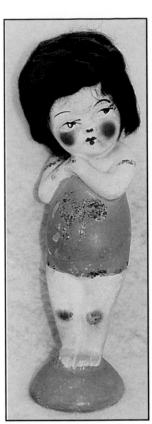

11½" flapper, blonde wig, large painted blue eyes, black painted lashes, rosy cheeks, blue base, pink crepe paper dress with matching ribbon in hair, circa 1920s, $180.00. *Courtesy Tom Morris.*

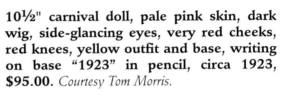

10½" carnival doll, pale pink skin, dark wig, side-glancing eyes, very red cheeks, red knees, yellow outfit and base, writing on base "1923" in pencil, circa 1923, $95.00. *Courtesy Tom Morris.*

13" carnival doll, very white chalkware, dark hair, very large blue painted eyes, black lashes, rosy cheeks, beaded hat, gold dress, green base marked "Portland, Miss," circa 1930s, $220.00. *Courtesy Tom Morris.*

13" Betty Boop type carnival doll, blonde mohair wig with gold band, blue painted side-glancing eyes, painted lashes, rosy cheeks, composition jointed arms, painted toenails, wearing pink and white crepe paper dress, on gold base, circa 1930s, $145.00. *Courtesy Tom Morris.*

13½" carnival doll lamp, painted blue side-glancing eyes, rosy cheeks, long eyelashes on bottom, eyeshadow, blonde mohair wig, all chalkware body with original bulb, jointed Kewpie-type arms, circa 1920s, $195.00. *Private collection.*

15" carnival Kewpie doll lamp (19" to top of shade), painted blue side-glancing eyes, painted eyelashes, rosy cheeks, closed painted smiling mouth, red nostrils, black horsehair wig, jointed at shoulders, black lace dress, black shade with bead fringe, circa 1920s, $350.00. *Courtesy Tom Morris.*

11¼" Multi Plastics, "Miss Victory," marked "Miss Victory" on front of base, "©//1942//The Multi Plastics//Chicago" on back of base, molded painted red hair with molded painted blue Navy cap and work outfit, painted brown eyes, eye shadow, thin painted eyebrows, standing at attention with hands held behind back, legs apart, circa 1942, $95.00. *Courtesy Tom Morris.*

9" military girl, molded painted blonde hair/blue and white military cap, heavily painted black side-glancing eyes with heavy eyeshadow, molded painted white outfit with pink, blue tie, yellow shoes, no paint on back, circa 1940s, $50.00. *Courtesy Tom Morris.*

9½" chalkware J. Y. Jenkins military carnival doll, marked "1946//copyright//J Y Jenkins" on base, molded painted brown hair with brown cap, side-glancing eyes, heavy painted upper lashes, rosy cheeks, brown military uniform, circa 1946, $60.00. *Courtesy Tom Morris.*

12½" military girl, molded painted blonde hair with white military cap, heavily painted black eyes with heavy upper lashes, blue eyeshadow, molded painted green jacket and white skirt, no paint on back, circa 1940s, $85.00. *Courtesy Tom Morris.*

13" J.Y. Jenkins military carnival doll, marked "U.S. Navy" on cap, "Copyrighted//1943//by J.Y. Jenkins," molded painted blonde hair, heavy black shadow around side-glancing eyes, blue eye-shadow above, white Navy cap, blue jacket, circa 1943, $145.00. *Courtesy Tom Morris.*

9½" J.Y. Jenkins military carnival doll, marked "U.S. Navy" on cap, "Copyrighted//1944//by J.Y. Jenkins," molded painted blonde hair, heavy black shadow and eyelashes around side-glancing eyes, blue eye-shadow above, rosy cheeks, white Navy cap, blue jacket, circa 1944, $110.00. *Courtesy Tom Morris.*

Cloth Dolls

Cloth dolls have recently gained immensely in popularity. Because the doll is made of cloth, children have always favored them for their soft, cuddly appearance. This category again presents a wide variety for the collector and while prices have skyrocketed in the past 10 years, there are still good buys to be found in some of the lesser known dolls collectors have overlooked in their pursuit of more well-known examples.

What to look for:

Clean dolls with high color on the cheeks, not soiled, ripped or torn, with original labels, tags, brochures, or boxes. A worn, dirty doll will retain little value, so the buyer should consider again that main factor, the condition, before purchasing. Do not pay huge prices for dolls that have rips, soil, fading or other flaws — even if you do love it.

Alphabetically by Manufacturer

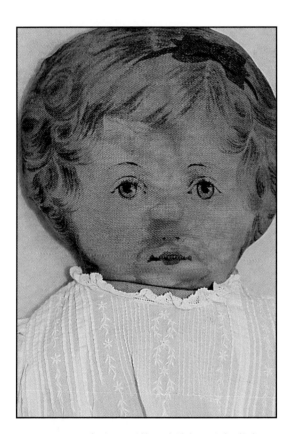

27" Art Fabric Mills child, with lithographed features, printed underwear, soiled, circa 1900s, $130.00. *Courtesy Debbie Crume.*

17" Erna Ahrens Puppe, tagged "Erna//Ahrens//Puppe//Gesetzl Geschutzt," oil painted mask face, painted hair, blue eyes, closed mouth, brown shorts and matching jacket, beige socks to knees, black shoes, circa 1920s, $195.00. *Courtesy Joan Sickler.*

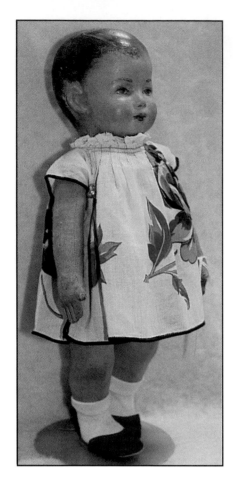

13½" Bing child, molded face, seamed head, painted brown eyes, closed mouth, painted hair, disk jointed sawdust filled body, stitched fingers and toes, white dress with big blue flowers, white socks, red slippers, circa 1921 – 1932, $485.00. *Courtesy Betty Warder.*

13" Chad Valley child, blonde mohair wig, painted side-glancing blue eyes, mask face, closed mouth, all velvet type cloth body, blue and white flower print dress with matching hat, blue felt shoes, circa 1930+, $325.00. *Courtesy June Allgeier.*

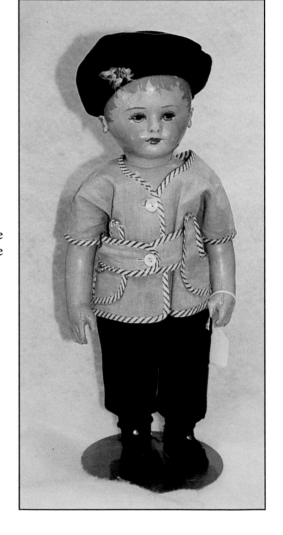

17" Martha Chase boy, painted hair and features, blue eyes, closed mouth, applied ears, in wool pants, light blue shirt, black hat, circa 1889+, $650.00. *Courtesy Betty Warder.*

17" Dutch girl, designed by Maud Tousey Fangel for Georgene Averill, printed features on stuffed cloth body, yellow painted hair with yellow yarn hair at bottom, wooden shoes, circa 1930s, $650.00. *Courtesy Joan Sickler.*

13" Georgene Averill doll, tagged "Spain//5095//Genuine//Georgene Doll," black hair, painted blue side-glancing eyes, closed mouth, in red, yellow, and black Spanish costume, circa 1930s – 1940s, $50.00. *Courtesy Jeanette Ortlieb.*

21" Hol-le Toy Co. Eloise, a literary character, from a book by Kay Thompson about a little girl who lived at NY Plaza Hotel; tagged "Eloise©//© Eloise, Ltd.//Hol-le Toy Co.//NY//10//NY," painted features, rosy cheeks, yellow yarn hair, red bow on top of head, stuffed cloth body, original tagged blue skirt and white blouse, black oilcloth shoes, box says "ELOISE DOLL//Style 60/22E//Presented to Mfg. By Hol-Le Toy Co.//New York 10 NY," MIB, circa 1955 – 1958+, $750.00. *Courtesy Elizabeth Surber.*

19" cloth Junel, with blue painted side-glancing eyes, thickly painted brown lashes, red dots at nostrils, closed mouth, rosy cheeks, with blonde yarn hair, original pink flower print dress and matching bonnet, MIB, circa 1920s – 1930s, $275.00. *Courtesy Kay Walimaa.*

17" Babyland Rag Buster Brown, E.I. Horsman, face lithographed on flesh colored sateen, blue eyes, blonde wig, cloth body, red knickers suit, white collar and cuffs, black tam, black stockings, lace shoes, circa 1904 – 1920, $550.00. *Courtesy Betty Warder.*

14" Richard Krueger Cuddle Kewpie, tagged "Kewpie//U.S. Pat. Off.//Rose O'Neill//Krueger N.Y.//U.S. Pat. Off//Made in USA," painted mask face with side-glancing eyes, red cloth body and head, topknot, and wings, circa 1931 – 1932, $200.00. *Courtesy Suzanne Prince.*

10½" Margaret Steiff French Soldier, painted hair, center seam in face, blue eyes, painted mustache, applied ears, no Steiff button, in soldier uniform with blue jacket, red cap and pants, black boots, all original, circa 1912 – 1917, $1,700.00. *Courtesy Lisa Vought.*

21" Russian Tea Cozy, stockinet head and hands, painted side-glancing eyes, mischievous smile, padded skirt to accommodate a teapot, flower print dress with white apron, cloth kerchief on her head, handmade, circa 1920s – 1930s, $275.00. *Courtesy Chan Jeschien.*

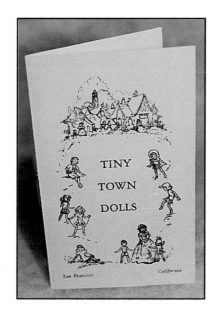

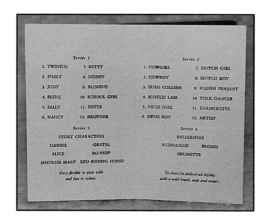

4" thread-wrapped Tiny Town Doll, red wig, painted features, pink thread-wrapped arms and legs, pink dress with blue trim, painted metal feet, in box that says "Tiny Town Dolls//San Francisco, California," circa 1940s, $25.00 – $75.00. *Courtesy Barbara Hull.*

17" unmarked girl, painted silk face, painted side-glancing eyes, jointed all-cloth body, orange satin dress and bonnet, circa 1920s, $95.00. *Private collection.*

3½" unmarked German miniature nursery rhyme characters Hansel and Gretel and 5½" Witch, felt-over-wire armature, painted features, embroidery floss hair, circa 1950s, $60.00/set. *Courtesy Pauline Flesher.*

4¾" unmarked German miniature Chimney Sweep, felt-over-wire armature, painted features, embroidery floss hair, black felt pants and top, black shoes, black top hat, circa 1950s, $35.00. *Courtesy Pauline Flesher.*

20½" unmarked boy, old lithographed doll with painted features, blue eyes, painted open/closed smiling mouth with teeth, brown coat and hat, extra wardrobe, circa 1920s – 1930s, $225.00. *Courtesy Amanda Hash.*

10" unmarked doll in suitcase with yellow yarn hair, painted blue eyes, black eyelashes, painted "O" shaped mouth with additional wardrobe of two dresses (one dimity), and pink seersucker pajamas, circa 1940s, $250.00. *Courtesy Marlys McPherson.*

Comic Dolls

Comic characters are great collectibles, and this category too presents a huge potential for the collector who is looking for something away from the mainstream. Not only characters from the comic pages of the newspapers, but comic books, movies, and television cartoon characters are included. These may come in many different mediums, and the collector may wish to include associated paper goods or other accessories with the dolls.

What to look for:

Again, condition is king when choosing collectibles. Dolls should be clean, with good color, little crazing if composition, and preferably with tags, boxes, labels, and original clothing all intact. Have fun looking for these dolls at garage and estate sales, on eBay, or thrift shops. Comic characters are a great collectible that men seem to like.

Alphabetically by Character

15" soft vinyl, Joe Palooka, Jr., molded painted yellow hair, large side-glancing painted eyes, hard vinyl body, closed mouth, wearing replaced red overalls and plaid shirt, marked "©," circa 1960s, $140.00. *Courtesy Fran Fabian.*

15½" all-composition, Herman Cohn and The House of Puzzy, Inc. comic character Puzzy, painted eyes to side, freckles, open/closed mouth, painted teeth, molded/painted red hair, known as the Good Habit kids (images used on soap, toothbrushes, other grooming items), black and white outfit, black ribbon tie, maroon socks, black shoes, marked "PUZZY©//H. of P.//U.S.A" on neck, circa 1948, $350.00. *Courtesy Joan Sickler.*

12½" vinyl Baby Barry comic character Pappy Yokum, with molded hair, beard, painted eyes, with heavy back molded eyebrows, two painted lashes at eye corners, closed smiling mouth, bare feet, dressed in red striped shirt and green pants with patch, marked "Baby Barry//Doll//2 S," from Al Capp's "Lil Abner" comic strip, circa 1957+, $200.00. *Courtesy Anna Bolejack.*

13½" vinyl Baby Barry comic character Mammy Yokum, with molded black hat, hair, painted eyes, one closed, with heavy black molded eyebrows, two painted lashes at eye corners, closed smiling mouth grips a corncob pipe, bare feet, dressed in green shirt, checked pants, has brown molded shoes, marked "Baby Barry//Doll//2 S", from Al Capp's "Lil Abner" comic strip, circa 1957+, $200.00. *Courtesy Anna Bolejack.*

Composition Dolls

Composition dolls have been made from the 1890s and possibly earlier. Cold press composition describes the method of putting a mixture of ingredients (composition) into molds. The recipe for composition varied with each manufacturer, but at first glue was used to bind together such substances as wood flour, shredded cardboard or paper, rags, and then later wood pulp as manufacturers learned how to bake the composition in multiple molds in the hot press method. The mixture was soupier when poured into molds than when pressed, and the ingredients also differed somewhat.

These doll heads were first described as "indestructible" or "Can't Break 'Em" as compared to the bisque and china heads that were easily broken. The dolls were dipped in tinted glue baths to give a flesh tone, and later the features and coloring were airbrushed. Humidity made it difficult for the dolls to dry correctly in early production procedures, but later techniques were refined to reduce this problem. The big problem with composition dolls was their glycerin and glue base; when the surface became saturated with water, it would disintegrate. Extremes of heat and humidity cause bacteria to grow on the surface and destroy the painted finish.

Collectors need to keep composition dolls clean and away from direct sunlight, avoid extremes of temperature, and keep a gauge in their cases to monitor the relative humidity. When the relative humidity exceeds 85%, bacteria have prime conditions to grow and destroy the painted surfaces. Composition dolls should not be stored in plastic, but wrapped in cotton fabric that has been washed and well rinsed to remove any soap or conditioner that may be present. However, collectors who had this type of doll as a plaything in their childhood can, with a little caution, enjoy some of the wide variety of dolls still available. Included in this category are composition dolls by unknown makers or little known companies.

What to look for:

Great composition dolls should have no crazing, cracking, peeling or lifting of paint, with rosy cheek color, original wig and clothes. They may have blush on knees, hands, and arms. Added incentives would be tags, labels, brochures or labeled boxes. Consider purchasing dolls with major flaws only if they have pluses like tagged original costumes, brochures, hang tags or boxes; flawed dolls should be priced accordingly.

13" unmarked carnival type doll, painted black side-glancing eyes, closed mouth, blonde mohair wig, one-piece composition body with jointed arms, painted black shoes, circa 1930s, $50.00. *Courtesy Sue Robertson.*

Composition Dolls

10" Eugenia baby, marked "Eugenia," with cloth body, composition hands, yarn hair; bodies purchased from Ideal, circa 1940s, $95.00. *Courtesy June Allgeier.*

8½" painted, Hollywood Doll Mfg. Miss Muffet Bride, box marked "Toyland Series//Miss Muffet//Hollywood Doll Mfg. Co. Glendale, Calif.," blue eyes, auburn hair, bridal gown and veil, white box with blue stars, circa 1950s, $50.00. *Courtesy Chan Jeschien.*

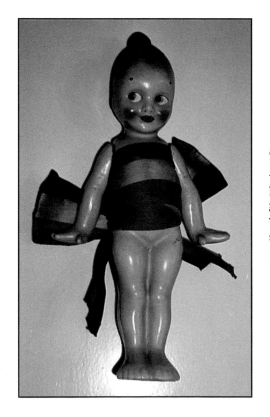

9" Maiden America Toy Mfg. Co., Maiden America, the National Doll, copyright by Kate Silverman, molded painted red hair in bun on top of head, painted side-glancing eyes, rosy cheeks, dressed in patriotic red, white, and blue ribbon, promoted as a good luck doll for servicemen, sold in WWI to promote war bonds, circa 1915, $150.00. *Courtesy Millie Busch.*

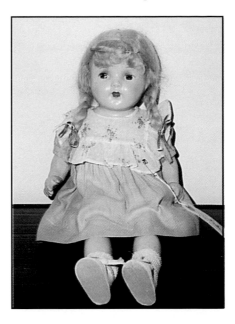

27" unmarked Mama Doll, brown sleep eyes, lashes, open mouth with four teeth, dimples, red wig, head turns on neck, cryer in back, composition arms/legs, cloth body, red dress with plaid trim, circa 1930s, $350.00. *Courtesy Kate Treber.*

18" unmarked girl, painted blue eyes, closed mouth, blonde braided mohair wig, composition arms and legs, cloth body, re-dressed, circa 1939 – 1940s, $140.00. *Courtesy Sue Robertson.*

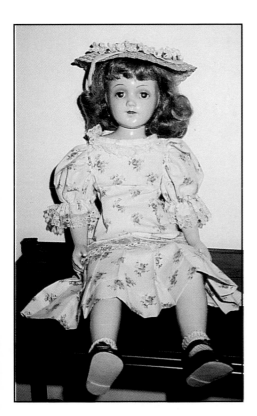

22" composition, unmarked shoulder plate, swivel neck, brown sleep eyes, closed mouth, brown wig, composition arms and legs, cloth body in sitting position, re-dressed, circa late 1930s to early 1940s, $200.00. *Courtesy Sue Robertson.*

21" girl, marked "22 over 8" under arms, "22" on back of legs, blue sleep eyes, closed mouth, blonde mohair wig, white dress with green ribbon and hairpiece, circa 1938 – 1941, $150.00. *Courtesy Kate Treber.*

11" unmarked girl, blue tin sleep eyes, real lashes, open mouth, four upper teeth, blonde mohair wig, 5-piece composition body, pink dress, coat and hat, one-piece underwear, socks and shoes, in original case with pink flannel robe, blue piqué sunsuit, red print sunsuit, blue print beach pajamas, yellow dress, blue print dress/matching hat, pink dress/matching hat, pink coat, two pairs shoes/socks, roller skates, blanket, underwear, circa 1930s, $375.00. *Courtesy McMasters Doll Auctions.*

15" unmarked girl, blue tin eyes, closed mouth, brown braided mohair wig, re-dressed in red and green plaid dress with red hat, circa 1930s, $125.00. *Courtesy Sue Robertson.*

13" girl, tin sleep eyes, closed mouth, auburn mohair wig, unmarked, pink checked dress and panties, straw hat, all original, circa late 1930s to early 1940s, $100.00. *Courtesy Gay Smedes.*

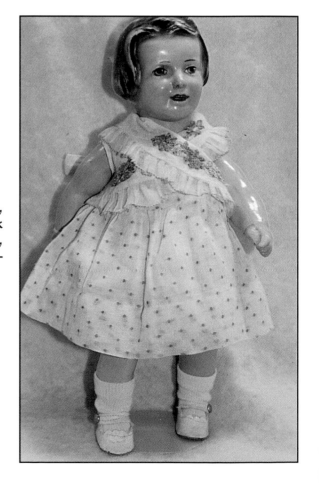

11½" Jessie M. Raleigh unmarked doll, painted blue eyes, closed mouth, molded painted hair, white dress with pink polka dots, white lace on top with embroidered pink flowers, white socks, white one-strap leatherette shoes, circa 1916 – 1920, $425.00. *Courtesy Betty Warder.*

15" Reliable Bride, marked "Reliable//Made in Canada," blue sleep eyes, real lashes, painted lower lashes, closed mouth, auburn mohair wig, long veil, long white dress trimmed in lace, circa late 1940s, $175.00. *Courtesy Taras Antonick.*

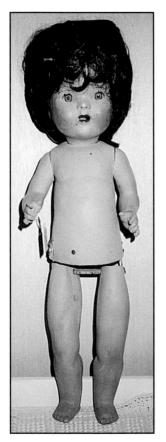

20" unmarked early walker, possibly European, unusual doll, blue glass sleep eyes, open mouth, head turns, segmented with wooden blocks in legs, circa 1930s – 1940s, $100.00. *Courtesy Sue Robertson.*

8½" ethnic girl, skater, brown painted side-glancing eyes, closed mouth, molded hair under blonde wig, flannel dress with yellow trim, gold shoes, white socks, flannel hat, 1939 World's Fair tourist doll, $100.00. *Courtesy Dorothy Bohlin.*

Deluxe Reading Dolls

Deluxe Reading manufactured dolls circa 1957 – 65 that were sold as supermarket premiums, rewards for purchasing some item or for groceries totaling a certain amount. These dolls were marketed under several names: Deluxe Premium Corp., Deluxe Reading, Deluxe Topper, Deluxe Toy Creations Topper Corp., and Topper Toys. Often made of stuffed vinyl, jointed at the neck only, with sleep eyes and rooted hair, the dolls were inexpensively dressed, often as brides, in long formals or in street wear which included a hat in the 1950s and 1960s. Deluxe also made 8" "Penny Brite," a vinyl doll with side-glancing eyes and vinyl carrying case.

What to look for:

More and more of these dolls are showing up, often still packed in their original box. Unfortunately those that were played with often had problems with the stuffed vinyl rupturing at the neck. The costumes and accessories with some of these dolls make them an interesting and often overlooked collectible.

8½" vinyl, Penny Brite, blonde rooted hair, painted side-glancing eyes, 5-piece jointed vinyl body, red and white dress with red plastic shoes, marked "Deluxe Reading Corp.//Elizabeth, N.J.//Pat. Pending," circa 1963+, $35.00. *Courtesy Bertha Melendez.*

30" vinyl, Darling Debbie, marked "Darling Debbie//$29.95//DE LUXE TOY CREATIONS, INC.//Newark, NJ" on wrist tag, sleep eyes, closed mouth, rooted hair, stuffed vinyl one-piece body, lacy blue dress, stole over shoulders, pearl necklace/earrings, 8½" x 4" Royal Coach jewelry box, gold plastic, clear plastic sides, box reads "DARLING DEBBIE//Soft Miracle Vinyl//bending arms and legs//washable rooted hair//high heel shoes," circa 1957, $90.00. *Courtesy Betty Strong.*

Disney Dolls

Walter Ellas Disney was born in 1902 in the Chicago area, grew up on a Missouri farm, and had his first art lessons at age 13. His family moved back to Chicago in 1917, and he entered the Chicago Academy of Fine Art and studied under cartoonist Leroy Gossitt. During World War I, at age 16 he was an ambulance driver in France. After the war, he worked for an advertising firm doing animation.

With his brother, Roy, Disney came to Hollywood where they set up their own animation studio and in 1927 had his first character, Oswald the Lucky Rabbit, in a silent cartoon series. Finding he did not own the rights to his cartoon — they were held by the distributor — Disney determined he would not lose control of his own creations again. He then created a new mouse character, first named Mortimer, but changed to Mickey by his wife.

Charlotte Clark designed and made the first Mickey Mouse doll and won Disney's approval for this copyrighted character. The demand soon overcame her production capabilities and the Disney brothers asked a major toy distributor George Borgfeldt in New York to mass-produce and market the doll. Unfortunately, these dolls proved inferior to Clark's dolls, so Disney got the idea for a pattern and have people make their own. McCalls offered pattern #91 to make a stuffed Mickey Mouse in 1932.

After Mickey and Minnie Mouse characters came Donald Duck, Pluto, Red Riding Hood, the Woof and the Three Little Pigs and then, Snow White and the Seven Dwarfs, Cinderella and Pinocchio. Some of the early firms who produced dolls for Disney include: Lenci and Lars of Italy; Steiff, Chad Valley, Dean's Rag, Gund , Crown, Knickerbocker, Ideal, Horsman, Borgfeldt, Krueger and Alexander. Because Disney retained the copyright for these dolls, he demanded high quality in the production and costuming of the dolls – and defended infringement on the use of his copyrights. Disney dolls are a great collectibles and their high quality has been appreciated over the years.

What to look for:

Because of the popularity of Disney theme parks and the related dolls sold in their gift shops, a collector could have a collection of just Disney dolls. The early cloth dolls should be clean and bright and have original clothing. Because early cloth dolls like Mickey Mouse were so loved, they are hard to find in excellent condition and even worn dolls have some value. These dolls still turn up in estate and garage sales — what child did not bring home a memento from their Disneyland visit?

12" cloth/velveteen, Knickerbocker Dopey from Snow White and the Seven Dwarfs, mask face with molded painted features, blue eyes to side looking upward, applied ears, head and body one piece, jointed arms, green jacket, boots, red hat, circa 1939+, $85.00. *Courtesy Kathy Smith.*

12" cloth/velveteen Knickerbocker Sleepy from Snow White and the Seven Dwarfs, mask face with molded painted features, head and body one piece, jointed arms, long plush fur beard, green jacket, red pants, circa 1939+, $75.00. *Courtesy Kathy Smith.*

19" cloth Snow White and 12" cloth Seven Dwarfs, unmarked, cloth mask faces, painted eyes, Snow White has real lashes, closed mouth, original black yarn wig, cloth body jointed at shoulders/hips, white socks/blue velvet shoes as part of legs, original dress; Dwarfs have brows and mouths of different types to represent different emotions of characters, bodies are colored velvet as clothing, black velvet feet for shoes, unplayed-with condition, circa 1938+, $2,200.00. *Courtesy McMasters Doll Auctions.*

11" cloth, Steiff Mickey Mouse, black oilcloth pie-shaped eyes, long thread whiskers, velvet body and clothes, black body, tan face, removable shoes, mother-of-pearl buttons on red pants, circa 1930s, $2,500.00. *Courtesy Susan L. Chase.*

12" cloth/velveteen, Knickerbocker Happy from Snow White and the Seven Dwarfs, mask face with painted features, head and body one piece, jointed arms, fur beard, green shirt is upper part of body, yellow pants and brown boots make up lower body, circa 1939+, $45.00. *Courtesy Kathy Smith.*

Effanbee Dolls

Bernard Fleishaker and Hugo Baum formed a partnership, Fleishaker and Baum, in 1910 in New York City that eventually become Effanbee. They began making rag and crude composition dolls and had Lenox produce bisque heads for them. They developed a very high quality composition doll with a high quality finish and this characterizes their dolls of the 1920s and 1930s, until after World War II, when the company was sold to Noma Electric.

The company declined with the death of Hugo Baum in 1940, but had remarkable success with a series of dolls, including Bubbles, Grumpy, Lovums, Patsy, and Dy-Dee. Effanbee was a very entrepreneurial company during its prominent years using the talents of freelance doll artist Bernard Lipfert who created Bubbles, Patsy, and Dy-Dee as well as Shirley Temple for Ideal, the Dionne Quintuplets for Alexander, and Ginny for Vogue. Effanbee Doll Company, with president Stanley and designer Irene Wahlberg, has reintroduced many of Effanbee's 1930s favorites in vinyl, painted to give a composition look.

What to look for:

Effanbee's early composition dolls are classics, and the painted finish was the finest available in its day. Unfortunately, the finish on played-with dolls was prone to scuffs and bumps, not to mention that these playthings have to have been stored for 70 years or more and subject to varying degrees of heat, cold and moisture. The biggest threat to composition dolls is changes in relative humidity. When the humidity is over 85 percent, conditions are ripe for the growth of bacteria that cause the paint to decompose, flake or peel. It is necessary to keep composition dolls clean and in a stable environment, avoiding high humidity. Also avoid direct sunlight to minimize fading.

Composition dolls should be clean, with rosy cheeks, and dressed in original or appropriate costume. These were some of the greatest dolls of the composition era and are a treasure when you find them.

Later hard plastic and vinyl dolls also have problems with cleanliness and high relative humidity that allows the growth of bacteria. You can, however, still find all-original dolls with labeled or tagged costumes and good color and condition.

Composition

14½" composition, Barbara Joan from the American Children collection designed by Dewees Cochran, marked "Effanbee" on back of head, "Effanbee//Anne-Shirley" on body, blonde human hair wig, brown sleep eyes, open mouth with four teeth, blue taffeta dress with wine trim, all original with box, circa 1936 – 1939+, $1,000.00. *Courtesy Janet Hill.*

19" composition, American Child designed by Dewees Cochran, marked "Effanbee//Anne Shirley" on back, original human hair wig, brown sleep eyes, real lashes, open mouth, four upper teeth, 5-piece composition child body, original blue flower print dress, matching underwear, original socks with blue trim, blue leatherette tie shoes, circa 1936 – 1939+, $900.00. *Courtesy McMasters Doll Auctions.*

15" composition, Baby Dainty, molded painted hair, painted blue eyes, closed mouth, composition arms and legs, cloth body, original blue and white flowered dress and matching hat, white socks and shoes, circa 1929, $400.00. *Courtesy Janet Hill.*

8" composition, Oriental Butin Nose, with black painted bangs and bob, side-glancing black eyes, with old specialty costume silk or satin finely made wardrobe (7) in wicker case, marked "Effanbee" on back of torso, perhaps a department store special, circa 1930s, $850.00. *Courtesy McMasters Doll Auctions.*

8" all composition, Oriental Butin Nose, painted side-glancing eyes, small nose, closed mouth, molded painted black hair, 5-piece composition body, in Oriental costume, circa 1936+, $400.00. *Courtesy Rae Klenke.*

Two 7½" compo, Vogue Toddles marked "Vogue," painted side-glancing eyes, closed mouths, little girl has molded painted hair, gypsy has black floss hair, 5-piece compo bodies, both in original clothing, circa 1937 – 1948, $300.00; right: 8" compo Butin-Nose, painted side-glancing eyes, closed mouth, molded painted hair, 5-piece compo body, original ethnic-type clothing, circa 1936, $395.00. *Courtesy McMasters Doll Auctions.*

12" composition, Black Grumpykins, painted side-glancing black eyes, closed mouth, molded painted hair with three floss braids, marked on back of shoulder plate "EFFAN-BEE//DOLLS//WALK.TALK.SLEEP," tagged red polka dot outfit, circa 1927, $600.00; right: 11" composition, Black Patsy Baby, painted side-glancing eyes, closed mouth, molded painted hair, three floss pigtails, 5-piece compo bent-leg baby body, red outfit/white rickrack, marked "Effanbee//Patsy Baby," circa 1931, $500.00. *Courtesy McMasters Doll Auctions.*

14" composition, Suzanne, marked "Suzanne" on back of head, human hair wig, blue sleep eyes, real lashes, painted lashes below, closed mouth, composition jointed body, blue and white dress, circa 1940, $225.00. *Courtesy Donna Hadley.*

18" composition, Little Lady, marked "EFFANBEE USA" on back and head, brown sleep eyes, closed mouth, brown human hair wig, black dress, metal heart bracelet, all-original, circa 1939+, $300.00. *Courtesy Lee Ann Beaumont.*

20" all-composition, Little Lady, marked "Effanbee//Anne Shirley" on back, sleep eyes, closed mouth, separated fingers, original yellow dress with yellow ribbon, matching hat trimmed with flowers, full slip, shoes, replaced stockings, circa 1936 – 1940, $375.00. *Courtesy Donna Nance.*

Hard Plastic

16" hard plastic, Honey, platinum blonde wig, sleep eyes, closed mouth, marked on head and back "Effanbee," jointed hard plastic body, checked dress, gold coat with brown trim and brown hat, brown shoes, with original box, circa 1949 – 1958, $550.00. *Courtesy Michelle Newby.*

18" composition, Little Lady with human hair wig, sleep eyes, original costume with long red plaid skirt, white blouse, marked "Effanbee" on head, "Effanbee U.S.A." on back, shown in 1943 Montgomery Wards catalog, $275.00. *Courtesy Debbie Crume.*

The Patsy Family

Another one of Effanbee's great success stories was the Patsy doll designed by Bernard Lipfert and advertised in 1928. She almost was not named Patsy. Identical ads in *Playthings* magazines advertised her as "Mimi" late in 1927 and then as "Patsy" in 1928. Patsy was one of the first dolls to have a wardrobe manufactured just for her by Effanbee and other manufacturers. She was made of all composition and her patent was hotly defended by Effanbee; what was actually patented was a neck joint that allowed the doll to pose and stand alone. She portrayed a 3-year-old girl with short bobbed red hair with a molded headband, painted side-glancing eyes, pouty mouth, bent right arm, and simple classic dresses closed with a safety pin. She had a golden heart charm bracelet and/or a gold paper heart tag with her name. Patsy was so popular she soon had several sisters, many variations, and even a boyfriend, Skippy.

Effanbee promoted Patsy sales with a newspaper, *The Patsytown News,* that went to a reported quarter million children. Effanbee also had an "Aunt Patsy" who toured the country promoting their dolls. In addition they formed a Patsy Doll Club and gave free pinback membership buttons to children who wrote in or bought a Patsy doll. Effanbee tied their doll line to popular current events, such as producing George and Martha Washington for the bicentennial of George's birth. They costumed a group of dolls like the traveling troupe, the White Horse Inn Operetta. During the war years, they fashioned military uniforms for the Skippy dolls and also costumed dolls in ethnic dress (Dutch) or after characters in books like *Alice In Wonderland.*

The death of Hugo Baum in 1940 and the loss of income during the war years threw the Effanbee success story into a decline. In 1946, Effanbee was sold to Noma Electric, and they reissued a 1946 Patsy and later a new 17" Patsy Joan. Since that time, the company has changed hands several more times, until reaching new owners with Stanley Wahlberg as president and Irene Wahlberg as designer. Limited editions of Patsy Ann and Skippy were issued during the 1970s, and Patsy reappeared in vinyl in the 1980s. Effanbee reissued Patsy Joan in 1995, and continued in 1996, 1997, and 1998 with a new group of Patsy, Skippy, and Wee Patsy dolls in vinyl painted to look like the old composition ones. These are already becoming collectibles for the modern collector.

5¾" Wee Patsy, head molded to body, painted blue eyes, molded painted hair, jointed arms and hips, molded painted black one-strap shoes and socks, marked "Effanbee//Wee Patsy" on body, long yellow dress with matching underwear, pinback button reads "Colleen Moore//Fairy Princess//an Eff an bee Doll," two extra red outfits in trousseau box, MIB circa 1935, $575.00. *Courtesy McMasters Doll Auctions.*

7" Baby Tinyette Toddler, $150.00; 6" Wee Patsy $305.00; and 9" Patsyette, $300.00, very good condition, light crazing. *Courtesy McMasters Doll Auctions*

7" Patsy Tinyette Toddler with trousseau, blue painted eyes, molded painted hair, 5-piece composition body, wearing red/white checked dress, red hooded cape, white apron, with extra outfits and shoes, marked "Effanbee" on head, "Effanbee//Patsy//Tinyette" on body, all original in suitcase, circa 1935, $1,200.00. *Courtesy McMasters Doll Auctions.*

7¾" Patsy Tinyette Toddler, painted side-glancing eyes, molded painted hair, 5-piece compo body, tagged original white with green polka dot dress, matching bonnet, all original, marked "Effanbee//Baby//Tinyette," circa 1935, $325.00; right: 11½" compo, Patsykin, painted side-glancing eyes, molded painted red bob, molded headband, 5-piece compo body, original green check dress, marked "Effanbee//Patsy Jr.//Doll," circa 1931, $375.00. *Courtesy McMasters Doll Auctions.*

7½" Baby Tinyette Kit and Kat, all original with gold paper hang tags that read: "We are the original//DUTCH TWINS//Kit and Kat//EFFANBEE DURABLE DOLLS," circa 1936+ $500.00+ for pair. *Courtesy Gay Smedes.*

9½" Patsyette Brother and Sister, painted brown side-glancing eyes, closed mouths, molded painted hair, 5-piece composition child bodies with bent right arms, "Effanbee//Patsyette Doll" on bodies, original matching brother and sister outfits of blue and white with matching tam, white leatherette shoes, circa 1931, $600.00. *Courtesy McMasters Doll Auctions.*

9½" Patsyette Dutch Girl, painted brown side-glancing eyes, closed mouth, long braided mohair wig, 5-piece composition body, metal heart bracelet, marked "Effanbee//Patsyette Doll" on body, Dutch outfit, wooden Dutch shoes, all original with box, circa 1931+, $675.00. *Courtesy McMasters Doll Auctions.*

9½" Patsyette Bridesmaid, painted brown side-glancing eyes, closed mouth, blonde wig, 5-piece jointed composition body, dressed in yellow bridesmaid outfit trimmed in pink, matching hat, all original in box, circa 1931, $425.00. *Courtesy Rae Klenke.*

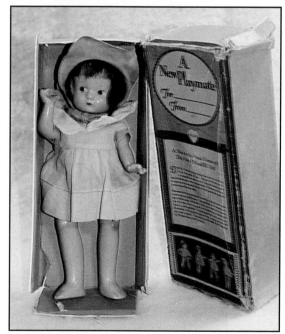

9½" Patsyette, marked "Effanbee//Patsyette Doll" on back, wig, painted brown side-glancing eyes, jointed arms and legs, tagged green dress with matching bonnet, all original with box, circa 1931, $300.00. *Courtesy Chlois Zumwalt.*

13½" Patsy, marked "Effanbee//Patsy" on head, red mohair wig, blue sleep eyes, closed mouth, tin wardrobe with clothes, wearing original green dress trimmed in pink, matching hat, black shoes, reproduction pin, circa 1932, $475.00. *Courtesy Donna Hadley.*

Two 16" Patsy Joans, green sleep eyes, real lashes, closed mouths, painted upper and lower lashes, 5-piece composition child bodies, left: original mohair wig, original pink silk dress, matching teddy, rabbit fur coat/hat, pink snap shoes, original box, circa 1946, $850.00; right: painted/molded side parted hair, original blue checked dress, matching bonnet, black one strap shoes, marked "Effandbee" (with extra "d" added), circa 1946, $550.00. *Courtesy McMasters Doll Auctions.*

19" Patsy Ann, sleep eyes, closed mouth, molded painted short red bob, 5-piece compo body, original print dress, red felt coat/matching tam, red leather shoes, marked "Effanbee//'Patsy-Ann'//©//Pat.#1283558," metal heart bracelet, circa 1929, $600.00; 16" Patsy Joan, sleep eyes, closed mouth, red mohair wig, 5-piece compo body, original blue felt coat/matching hat, organdy dress, red shoes, marked "Effanbee//Patsy Joan," circa 1931, $550.00. *Courtesy McMasters Doll Auctions.*

19" Patsy Ann dressed in original red/white pleated dress, matching undergarments and red/white socks, red shoes, circa 1929, $375.00. *Courtesy McMasters Doll Auctions.*

19" Patsy Ann, marked "Effanbee//"Patsy Ann"//©//Pat. #1283558," molded painted short red bob, blue tin sleep eyes, real lashes, closed mouth, 5-piece compo child body, original blue flowered dress, white collar/cuffs, white teddy, leatherette shoes, metal heart pinned to dress, original box with extra clothing, circa 1929, $1,200.00. *Courtesy McMasters Doll Auctions.*

9" vinyl Patsy Babyette twins, circa 1997, retail $54.00. *Courtesy Lilian Booth.*

22" Patsy Lou, green sleep eyes, closed mouth, molded painted hair, 5-piece composition body, metal heart bracelet, rust old pattern pleated wool skirt and rust colored tam with matching beige and rust wool sweater, panties, socks, leather shoes, marked "EFFAN-BEE//PATSY LOU" on body, circa 1930, $500.00. *Courtesy McMasters Doll Auctions.*

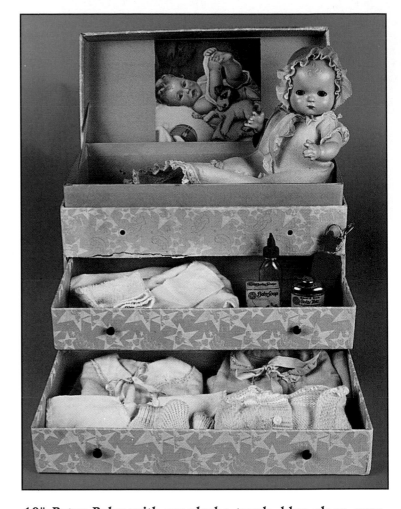

29" Patsy Mae, crazed brown sleep eyes, real lashes, painted upper and lower lashes, closed mouth, auburn human hair wig, a mama-style body with cloth torso, crier, swing legs, composition arms and lower legs, all original, gold metal heart bracelet, marked "Effanbee//Patsy Mae" on head, "Effanbee//Lovums//©//Pat. No. 1283558" on shoulder plate, circa 1934, $950.00. *Courtesy McMasters Doll Auctions.*

10" Patsy Baby with wardrobe trunk, blue sleep eyes, molded painted hair, closed mouth, 5-piece composition bent-leg baby body, original white baby dress, matching bonnet, metal heart name bracelet, trunk, pillow, white flannel blanket, glass baby bottle, rubber hot water bottle, B&B baby talc, kimono, wash cloth, white baby sacque, naval band, yellow sweater, pink kimono, B&B baby soap, marked "Effanbee//Patsy Baby," circa 1931+, $1,400.00. *Courtesy McMasters Doll Auctions.*

9" Patsy Babyette, blue sleep eyes, closed mouth, molded painted hair, 5-piece bent-leg composition baby body, white baby dress with matching bonnet, marked "Effanbee" on head, "Effanbee//Patsy//Babyette" on body, all original, circa 1940s, $400.00. *Courtesy McMasters Doll Auctions.*

6¾" set of five Patsy Baby Tinyette Quints, blue painted eyes (one side-glancing), molded painted hair, bent-leg compo baby bodies, marked "Effanbee" on heads, "Effanbee//Baby Tinyette" on backs, all dressed in original pastel dresses with matching bonnets, white one-piece underwear, cotton socks tied with ribbons, original case with tray, five flannel gowns, flannel pink-edged diapers, circa 1935, $1,400.00. *Courtesy McMasters Doll Auctions.*

7¾" White Horse Inn Tyrolean Tinyette Toddler, painted brown eyes, closed mouth, molded painted hair, jointed composition body, in original costume, wears White Horse Inn pin, circa 1936, all original, $400.00. *Courtesy Rae Klenke.*

14" Patsy/Patricia variant, with a marked Patsy head and Patricia body, molded painted hair, sleep eyes, closed mouth, original plaid dress, red shoes, circa 1940, $600.00. *Courtesy Georgine Cadwallader.*

15" Patsy/Patricia variant, marked Patsy head on a marked Patricia body, painted blue side-glancing eyes, closed mouth, molded painted hair, magnets in hands to hold accessories, body marked "Effanbee//'Patricia'," pale pink organdy dress, matching bonnet, metal heart bracelet, circa 1940, $950.00. *Courtesy McMasters Doll Auctions.*

15" Patricia as Anne Shirley, crazed green sleep eyes, closed mouth, dark blonde braids, five-piece compo body, celluloid fingernails, marked on back "PATRICIA," wearing original Anne Shirley costume, blue checked dress with attached panties, dark blue jacket, dark blue felt hat, from the 1934 movie "Anne of Green Gables," circa 1935, $700.00. *Courtesy McMasters Doll Auctions.*

16" Mary-Lee, green sleep eyes, open mouth, four teeth, original skin, tousled wig, circa 1932, $300.00. *Courtesy McMasters Doll Auctions.*

27" Patricia Ruth, brown sleep eyes, real lashes, painted upper and lower lashes, closed mouth, auburn human hair wig, all-composition slimmer style body, all original in white rabbit fur hat and coat, peach silk dress and teddy, white leather shoes, white socks, gold metal heart bracelet, marked "Effanbee//Patsy Ruth" on head, circa 1935, $1,700.00. *Courtesy McMasters Doll Auctions.*

14" Skippy Cowboy, painted blue side-glancing eyes, molded painted brown hair, cloth torso with compo legs and arms, molded painted feet, wearing a cowboy outfit, has gun in holster, marked "Effanbee//Skippy//©//P.L. Crosby" on head, circa 1936, $1,200.00. *Courtesy McMasters Doll Auctions.*

12" composition, Madame Alexander Betty, all original with red mohair wig, tagged dress, $300.00; and 13" Effanbee Skippy in soldier uniform, circa 1940s, $300.00. *Courtesy McMasters Doll Auctions.*

Ethnic Dolls

Collectors sometimes refer to dolls dressed in regional or national costumes as ethnic or tourist dolls. These were commonly available for sale in shops to tourists who wanted souvenirs of the country they visited. Dolls dressed in national costume were touted as "educational" by showing the costume or dress of that country.

Today some collectors are trying to identify many of these ethnic dolls that are often quite charming and passed over for the better-known collectible dolls. One doll club has taken on the project of researching certain groups of dolls. After one year's study efforts, they became so engrossed, they decided to continue for another year. This is an area with little research and worthy of continued interest. Dolls in national costume were made of many mediums, including bisque, cloth, composition, hard plastic, and vinyl. During the 1930s, 1940s, and 1950s and later, many dolls dressed in regional costumes could be purchased cheaply in different areas. A wide variety of these dolls are unmarked or made by little-known companies. This category is sometimes a catch-all for dolls that have little history and no category. Many were cheaply made and mass-produced for the tourist market, but some were extremely well made and are whimsical and charming and make an interesting and eclectic collection.

What to look for:

The workmanship and the costuming make these dolls valuable. Look for clean, all original dolls with boxes, labels and or tagged clothing. Try for dolls with very well-made clothing that is clean, has bright colors, no fading or soil. This category had a big potential for collectors as it is not as popular with older collectors, who seek more conventional dolls in ethnic costumes, so the dolls of little known or unknown manufacturers may be passed by. Acquire dolls that are appealing to you, but always look for well-made dolls of good color and original costume.

American Indian

7½" painted bisque (possibly Averill), Indian baby in cradleboard, painted side-glancing eyes, molded painted hair, closed mouth, in cradleboard made of felt, circa 1920s, $45.00. *Courtesy Lee Ferguson.*

11½" hard plastic, Plastic Molded Arts Indian girl, brown sleep eyes, painted lashes below, closed mouth, black mohair braided wig, brown Indian dress with beads, trimmed in green fringe, matching green moccasins with beads, circa 1950s, $25.00. *Courtesy Lee Ferguson.*

11½" hard plastic, Plastic Molded Arts Indian girl, brown sleep eyes, painted lashes below, closed mouth, black mohair wig, red plaid shawl, red top, floral skirt, beaded necklace, circa 1950s, $25.00. *Courtesy Lee Ferguson.*

13" cloth unmarked ethnic Indian, made by modern Indians, painted features, wig with beaded barrettes, turquoise beaded necklace and earrings, silver conchos on velveteen clothing, circa 1970s, $30.00. *Courtesy Betty Strong.*

Skookums, 1914 – 1950+

Skookums was designed and patented by Mary McAboy in 1914 and the first doll heads were reported to be made of dried apples, made later in composition and plastic. They were manufactured first as a cottage industry for the Denver H.H. Tammen Company and then by Arrow Novelty Co. With side-glancing painted eyes, they had molded and painted features, horsehair wigs, and padded cloth over stick bodies, formed by wrapping and folding an Indian blanket to suggest arms. The label on the bottom of the flat wooden feet reads, "Trade Mark Registered (Bully Good) Indian//U.S.A.//Patented." Later dolls had plastic molded feet. Dolls range in size from 6" to 36" store displays. Typical figures represent a chief, a squaw with papoose, and a child. The dolls were made for the tourist markets and sold through the Tammen Company catalogs and elsewhere and are a nostalgic piece of Americana tourist dolls.

3½" composition, Skookum Baby in cradleboard, designed by Mary McAboy, painted features, side-glancing eyes, black mohair wig, cloth figure wrapped in Indian blanket, circa 1940s, $35.00. *Courtesy Lee Ferguson.*

7¾" composition, Skookum girl, designed by Mary McAboy, painted features, side-glancing eyes, black mohair wig, cloth figure wrapped in Indian blanket, folds represent arms, beaded necklace, circa 1940s, $45.00. *Courtesy Lee Ferguson.*

8½" composition, Indian, designed by Mary McAboy, painted features, side-glancing eyes, black mohair wig in braids, cloth figure wrapped in Indian blanket, paper label on bottom of foot reads "TRADEMARK REGISTERED//SKOOKUM//(BULLY GOOD)//INDIAN//U.S.A.//PATENTED," box reads "SKOOKUM//(BULLY GOOD)//The Great Indian Character Doll//No. 4030//$1.50," all original with box, circa 1930s – 1940s, $85.00. *Courtesy Betty Strong.*

11½" composition, Indian squaw and child, designed by Mary McAboy, black mohair wigs, painted features, painted side-glancing eyes, yellow headband, cloth figure wrapped in Indian blanket, folds representing arms holding child, leather boots, left foot has oval paper tag reading "Trade Mark Registered//Skookum//(Bully Good)//Indian," circa 1930s – 1940s, $275.00. *Courtesy Derra Hunt.*

11½" composition, Indian, designed by Mary McAboy, painted features, side-glancing eyes, black mohair wig in braids, cloth figure wrapped in Indian blanket, fuchsia colored wooden beads around neck, paper label on bottom of foot reads "TRADEMARKREGISTERED//SKOOKUM//(BULLY GOOD)//INDIAN//U.S.A.//PATENTED," circa 1930s – 1940s, $125.00. *Courtesy Betty Strong.*

16" stockinet Ethnic Seminole Indian with mask face, glass eyes, open mouth, earrings, yarn wig, handcrafted, stitched fingers and toes, circa 1940s – 1950s, $275.00. *Courtesy Oleta Woodside.*

Baitz

The Baitz firm started in Germany in 1912. After World War II, the company moved to Austria where it became Camillo Gardtner and Company in 1963. They are still producing well-made dolls dressed in regional costumes.

Baitz dolls are good examples of attractive, well-made dolls nicely dressed. They are 9" tall, and the head appears to be painted hard plastic but could also be described as composition; we are unsure of the material used. Since *Colemans' Collector's Encyclopedia of Dolls* refers to composition as "made of various ingredients," most collectors equate the term "composition" with heads made of sawdust or wood pulp mixtures.

Baitz dolls are very appealing with their side-glancing painted brown eyes, open round surprise or kissing mouths, and attractive costumes. They have single line painted eyebrows, and two brown eyelashes painted from the upper corner of the eye, glued-on mohair wigs with curls or braids for the girls, and shorter hair for the boys. Their bodies are felt-over-wire armature with simple mitt felt hands with a red and black heart-shaped paper hang tag marked BAITZ. On the back of the tag is a gold foil sticker that reads "Made in Austria" and the name of the doll or region it

Austria

represents. Dolls come in cream floral pattern boxes, also with a gold foil sticker. Clothing is cotton with no fasteners or openings with felt accents and felt hats. All known dolls have head coverings. The feet have simple black gathered cloth shoes and white cotton knit stockings. They come dressed both as boys and girls.

Dutch – Holland

9" painted hard plastic, Tessin girl, painted features, mohair wig, side-glancing eyes, round open/closed mouth, felt-over-wire body, original regional outfit, Baitz heart tag, sticker "Made in Austria," circa 1970s, $75.00. *Private collection.*

10½" hard plastic, Rozetta Holland boy and girl, tagged "Genuine Rozetta Dolls//Amsterdam (Holland)," painted eyes, red and black outfit, black hat on boy, white cloth hat on girl, wooden shoes, circa 1950s, $50.00. *Courtesy Sandy Sumner.*

France

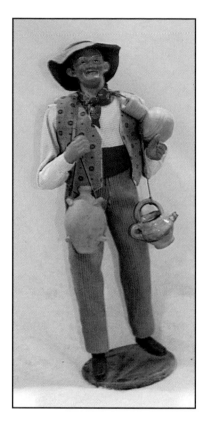

8½" terra cotta, Santon, Old Woman Carding Wool, seated in wooden chair, signed on base (unreadable), painted molded gray hair, painted eyes, closed smiling mouth, lace cap, red shawl, green floral dress, blue print apron, holds wool and wooden sticks with yarn; Santons (little saints) have been made for many generations by people of Provence in southern France to represent themselves and join with the Wise Men on their journey to see the Christ Child, circa 1930, $100.00. *Courtesy Connie Bedenkop.*

12" terra cotta, Santon, Olive Oil Seller, signed "S. Jouglas" on base, with painted molded hair, painted eyes, closed smiling mouth, molded ears, original in blue shirt, tan print vest, red scarf, tan hat, pants, holding clay pots, one olive oil pot over shoulders; Santons (little saints) have been made for many generations by people of Provence in southern France to represent themselves and join with the Wise Men on their journey to see the Christ Child, circa 1930, $125.00. *Courtesy Connie Bedenkop.*

12" cloth doll, unmarked, painted features, wigged, old fabric used on costume, stitched fingers, circa 1960s or later, $50.00. *Courtesy Terri Parker.*

10" terra cotta, Santon, Old Woman with Basket, signed Vevizez on base, with painted molded hair, painted eyes, closed smiling mouth, molded ears, original straw hat, red jacket, print scarf, black print apron, multicolored print long skirt; Santons (little saints) have been made for many generations by people of Provence in southern France to represent themselves and join with the Wise Men on their journey to see the Christ Child, circa 1930, $100.00. *Courtesy Connie Bedenkop.*

Petticollin produced celluloid dolls for various companies that dressed them in regional costumes. Madame Le Minor, a French designer, bought composition and celluloid dolls, costumed them, and sold them under her label. Other companies followed her lead, dressing dolls from different regions of France.

India

4½" celluloid, pincushion doll, painted blue eyes, rosy cheeks, closed mouth, celluloid head and hands, all original, circa 1930s, $35.00. *Private collection.*

19½" bisque, ethnic girl, tagged "Village Girl//of Delhi," painted brown eyes, cloth hands, original ethnic outfit, carrying pottery bowls, circa 1930s, $120.00. *Courtesy Thelma Williams.*

Russia

Two 14" cloth, men, stockinet faces, painted features, strange hair, circa 1930s, $225.00 pair. *Courtesy June Allgeier.*

Spain

22" celluloid, unknown German Spanish Lady, black floss hair with curl down center, brown set glass eyes, open/closed mouth, teeth, celluloid lower arms, legs, lower left leg broken, cloth body, long tan flowered dress, marked "Germany//(turtle inside diamond)//Germany," circa 1920s – 1930s, $225.00. *Courtesy Judy Dunn.*

World's Fair Tourist Dolls

In Judds' *Compo Dolls, 1928 – 1985,* they report finding a 13" composition doll tagged, "A Doll Craft Product." The Judds believe the dolls were made in the late 1930s by a factory that sold them to marketing firms who dressed and sold them to different stores and catalog companies. It has been reported that the dolls were offered for sale at the 1939 New York World's Fair at the pavilions representing various countries participating in the Fair.

These dolls were 8½" or 13" tall, with painted side-glancing eyes, molded hair under mohair wigs, and original costumes with hang tags. The dolls are jointed, all-composition with gently curved arms, pouty mouths, single line painted eyebrows, and eyelashes painted above their brown irises. A dot of white accents the right of each black pupil. The fingers are molded together and the composition is well finished, but cruder than Effanbee's Patsy family. Each has a yellow hang tag stating her name and the country that her costume represents, such as "I am Katrinka from Holland," "I am Marguerita from Roumania," or "I am Maria from Italy."

All-composition 13" dolls such as these with clean, bright, original costumes, little or no crazing, good color, complete with hang tags, and in excellent condition would be priced at $250.00 or more if the costume is elaborate or with accessories, much less if no tag, not original, or faded with heavy crazing. The 8" dolls would be priced at $175.00 or less for played-with or soiled condition.

What to look for:

These examples of tourist dolls from the late 1939 World's Fair are charming and great collectibles. Revived interests in ethnic and tourist dolls make them a nifty collecting niche. Dolls with fine costuming with intricate details are more in demand. Look for composition dolls with little crazing, good facial color and, original costumes, hang tags, boxes, or labels. This remains a category that needs more study and research and poses a good avenue for new collectors to pursue and enjoy.

8½" composition, Bolivia, brown painted side-glancing eyes, closed mouth, molded painted hair, molded shoes/socks, white pants, vest with embroidery, black hat, 1939 World's Fair tourist doll, $100.00. *Courtesy Dorothy Bohlin.*

8½" composition, hang tag reads "I am a Flower Girl from France," painted eyes, closed mouth, molded hair/wig, molded shoes, provenance reads "Faustine sent to me from N.Y. World's Fair Aug. 1, 1940 by Claude James," $150.00. *Courtesy Dorothy Bohlin.*

8½" composition, France, brown painted side-glancing eyes, closed mouth, molded hair under red wig, molded shoes/socks, red skirt and scarf in hair, black vest, 1939 World's Fair tourist doll, $100.00. *Courtesy Dorothy Bohlin.*

8½" composition, Hawaii, green painted side-glancing eyes, closed mouth, molded hair under black wig, molded socks/shoes, grass skirt, 1939 World's Fair tourist doll, $135.00. *Courtesy Dorothy Bohlin.*

8½" composition, hang tag reads "I am Carlotta of Portugal," brown painted side-glancing eyes, closed mouth, molded hair under red wig, red flowered skirt, black vest, 1939 World's Fair tourist doll, $125.00. *Courtesy Dorothy Bohlin.*

8½" composition, girl, hang tag reads "I am Sophie of Poland," brown painted side-glancing eyes, closed mouth, molded hair under blonde wig, molded socks/shoes, scarf, striped skirt, tourist doll for 1939 World's Fair, $125.00. *Courtesy Dorothy Bohlin.*

8½" composition, Russia, brown painted side-glancing eyes, closed mouth, molded painted hair, orange top, white pants/hat, black boots/sash, replaced gold trim around neck, 1939 World's Fair tourist doll, $100.00. *Courtesy Dorothy Bohlin.*

8½" composition, hang tag reads "I am Sonya of Russia," brown painted side-glancing eyes, closed mouth, molded hair under black wig, molded socks/shoes, 1939 World's Fair tourist doll, $125.00. *Courtesy Dorothy Bohlin.*

8½" composition, hang tag reads "I am Lassie of Scotland," painted side-glancing eyes, closed mouth, molded hair under blonde wig, short plaid outfit, shoes and socks, 1939 World's Fair tourist doll, $125.00. *Courtesy Dorothy Bohlin.*

8½" composition, hang tag reads "I am Chiquita of South American Rhumba," brown painted side-glancing eyes, closed mouth, molded hair under auburn wig, molded socks/shoes, 1939 World's Fair tourist doll, $125.00. *Courtesy Dorothy Bohlin.*

8½" composition, Kasmira of Turkey, brown painted side-glancing eyes, closed mouth, molded hair under black wig, red felt hat/shoes, 1939 World's Fair tourist doll, $100.00. *Courtesy Dorothy Bohlin.*

8½" composition, ethnic girl from unknown country, brown painted side-glancing eyes, closed mouth, molded hair under blonde wig, molded shoes/socks, red tam, blue and white print stripes on skirt, green vest, 1939 World's Fair tourist doll, $85.00. *Courtesy Dorothy Bohlin.*

8½" composition, ethnic girl from unknown country, brown painted side-glancing eyes, closed mouth, molded hair under red wig, molded socks/shoes, black felt hat and vest, blue skirt with white stripes, 1939 World's Fair Tourist doll, $100.00. *Courtesy Dorothy Bohlin.*

Gene Dolls

Created by magazine illustrator, Mel Odom, a North Carolina native now living in New York and marketed by Ashton-Drake Galleries, Gene is a 15½" vinyl fashion doll and comes complete with her own history. Making her debut in 1995 as Gene Marshall, an actress of the 1940s and 1950s, she is reminiscent of Betty Grable, Rita Hayworth or Gene Tierney. Born in the East, Gene comes west to Hollywood and wins starring roles as well as performs on USO tours. Glamor and personality make Gene a favorite among collectors, but the well-made clothing, accessories, and presentations make her one of the hottest competitors for Barbie for the new millennium.

The Gene Team leader is Joan Greene who says the making of Gene is a labor of love — something few large corporations ever claim. Besides the excellent presentation of the doll, costumes, and accessories in 1996, the Gene Team came up with an inspiring new program, Young Designers of America. This concept encourages young high school students, who receive a Gene doll and are challenged to create a scenario and costume. Each participant is honored with a special certificate of achievement and a sterling silver pin. Winners receive a cash prize and the possibility of seeing their design produced and collecting professional royalties. This program alone makes Gene a winner for collectors and young designers and also for Ashton-Drake. Fun to dress, fun to costume, and a great collectible, eight to ten dolls are introduced annually and about the same number of new costumes. Dressed dolls retail for $79.95 and up, with "Simply Gene" offered for $54.95. It has been a long time since a doll offered so much excitement to the doll-collecting world.

What to look for:
Check eBay, the Internet, doll shows, and your local doll shop for the latest dolls and costumes.

15½" vinyl, marked "Gene ™//© 1995 Mel Odom" on head, painted eyes, auburn rooted synthetic wig, jointed fashion type body, bendable knees, wearing "Shooting Star," blue fringe skirt and matching jacket with rhinestone decoration, yellow Western trim shirt, brown belt with lariat around waist, black cowboy hat, boots, pink scarf tied around neck, limited to 5,000, circa 2000, $84.95. *Photo courtesy Ashton-Drake Galleries.*

15½" vinyl, marked "Gene ™//© 1995 Mel Odom" on head, painted eyes, blonde rooted synthetic wig, jointed fashion type body, bendable knees, wearing "First Stop: Chicago," blue two-piece suit with fur collar, matching fur mitt, brown gloves, brown high-heel shoes, hose, hat, limited to 5,000, circa 2000, costume only, $44.95. *Photo courtesy Ashton-Drake Galleries.*

15½" vinyl, marked "Gene ™//© 1995 Mel Odom" on head, painted eyes, blonde rooted synthetic wig, jointed fashion type body, bendable knees, wearing "First Close-Up," yellow gold satin dress with full skirt, off the shoulder sleeves with white cuffs, buttons, white short apron, carrying box around neck, flowered choker, pink tie high-heel sandals, hose, limited to 5,000, circa 2000, costume only, $39.95. *Photo courtesy Ashton-Drake Galleries.*

15½" vinyl, marked "Gene ™//© 1995 Mel Odom" on head, painted eyes, brown rooted synthetic wig, jointed fashion type body, bendable knees, wearing "Hacienda," blue gown with black and gold zigzag trim on lower part of skirt, short black jacket, earrings, hose, shoes, limited to 5,000, circa 2000, costume only, $44.95. *Photo courtesy Ashton-Drake Galleries.*

15½" vinyl, designed by Mel Odom, marked "Gene ™//© 1995 Mel Odom" on head, painted eyes, blonde rooted synthetic wig, jointed fashion type body, bendable knees, wearing "Jazz Note," long black fitted gown with lace insert in front and back, blue ribbon in back, lace hat, black purse, black high-heels, hose, limited to 5000, circa 2000, costume only, $44.95. *Photo courtesy Ashton-Drake Galleries.*

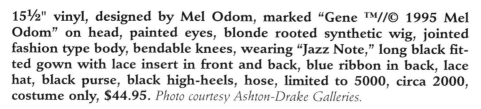

15½" vinyl, designed by Mel Odom, marked "Gene ™//© 1995 Mel Odom" on head, painted eyes, platinum rooted synthetic wig, jointed fashion type body, bendable knees, wearing "The Spirit of Truth," gold and silver outfit with pleated skirt, silver gloves, shield and sword, silver boots, silver net stockings, hoop earrings, limited to 5,000, circa 2000, costume only, $44.95. *Photo courtesy Ashton-Drake Galleries.*

15½" vinyl, designed by Mel Odom, marked "Gene ™//© 1995 Mel Odom" on head, painted eyes, red rooted synthetic wig, jointed fashion type body, bendable knees, wearing "It's A Wrap," blue baby doll outfit, white house-coat, white mules, earrings, limited to 5,000, circa 2000, costume only, $32.95. *Photo courtesy Ashton-Drake Galleries.*

15½" vinyl, designed by Mel Odom, marked "Gene ™//© 1995 Mel Odom" on head, painted eyes, brown rooted synthetic wig, jointed fashion type body, bendable knees, wearing "Table For Two," pink two-piece suit with fitted top, buttons down front, mid-length sleeves, matching A-line skirt, pink purse, pink hat, pink ribbon tie high-heel sandals, hose, white gloves, pink beaded necklace, limited to 5,000, circa 2000, costume only, $34.95. *Photo courtesy Ashton-Drake Galleries.*

15½" vinyl, designed by Mel Odom, marked "Gene ™//© 1995 Mel Odom" on head, painted eyes, brown rooted synthetic wig, jointed fashion type body, bendable knees, wearing "Love Letters," red two-piece outfit with matching lace tie high-heel sandals, red hat with red net lace, short red gloves, matching purse, rhinestone pin, limited to 5,000, circa 2000, costume only, $39.95. *Photo courtesy Ashton-Drake Galleries.*

15½" vinyl, designed by Mel Odom, marked "Gene ™//© 1995 Mel Odom" on head, painted eyes, brown rooted synthetic wig, jointed fashion type body, bendable knees, wearing "Shorts Story," blue two-piece outfit with red and white flower print, midriff top, shorts, strap sandals, matching flat large brim hat, purse, white sunglasses, bracelet, limited to 5,000, circa 2000, costume only, $32.95. *Photo courtesy Ashton-Drake Galleries.*

15½" vinyl, marked "Gene ™//© 1995 Mel Odom" on head, painted eyes, brown rooted synthetic wig, jointed fashion type body, bendable knees, wearing "Don't Fence Me In," white Western shirt with red trim, blue jeans, brown belt, boots, earrings, limited to 5,000, circa 2000, costume only, $34.95. *Photo courtesy Ashton-Drake Galleries.*

15½" vinyl, marked "Gene ™//© 1995 Mel Odom" on head, painted eyes, blonde rooted synthetic wig, jointed fashion type body, bendable knees, wearing "Dance with Me," limited to 5,000, with long evening gown with straps across shoulders, matching shawl, circa 2000, $84.95. *Photo courtesy Ashton-Drake Galleries.*

15½" vinyl, marked "Gene ™//© 1995 Mel Odom" on head, painted eyes, brown rooted synthetic wig, jointed fashion type body, bendable knees, wearing "Encore," retailer exclusive doll, limited to 5,000, cerise evening gown with matching cape, circa 2000, $99.95. *Photo courtesy Ashton-Drake Galleries.*

15½" vinyl, marked "Gene ™//© 1995 Mel Odom" on head, painted eyes, red rooted synthetic wig, jointed fashion type body, bendable knees, wearing "Twighlight Rumba," 5th Anniversary Annual Edition, limited to the year 2000, wearing lilac midrift top with long sleeves, matching skirt, both with beaded trim, pink flowers at top of skirt, matching flowers in hair, high heels, circa 2000, $99.95. *Photo courtesy Ashton-Drake Galleries.*

15½" vinyl, marked "Gene ™//© 1995 Mel Odom" on head, painted eyes, brown rooted synthetic wig, jointed fashion type body, bendable knees, wearing "Encore," retailer exclusive doll, limited to 5,000, dark purple evening gown with lilac trim at bodice and shoulders, long lilac ribbon bow in back, matching lilac long evening gloves, circa 2000, $99.95. *Photo courtesy Ashton-Drake Galleries.*

15½" vinyl, marked "Gene ™//© 1995 Mel Odom" on head, painted eyes, blonde rooted synthetic wig, jointed fashion type body, bendable knees, wearing "I Do", white wedding dress, long veil, white high heels, short white gloves, holding bouquet of flowers, limited to 5,000, circa 2000, $84.95. *Photo courtesy Ashton-Drake Galleries.*

15½" vinyl, marked "Gene ™//© 1995 Mel Odom" on head, painted eyes, brown rooted synthetic wig, jointed fashion type body, bendable knees, wearing "Love At First Sight," rust colored long top fitted at waist, matching skirt with slit in front, lace collar, matching high heels, bracelet, limited to 5,000, circa 2000, $84.95. *Photo courtesy Ashton-Drake Galleries.*

15½" vinyl, Simply Gene, designed by Mel Odom, marked "Gene ™//© 1995 Mel Odom" on head, painted eyes, platinum rooted synthetic wig, jointed fashion type body, bendable knees, twists at the waist, black and white short outfit, black high heels, open edition, circa 2000, retail $54.95. *Photo courtesy Ashton-Drake Galleries.*

15½" vinyl, marked "Gene ™//© 1995 Mel Odom" on head, painted eyes, blonde rooted synthetic wig, jointed fashion type body, bendable knees, wearing "Little Black Dress," black dress with black jacket, pin, black hat, black purse, black high-heel sandals, limited to 5,000, circa 2000, costume only, $49.95. *Photo courtesy Ashton-Drake Galleries.*

15½" vinyl, marked "Gene ™//© 1995 Mel Odom" on head, painted eyes, blonde rooted synthetic wig, jointed fashion type body, bendable knees, wearing "Little Black Dress," black dress, gold chain around waist, gold chain necklaces with pearls, black hat with pink rose, black high-heel sandals, limited to 5,000, circa 2000, costume only, $49.95. *Photo courtesy Ashton-Drake Galleries.*

15½" vinyl, marked "Gene ™//© 1995 Mel Odom" on head, painted eyes, blonde rooted synthetic wig, jointed fashion type body, bendable knees, wearing "Croquet, Anyone?," dress with belt and matching jacket, blue stitch trim, two pleats on skirt, matching high heels, hose, hat, limited to 5,000, circa 2000, costume only, $34.95. *Photo courtesy Ashton-Drake Galleries.*

Gene's Croquet Set, circa 2000, $29.95. *Photo courtesy Ashton-Drake Galleries.*

15½" vinyl, marked "Gene ™//©
1995 Mel Odom" on head, painted
eyes, blonde rooted synthetic wig,
jointed fashion type body, bendable
knees, wearing "The Perfect Gift,"
two-piece emerald green suit, red
flower corsage, matching flowered
hat and purse, black high heels,
hose, necklace, limited to 5,000,
circa 2000, costume only, $44.95.
Photo courtesy Ashton-Drake Galleries.

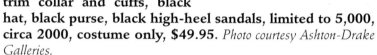

15½" vinyl, marked "Gene
™//© 1995 Mel Odom" on
head, painted eyes, blonde
rooted synthetic wig, jointed
fashion type body, bendable
knees, wearing "Little Black
Dress," black dress with lace
trim collar and cuffs, black
hat, black purse, black high-heel sandals, limited to 5,000,
circa 2000, costume only, $49.95. *Photo courtesy Ashton-Drake
Galleries.*

15½" vinyl, marked "Gene ™//© 1995
Mel Odom" on head, painted eyes,
blonde rooted synthetic wig, jointed
fashion type body, bendable knees,
wearing "Little Black Dress," black
dress with red and black plaid hat, tie
around waist, matching plaid gloves,
black high-heel sandals, limited to
5,000, circa 2000, costume only, $49.95.
Photo courtesy Ashton-Drake Galleries.

15½" vinyl, marked "Gene ™//© 1995 Mel Odom" on head,
painted eyes, blonde rooted synthetic wig, jointed fashion type
body, bendable knees, wearing "Will You Marry Me?," blue
satin dress with sheer blue overlay, blue satin ribbon around
waist, trimmed with pink flowers, white straw hat, white high-
heel sandals, gloves, limited to 5,000, circa 2000, costume only,
$44.95. *Photo courtesy Ashton-Drake Galleries.*

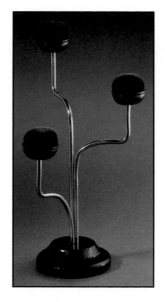

Gene's Hat Stand, Item
92255, circa 2000, $14.95.
*Photo courtesy Ashton-Drake
Galleries.*

15½" vinyl, marked "Gene ™//©
1995 Mel Odom" on head, painted
eyes, auburn rooted synthetic wig,
jointed fashion type body, bendable
knees, wearing "Baking Cookies,"
yellow and white checked dress
with puffed sleeves, matching mitt,
white apron with blue rickrack trim,
yellow ribbon in hair, limited to
5,000, circa 2000, costume only,
$34.95. *Photo courtesy Ashton-Drake Galleries.*

Gene's "Hat/Purse Set No. 1," Item
92940, intricately detailed and crafted
pieces, each a perfectly scaled wearable work of art, circa 2000, **$44.95.**
Photo courtesy Ashton-Drake Galleries.

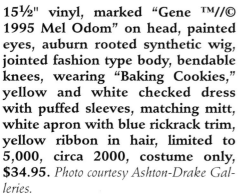

Gene's "Hat/Purse Set No. 1," Item 92940, intricately detailed and crafted pieces, each a
perfectly scaled wearable work of art, circa 2000, **$44.95.** *Photo courtesy Ashton-Drake Gal-
leries.*

Gene's "Hat/Purse Set No. 1," Item 92940, intricately detailed and crafted pieces, each a perfectly scaled wearable work of art, circa 2000, $44.95. *Photo courtesy Ashton-Drake Galleries.*

Gene's "Hat/Purse Set No. 4," Item 96319, intricately detailed and crafted pieces, each a perfectly scaled wearable work of art, circa 2000, $44.95. *Photo courtesy Ashton-Drake Galleries.*

Gene's "Hat/Purse Set No. 4," Item 96319, intricately detailed and crafted pieces, each a perfectly scaled wearable work of art, circa 2000, $44.95. *Photo courtesy Ashton-Drake Galleries.*

Gene's "Hat/Purse Set No. 3," Item 96314, intricately detailed and crafted pieces, each a perfectly scaled wearable work of art, circa 2000, $44.95. *Photo courtesy Ashton-Drake Galleries.*

Gene's "Hat/Purse Set No. 3," Item 96314, intricately detailed and crafted pieces, each a perfectly scaled wearable work of art, circa 2000, $44.95. *Photo courtesy Ashton-Drake Galleries.*

Gene's "Hat/Purse Set No. 3," Item 96314, intricately detailed and crafted pieces, each a perfectly scaled wearable work of art, circa 2000, $44.95. *Photo courtesy Ashton-Drake Galleries.*

Gene's "Hat/Purse Set No. 2," Item 93324, intricately detailed and crafted pieces, each a perfectly scaled wearable work of art, circa 2000, $44.95. *Photo courtesy Ashton-Drake Galleries.*

Gene's "Hat/Purse Set No. 2," Item 93324, intricately detailed and crafted pieces, each a perfectly scaled wearable work of art, circa 2000, $44.95. *Photo courtesy Ashton-Drake Galleries.*

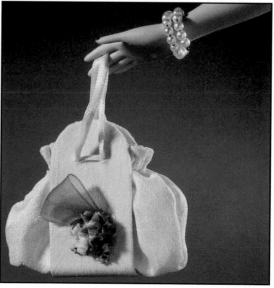

Gene's "Hat/Purse Set No. 2," Item 93324, intricately detailed and crafted pieces, each a perfectly scaled wearable work of art, circa 2000, $44.95. *Photo courtesy Ashton-Drake Galleries.*

 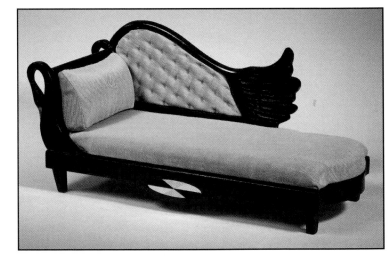

Gene's "Hearts and Flowers," circa 2000, $34.95. *Photo courtesy Ashton-Drake Galleries.*

"Gene's Chaise Lounge," handcrafted lounge features an elegant swan motif, includes "inlaid" wood panels, exquisite carving, circa 2000, $74.95. *Photo courtesy Ashton-Drake Galleries.*

"Gene's Dressing Screen," circa 2000, $44.95.
Photo courtesy Ashton-Drake Galleries.

"Gene's Wardrobe Rack," handcrafted with swan motif, six hang-
ers, circa 2000, $44.95. *Photo courtesy
Ashton-Drake Galleries.*

"Gene's Swan Lamp,"
handcrafted, circa 2000,
$49.95. *Photo courtesy Ashton-
Drake Galleries.*

"Gene's Gazebo," circa
2000, $44.95. *Photo courtesy
Ashton-Drake Galleries.*

Hard Plastic Dolls

Plastics came into use during World War II. The war and shortages of some materials caused great upheavals in the toy industry since many plants had been converted to make items for the war effort. After the war, some companies began to use plastic for dolls. Hard plastic seems to have been a good material for doll use. Relatively unbreakable, it seems not to deteriorate with time, as had been the case with "magic skin" and other materials that were tried and discarded. The prime years of plastic use, roughly 1940 – 1950, produced a wide variety of beautiful dolls that Baby Boomers still remember fondly. With the advent of vinyl in the late 1950s and early 1960s, fewer hard plastic dolls were made, although occasionally some manufacturers today still present hard plastic.

What to look for:

Look for clean dolls with rosy cheek color, in original clothing, with labels, boxes, hang tags or brochures. Dirt on dolls may cause the plastic to change chemically with the growth of bacteria in high relative humidity. Another niche where collectors may find inexpensive dolls is dolls unmarked or by little known companies.

7", doll in plastic bell, tag says "Diamond April Birthstone Doll," bottom of bell says "A & H//Woodside, NY," in blue dress with ring on tag around wrist, circa 1950s, $15.00. *Courtesy Betty Strong.*

8", "Lady Alice," by Admiration Toy Co., NY, jointed arms, neck, sleep eyes, MIB. Circa 1950s, $30.00. *Courtesy Carolyn Haynes.*

10½", Block Doll Corp. "Baby Walker," blue sleep eyes, closed mouth, blonde braided wig, straight leg walker, white flowered dress with pink skirt, black band around waist, circa 1955, $55.00. *Courtesy Sue Robertson.*

12", unmarked nun, "Our Lady of Fatima," label reads "D & D Mfg.," sleep eyes, closed mouth, black habit, black and white beaded rosary, plastic headband and collar, circa 1950s, $50.00. *Private collection.*

11½", Gura girl, tag reads "Gura//This is an original costume doll//as worn in the age of//Biedermeier//(worn 1815 – 1850)," brown synthetic hair, blue sleep eyes, closed mouth, wearing long blue dress with pink shawl, straw hat with flowers, pink ribbon, circa 1950s, $75.00. *Courtesy Sandy Sumner.*

5", Hollywood Doll Co. "Nun," marked "Star//Hollywood Doll Co.", sleep eyes, closed mouth, molded painted hair, fingers molded together, original nun habit, circa 1950s, $25.00. *Courtesy Nelda Shelton.*

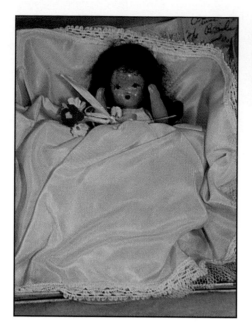

5½", Hollywood Doll Co., Bride, box says "A HOLLYWOOD DOLL//PRINCESS SERIES//The Bride," painted eyes, brown hair, in white dress, white satin sash with flowers at waist, MIB, circa 1953, $35.00. *Courtesy Betty Strong.*

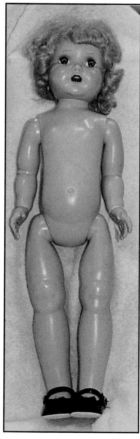

28", Paris Doll Company, Rita, blonde saran hair, blue sleep eyes, painted lashes below eyes, eyeshadow, open mouth with teeth, 5-piece hard plastic body; an identification tip for these unmarked dolls, the square knobby knees indicate Rita, circa 1951 – 1953, $175.00. *Courtesy Eileen Hanrahan.*

12", D.G. Todd & Co. Ltd., of Southport, England, girl marked "Roddy//Made in England," blue sleep eyes, blonde wig, pink lace dress circa 1950s – 1960s, $50.00. *Courtesy Betty Crosby.*

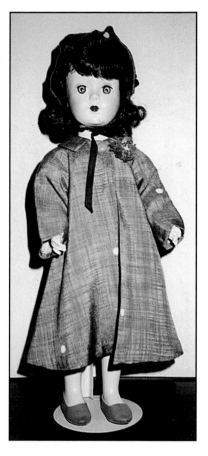

7½", Rosebud Ltd., "Miss Rosebud," marked "Rosebud" in script on head and "Miss Rosebud(script)//MADE IN ENGLAND" on body, strung, blue sleep eyes, painted lashes, curly blonde mohair wig, dressed in Scottish costume, circa mid 1950s, $125.00+. *Courtesy Lee Ann Beaumont.*

18", Bride, sleep eyes, closed mouth, rosy cheeks, no tags, circa late 1940s, $300.00. *Courtesy Cherie Gervais.*

19", unmarked walker, blue sleep eyes, closed mouth, brunette wig, redressed in light brown coat with pink corsage, circa 1950s, $475.00. *Courtesy Sue Robertson.*

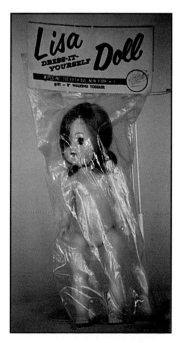

8", Wipco Lisa Doll, reads on package "Dress-It-Yourself Doll," walking toddler, still in package, circa 1955, $25.00. *Courtesy Peggy Millhouse.*

G.I. Joe

One of the major developments in the doll field has been the action figure, which has produced its own cadre of doll collectors. The most famous of those figures has to be G.I. Joe who spawned a whole new generation of collectors.

G.I. Joe, 1964 – 1976, 11½" tall
Super Joes, 1976 – 1978, 8½" tall
G.I. Joe, 1982 – on, 3½" tall

18" vinyl, "Real Baby," marked "C 1984//J. Turner," original yellow baby outfit with matching hair bow, circa 1984, $55.00. *Courtesy Phyllis Chrestman.*

12" vinyl, "Talking GI Joe Adventure Team Commander," flocked hair and beard, circa 1970, some accessories missing, $115.00. *Private collection.*

11½" vinyl, "Air Adventurer G.I. Joe" from the Adventure Team, blonde flocked hair and beard, brown eyes, facial scar, wearing original orange flight suit with AT decal, black boots, kung fu grip, NMIB, circa 1975, $145.00. *Courtesy McMasters Doll Auctions.*

Jem

Hasbro produced Jem dolls in 1985 and 1986. They were patterned after characters in the Jem cartoon television series, which aired in 1985 – 1988 and was later available as reruns. The complete line of Jem dolls consists of 21 dolls, but there are lots of variations and rare fashions to keep the collector hunting. All dolls are 12" tall (except Starlight who is 11") and totally posable since the knees and elbows bend, the waist and head turn, and the wrists swivel. The dolls are realistically proportioned like a human figure. They are made of vinyl with rooted hair, marked on head "Hasbro, Inc.," and some backs are marked "COPYRIGHT 1985 HASBRO, INC.//CHINA," some are marked "COPYRIGHT 1987 HASBRO//MADE IN HONG KONG." Starlight girls are unmarked. Their appeal to the public may have been the "truly outrageous" flashy mod fashions and startling hair colors that made them so different from other fashion type dolls of this era.

G.I. Joe Action Sailor #7606 "Frogman Scuba Tanks," dual oxygen tanks that strapped to Action Sailor's back, plus air hose and connecting mouth piece, NRFP, circa 1964, $25.00. *Courtesy McMasters Doll Auctions.*

12" vinyl, Roxy, has platinum hair, facial painting, black and multicolor "Truly Outrageous" costume, music cassette and guitar, MIB, stock #4206, circa 1985, $50.00. *Courtesy Cornelia Ford.*

12" vinyl, Aja, has blue hair, guitar, pink and silver "Truly Outrageous" costume, MIB, stock #4101, with music cassette and guitar, circa 1985, $45.00. *Courtesy Cornelia Ford.*

12" vinyl, Kimber, has red hair, guitar, in silver, white, and pink costume, "Truly Outrageous," MIB, #4202, with music cassette, circa 1985, $45.00. *Courtesy Cornelia Ford.*

Hitty Dolls

Hitty is major character in the book, *Hitty, Her First Hundred Years* by Rachel Field, published in 1929. It is a story of a 6" doll, Hitty, and her adventures through 100 years. The story remains popular with people who read it as children and gave the book to their children and grandchildren. It is charmingly illustrated with pen and ink drawings, and early editions also contain some color plates. The original Hitty makes her home in the Sturbridge, Massachusetts, library, while today's artists recreate Hitty for collectors. A *Hitty Newsletter* is published and Hitty get-togethers happen at doll conventions and conferences. See Collector's Network for information on the *Hitty Newsletter* to keep abreast of latest artist creations.

What to look for:

Reread the Hitty book to fix in your mind your ideal Hitty and then look for the many artist interpretations available today. You can find them nude or dressed, giving you options on price and the opportunity to make a wardrobe for your own Hitty. You may even wish to try carving your own.

6¼" wood, carved by Judy Brown, painted features, jointed hips and arms, dressed white flower print dress by chair with two small wooden dolls, circa 1999, prices range from $310.00 to $425.00 for Hitty and outfit. *Courtesy Judy Brown.*

6¼" wood, carved by Judy Brown, painted features, jointed hips and arms, dressed in blue pleated skirt and jacket with gold trim, matching hat, circa 1999, prices range from $310.00 to $425.00 for Hitty and outfit. *Courtesy Judy Brown.*

6¼" wood, carved by Ruth Brown, dark ash, painted features, jointed hips and arms, painted-on black boots and white socks, dressed in blue floral print dress with white lace petticoat, red bead necklace, circa 1999, $175.00. *Photo courtesy Ruth Brown.*

6¼" wood, carved by Ruth Brown, light ash, painted features, jointed hips and arms, painted-on black boots and white socks, dressed in beige print dress with puff sleeves trimmed in white lace, circa 1999, $175.00. *Photo courtesy Ruth Brown.*

6¼" wood, carved by Ruth Brown, light ash, painted features, jointed hips and arms, painted-on black boots and white socks, dressed in white dress with pink flower print and blue line print, circa 1999, $175.00. *Photo courtesy Ruth Brown.*

6¼" wood, carved by Ruth Brown, light ash, painted features, jointed hips and arms, painted-on black boots and white socks, dressed in blue and white print dress with full skirt, circa 1999, $175.00. *Photo courtesy Ruth Brown.*

6¼" basswood, "Hittybel and Friends," by doll artist DeAnn Cote, handcarved replicas using digital caliper measurements taken from the original Hitty to ensure authenticity, painted with old-fashioned oil base paints, antiqued with a coat of beeswax, Friends designed with unique hairstyles, boots, hair and eye color, dressed in vintage fabric chemise and pantalets, numbered, dated, and signed birth and authenticity certificates, circa 1999, Hittybel $450.00, Friends $400.00. *Courtesy DRC Design.*

6¼" white ash, by doll artist DeAnn Cote, handcarved replicas using digital caliper measurements taken from the original Hitty to ensure authenticity, painted with old-fashioned oil base paints, antiqued with a coat of beeswax, blue and lilac flower print dress, pink apron with lace, bead necklace, circa 1990s, $650.00; fossilized ivory (walrus tooth) 1³⁄₁₆" carved Hitty by DeAnn Cote, sitting by cat, $350.00, on book 1¼", $300.00. *Courtesy Betty Fronefield.*

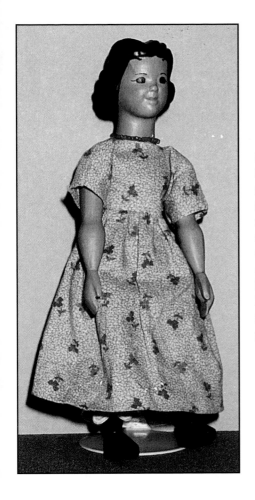

6¼" white ash, by doll artist DeAnn Cote, handcarved replicas using digital caliper measurements taken from the original Hitty to ensure authenticity, painted with old-fashioned oil base paints, antiqued with a coat of beeswax, orange print dress, bead necklace, circa 1990s, $650.00. *Courtesy Betty Fronefield.*

6¼" wooden jointed Hitty, handcarved by Janci doll artists Jill Sanders and Nancy Elliot, painted features, one-of-a-kind, circa 1999, $395.00. *Courtesy Jill Sanders.*

6¼" wooden jointed Hitty, handcarved by Janci doll artists Jill Sanders and Nancy Elliot, painted features, calico dress, hang tag reads "Janci Dolls//Hand painted & carved wooden dolls made one at a time with love in Michigan, USA," circa 1999, $295.00. *Courtesy Jill Sanders.*

Horsman Dolls

Horsman was founded by Edward Imeson Horsman in New York City in 1865. The E.I. Horsman Company distributed, assembled, and made dolls, merged with Aetna Doll and Toy Co. and in 1909 obtained its first copyright for a complete doll, "Billiken." Horsman later made hard plastic and vinyl dolls, many of which are unmarked; some have only a number or they may be marked Horsman. *Judd's* reports that painted inset pins on the doll's walking mechanism are one means of identification of these hard plastic dolls. Some of the hard plastic dolls had either a child or fashion type body.

What to look for:

Composition dolls should have minimal crazing, rosy cheeks, original clothing, and labels or tags when possible. Great characters like the Campbell Kids are always charming. Later dolls should be much more perfect and all original. This company offers a nifty collecting niche; collectors may find bargains, since Horsman's later dolls have not been as popular.

11" composition, "Tynie Baby," marked "© 1924//E.I.H. Co. Inc." on head, blue sleep eyes, closed mouth, painted molded hair, composition arms and hands, cloth body and legs, tagged baby dress, white bonnet, pin reads "TINIE//HORSMAN'S//BABY," Tynie spelled "TINIE" on pin, circa 1924, $325.00. *Courtesy Robert V. Hardy.*

16½" composition, "Baby Darling," marked "E.I.H." on back of head, sleep eyes, open mouth, no teeth, molded painted hair, disc jointed arms and bent baby legs, cloth body, dressed in pink baby dress and matching bonnet, dress tagged "Baby Darling//MADE BY//HORSMAN," circa 1930s, $250.00. *Courtesy Myra Boyd.*

18" all-composition, "Bright Star Skater," long, blonde braided wig with curled bangs, blue sleep eyes, open mouth, teeth, red and white outfit, white skates, MIB, circa 1937 – 1946, $500.00. *Courtesy Iva Mae Jones.*

14" composition, "Peterkins" marked "EIH" on back of head, cloth body, composition arms and legs, original blue print dress, blue painted eyes, closed mouth, molded and painted reddish hair, crazing, circa 1929, $250.00. *Courtesy Elizabeth Surber.*

18" composition, toddler, brown tin sleep eyes, real lashes, open mouth with two upper teeth, molded tongue, blonde mohair wig, chubby 5-piece composition toddler body, original dark blue print dress with white felt dog, matching bonnet, white romper, rayon socks, white leatherette shoes, all original with box, circa 1930s, $255.00. *Courtesy McMasters Doll Auctions.*

17" composition, "Rosebud," marked "Rosebud" on back of head, brown sleep eyes, real lashes, painted lashes, open mouth with four upper teeth, original mohair wig, 5-piece composition body, original pleated blue organdy dress, underwear combination, socks and white leatherette shoes, original box with extra pink flowered dress, box label "Horsman//Genuine Horsman Art Doll//Made in U.S.A.//Horsman Dolls Inc.," circa 1930s, $325.00. *Courtesy McMasters Doll Auctions.*

17" vinyl, "Poor Pitiful Pearl," blue sleep eyes, rosy cheeks, red scarf, flowered dress, black stockings, MIB, circa 1959 – 1963, $195.00. *Courtesy Betty Strong.*

24" vinyl, "Jackie," marked "Horsman//19©61//JK25," sleep eyes, closed mouth, rooted dark brown curly hair, pierced ears, rigid vinyl jointed body, tall slender fashion body, slim legs, high-heeled feet, lacy dress with stole, circa 1961, $25.00. *Courtesy Betty Strong.*

9" vinyl, "Mickey Mouse Club" doll, marked "Horsman Doll Inc.//©//1971" on back, blue sleep eyes, closed mouth, rosy cheeks, blonde synthetic wig, dressed in Mickey Mouse Club dress and ears, circa 1971, $25.00. *Courtesy Betty Strong.*

11" vinyl, "Pippi Longstocking," marked "Horsman Doll Co.//1972," apron reads "Pippi," painted side-glancing eyes, freckles, open/closed mouth with painted teeth, long rooted red hair with bangs, center part, green dress with orange checked apron, one orange and one green stocking, circa 1972, $25.00. *Courtesy Betty Strong.*

17½" vinyl, "Tessie Talk," marked "Horsman Dolls Inc.//19©74," painted features, freckles, rooted hair, pull string to make mouth move, large hands and feet, black and white striped dress with red and white polka dot sleeves, circa 1974, $25.00. *Courtesy Betty Strong.*

Mary Hoyer Dolls

Mary Sensenig Hoyer was born October 21, 1901, in Lancaster County, Pennsylvania, to Sallie Whitman and Daniel Sensenig, the youngest of 14 children. Her father had a general store and post office in Lancaster, but moved when Mary was six months of age to Mohnton, Pennsylvania, where her father again ran a store. When she was seven years old, the family moved to Reading, Pennsylvania, and she has lived in this area ever since. Her oldest sister, Alice, who did piece work and made cotton sunbonnets with brims of real straw, influenced her.

At age eight, Mary was hospitalized with appendicitis, and Alice told her to hurry and get well and she would buy Mary a beautiful doll. When she left the hospital, she went home to Alice's house, and the doll was waiting for her. Mary remembers the doll being the most beautiful doll she had ever seen. It had a bisque head with long, golden, finger curls of human hair, blue eyes, and a smiling mouth with little teeth. The doll was made in Germany, had a jointed body, and wore a dress Alice had made of blue China silk.

While Mary was recovering, Alice taught her how to knit and crochet and do some simple sewing. Alice eventually opened a store selling yarn, needles, and other related sewing items. Mary, at age 18 attended McCanns Business School and later worked for Alice, designing and writing knitting instructions.

Mary met William Hoyer in 1923, and they married in 1926, driving to their first home in Canada in 1926 in a Model T. The honeymooners lived in an apartment until they could build a house nearby in Springmont where daughter Arlene was born.

Mary's career began as a designer of knit and crochet fashions for children and babies. It seemed a natural outgrowth of that to extend her talents to designing fashions for children's dolls. She first made clothes for her daughter Arlene's doll, a 14" heavy composition of unknown maker. Mary soon began dreaming about having an artist make a doll to her own specifications, 14" tall and shaped like a little girl. She first used 13" dolls from Ideal Novelty and Toy Company. Her idea was to sell the undressed doll with accompanying instruction booklet with patterns for knit and crochet outfits.

About 2,000 of these unmarked Ideal 13" jointed composition dolls were sold before this model was discontinued by Ideal. They had sleep eyes and mohair wigs that came in three different shades, blonde, dark brown, and auburn. The composition bodies had a segmented torso joint just below the arms. The undressed doll sold for $1.50 or dressed for $3.00.

In late 1937 Mary met with doll sculptor Bernard Lipfert who had already designed Patsy, Shirley Temple, the Dionne Quintuplets, Ginny, and many other dolls. She said he did not want to sculpt the doll she wanted, but after some conversation and a glass of wine, they came to an agreement. The Fiberoid Doll Company in New York produced the Mary Hoyer doll, but Mary retained ownership of the molds. She estimates approximately 6,500 of the composition dolls were made before production was discontinued in 1946. The molds were later sold without the company's knowledge to someone in South America.

Mary Hoyer dolls were unmarked and had painted eyes, with mohair wigs in four shades. The next 5,000 dolls were incised with the mark "THE//MARY HOYER//DOLL." As soon as sleep eyes were available for the composition dolls, they were used, but painted eyes were used first.

With World War II and the use of plastic for the war effort, hard plastic became a popular material for use in dolls. It was new; it was different; it was MODERN! And it appealed to mothers and children. Hoyer began using this new material on the new Mary Hoyer dolls. They were also 14" tall, and had a walking mechanism. This doll was marked in a circle on the back, "ORIGINAL//MARY HOYER//DOLL." The walker type of body proved troublesome and was removed, leaving those models with two slits in the head.

A variation was introduced in 1950, an 18" Mary Hoyer named "Gigi" with the same hard plastic mark as the 14" dolls. The Frisch Doll Company made only about 2,000 of these dolls, and they never gained the popularity of the 14" dolls.

Another variant made in the middle 1950s by Ideal had a vinyl head, rooted hair in a ponytail, and high-heeled feet. This doll was discontinued after only one shipment was made. She originally sold for $6.95.

Mary placed ads in *McCall's Needlework and Crafts* magazine and by 1945, Mr. Hoyer quit his job as purchasing agent for Berkshire Knitting Mills to spend full time managing the mail order business, opening a plant and shipping department. Mary also had a retail shop on Penn Street in Reading and another on the Boardwalk in Ocean City, New Jersey, where granddaughter Mary Lynne Sanders remembers playing under the Boardwalk in the summer as a little girl.

Another variation was the all-vinyl "Vicky" doll made in 1957 for Hoyer by Ideal. She came in three sizes, 10½", 12", and 14". The two larger sizes were discontinued and only the 10½" was continued for any length of time. She was described as having a body that bent at the waist, sleep eyes, and rooted saran hair and was a high-heeled doll. She came dressed in a bra and panties, high heels, and earrings.

The next year, 1958, an all-vinyl 10" toddler, the Unique Doll Company made Margie with rooted hair and sleep eyes for Hoyer. In 1961 they added a 10" Cathy, an all-vinyl infant made by the same company. Next came an 8" vinyl baby, Janie. Hoyer continued her main marketing thrust with knitted and crocheted patterns, kits, and dressed dolls that came to be her trademark in the doll world as well as her custom-made costumes sold mail order and the costumes sold in retail shops. The labels read "Mary Hoyer//Reading//PA."

In 1960, the Fiberoid Doll Company folded after producing approximately 72,000 of the 14" hard plastic dolls, Mary Hoyer's personal favorite of all her dolls. Hoyer next had the 14" doll copied in vinyl, with rooted hair and some face changes. She was called "Becky." Becky had long straight, curly or upswept hairstyles. The hair could be combed, washed, and set and came in four shades. The Becky doll was unmarked and was discontinued in 1968.

Granddaughter Mary Lynne Saunders continued the Mary Hoyer Doll Company in the 1980s with a vinyl play doll and characters from a fairy tale, "The Doll with the Magic Wand," written by Mary Hoyer. Her 1990s dolls are now more of a basic play doll with a variety of eye colors, hairstyles, and wardrobes. Some of the more intriguing pieces available include hiking boots, shorts, camping gear, and realistic accessories for the modern girls of today. The dolls, clothing, and accessories are forever popular.

A delightful, talented lady who turned her designing talents into a wonderful career, Mary Hoyer has given the doll world a treat with her designs, dolls, and patterns that will carry on for generations. The Mary Hoyer Doll Company and mail order business is still thriving: Mary Hoyer Doll Company, PO Box 1608, Lancaster, PA 17603, (717) 393 – 4121.

What to look for:

One of the hot collectible dolls has been the 18" hard plastic "Gigi" with the round Mary Hoyer mark on her back. Prices are high for dolls with original clothing in excellent condition. Mary Hoyer dolls are a great delight for knitters who can use all the patterns in Mary Hoyer pattern books that have been reissued. Mary Hoyer dolls are a great collectible to look for in composition and hard plastic, but do not pass up the new ones produced by the family business headed by Mary's granddaughter. Look for rosy cheeks, little crazing if composition, clean hard plastic, and original outfits when possible.

14" composition, marked "The//Mary Hoyer//Doll," blonde curly mohair wig, painted blue side-glancing eyes, closed mouth, 5-piece composition body, perhaps original ballerina costume, circa 1940s, $250.00. *Courtesy Martha Cotta.*

14" composition, marked "ORIGINAL//Mary Hoyer//DOLL" in circle, sleep eyes, real lashes, painted lower lashes, closed mouth, blonde mohair wig, pink crocheted skating outfit trimmed in white with matching hat, white roller skates, circa 1940s, $375.00. *Courtesy Kris Lundquist.*

14" hard plastic, marked "Original Mary//Hoyer Doll" in circle, blonde synthetic wig, blue sleep eyes, closed mouth, in blue knit skating outfit trimmed in white, matching hat, white skates, circa mid 1940s to 1950, $300.00. *Courtesy Donna Hadley.*

14" hard plastic type, auburn synthetic wig, sleep eyes, closed mouth, gold knit skating outfit and matching hat, white skates, gold socks, circa 1950+, $200.00. *Courtesy Donna Hadley.*

14" hard plastic, marked "Made in U.S.A.," blonde synthetic wig, sleep eyes, closed mouth, red knit dress, plaid tam, black shoes, circa mid to late 1940s, $225.00. *Courtesy Donna Hadley.*

14" composition in 5-piece crocheted ice skating costume, from Mary Hoyer pattern "Delores," auburn mohair wig, blue sleep eyes, $525.00. *Courtesy Sue Robertson.*

Ideal Dolls

The Ideal Novelty and Toy Co., begun 1906 in Brooklyn, New York, produced their own composition dolls in their early years. Morris Michtom started the business by making "Teddy" bears in 1906 with his wife, Rose, after the incident in which President Teddy Roosevelt refused to shoot a bear cub during a hunting expedition. Michtom also began making composition "unbreakable" dolls about this time. His early comic characters were popular, and Ideal also produced licensed dolls for companies to help promote their products such as "Uneeda Kid" that carried a small box of crackers for the Uneeda Biscuit Company. Some of their big successes were Shirley Temple in composition, Saucy Walker and Toni in hard plastic, and Miss Revlon in vinyl. They also made dolls of cloth and rubber.

Marks: Various including IDEAL in a diamond; US of A; IDEAL Novelty and Toy Co., Brooklyn, New York, and others.

What to look for:

Look for dolls with minimal crazing in composition, good color, and original clothing. Hard plastic and vinyl dolls should be better, with very good color, clean, bright, and perhaps tagged original clothing. A wide variety of Ideal dolls are available since they were in business into the 1990s.

18" composition, marked "Ideal Doll//Made in USA//Pat. No. 2252077," molded painted hair, blue sleep eyes, closed mouth, cloth bent leg baby body, composition limbs, some fingers missing, in baby dress with matching bonnet, circa 1940s, $100.00. *Courtesy Michele Newby.*

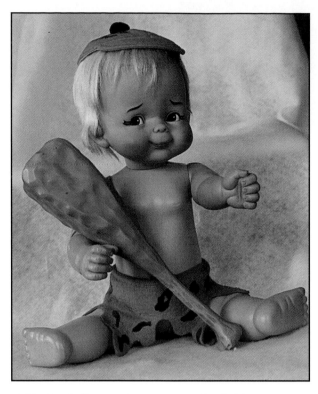

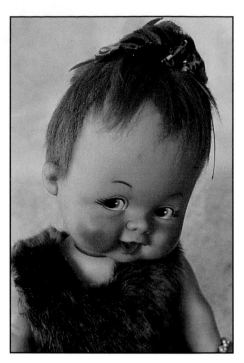

16" vinyl, Bamm-Bamm, marked "©HANNA-BARBERA PRODS., INC.//IDEAL TOY CORP.//BB-17//2" on head, character from Flintstones TV cartoon, painted brown side-glancing eyes, rooted blonde saran hair, jointed body, leopard skin suit and cap, original club, circa 1964, $100.00. *Courtesy Betty Strong.*

16" vinyl, Pebbles, marked "©HANNA-BARBERA PRODUC-TIONS, INC." on head, character from Flintstones TV cartoon, painted blue side-glancing eyes, rooted saran hair with topknot, jointed body, redressed, circa 1964, $50.00. *Courtesy Betty Strong.*

9½" vinyl, Belly Button Baby Me So Glad, marked "© 1970//Ideal Toy Corp//E 9-2-H185//Hong Kong," rooted blonde hair, green decal eyes, press button in belly makes arms, legs, and head move, curved legs, blue dotted Swiss dress, circa 1971, $7.00. *Courtesy Adrienne Hagey.*

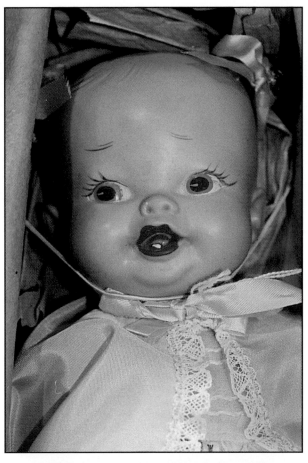

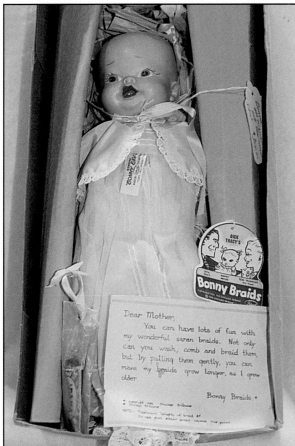

14" vinyl, Bonny Braids, painted blue eyes, open/closed mouth, one tooth, painted yellow hair, two pigtail tufts, magic skin latex rubber one-piece body, came with tube of Ipana toothpaste and toothbrush, wearing pink tagged gown, marked on back of neck "© 1951//CHI. Tribune//Ideal Doll//U.S.A." Braids would grow to 4" according to letter included in box. Bonny Braids Baby was the daughter of comic strip Dick Tracy & Tess Truheart, circa 1953, $250.00+. *Courtesy Geri Teeter.*

24" vinyl, Cream Puff, marked "Ideal Doll//B-23-L" on head, rooted saran hair, sleep eyes, lashes, watermelon mouth, dimpled cheeks, yellow nylon dress and matching bonnet with blue ribbon trim, all original with box, circa 1959 – 1962, $140.00. *Courtesy Chan Jeschien.*

20½" composition, Deanna Durbin, mohair wig, brown sleep eyes, open mouth, six teeth, wearing tagged long white gown with blue, yellow, and orange flowers, circa 1938, $695.00. *Courtesy June Allgeier.*

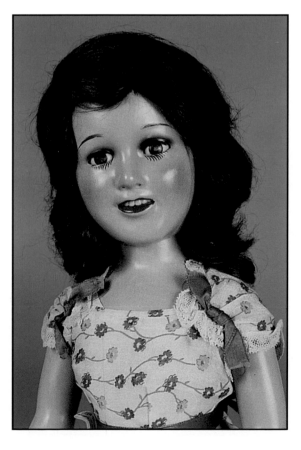

20" composition, Deanna Durbin, marked "Deanna Durbin//Ideal Doll" on head, "Ideal Doll" on back, hazel sleep eyes, eye shadow, painted lower lashes, open mouth with six upper teeth, original human hair wig, 5-piece composition body, original floral tagged dress, underclothing, socks and shoes, circa 1938, $550.00. *Courtesy McMasters Doll Auctions.*

17½" all-vinyl, Diana Ross, marked "©1969//Ideal Toy Co.//D B-18-ME4-1," dark brown sleep eyes, real lashes, painted lower lashes, open/closed smiling mouth with painted teeth, "On Stage" in a gold fabric sheath with feathers and gold shoes, all original mint, circa 1969, $200.00. *Courtesy Sharon Kolibaba.*

20" composition, Deanna Durbin, marked "Deanna Durbin//Ideal Doll" on back of head, "Ideal Doll" on back, hazel sleep eyes, real lashes, eye shadow, painted lower lashes, open mouth with six upper teeth, original human hair wig, 5-piece composition body, original maroon short dress with white trim, original teddy and slip, socks and black shoes with fringe trim, circa 1938, $275.00. *Courtesy McMasters Doll Auctions.*

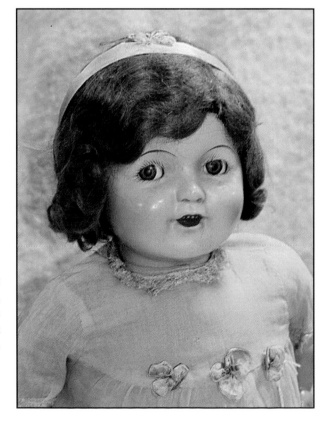

22" composition, Flossie Flirt, marked "Ideal" (inside diamond), brown mohair wig, blue tin flirty eyes, open mouth with two painted upper teeth, compo limbs, cloth body, original pink dress and pink bow in hair, pink slip, all original, circa 1924 – 1931, $200.00. *Courtesy Angie Gonzales.*

24" hard plastic, Howdy Doody, marked "IDEAL" on head, scarf reads "HOWDY DOODY," signed by Buffalo Bob Smith on the neck when the doll was brought to St. Petersburg, Florida, by the owner, television personality, red painted molded hair, freckles, ventriloquist doll, mouth operated by a pull string, cloth body and limbs, dressed in cowboy outfit, circa 1950 – 1953, $450.00. *Courtesy Iva Mae Jones.*

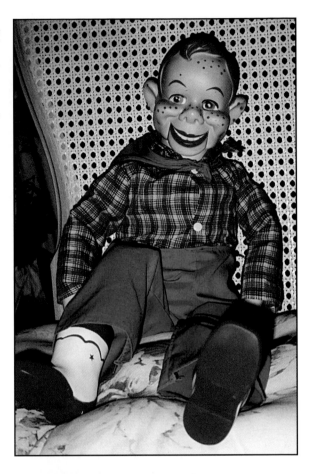

22" vinyl, Kissy, with rigid vinyl body. Press her hands together and her mouth puckers up with a noisy kiss. Rooted blond saran hair, sleep eyes, jointed wrists, original red and white checked dress/bloomers, matching red vinyl sandals, in box, circa 1961 – 1964, marked on head "© Ideal Corp//K-21-L," marked on body "Ideal Toy Corp.//K22//Pat. Pend.", $145.00. *Courtesy McMasters Doll Auctions.*

18" vinyl, Miss Revlon, marked "Ideal Doll//VT-18" on head, swivel head, blue sleep eyes, real lashes, closed mouth, pierced ears, rooted nylon hair, vinyl lady body jointed at waist, shoulders, and hips, high-heeled feet, original tagged red print dress with matching reverse jacket, panties, nylon stockings, high heel shoes, unplayed-with condition, wrist booklet, circa 1957, $310.00. *Courtesy McMasters Doll Auctions.*

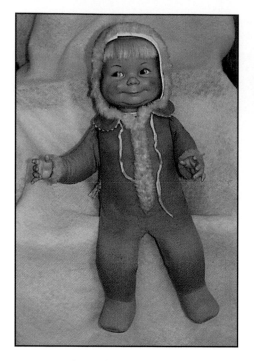

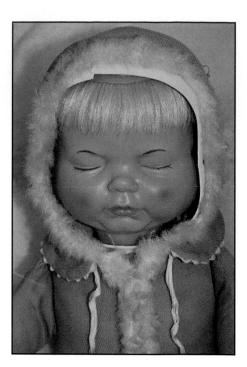

22" vinyl, Little Lost Baby, vinyl head with three faces, soft body, cries, coos, laughs, sleeps, head changes mechanically, voice operates on battery, MIB, circa 1968, $65.00. *Courtesy Susan Dubow.*

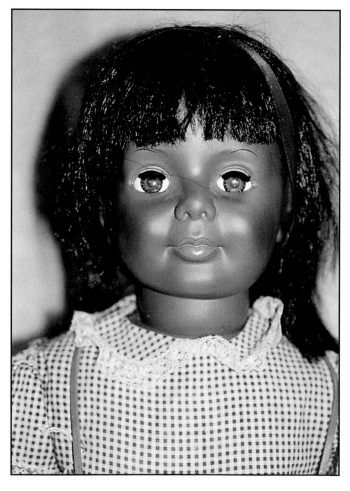

35" vinyl, black Patti Play Pal, marked "Ideal//M 346," brown sleep eyes, black rooted hair with bangs, closed mouth, individual fingers, size of a three-year-old, wears original red and white dress, circa 1959, $400.00. *Courtesy Angie Gonzales.*

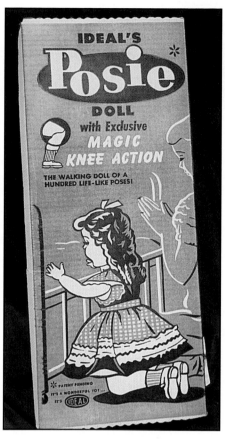

17" vinyl, Posie, marked "IDEAL DOLL//VP-17" on head, "IDEAL DOLL" on back, soft vinyl head, hard plastic body, jointed bent knees, walker, rooted saran hair, flirty blue sleep eyes, came with curlers, wears short blue dress, white socks/shoes, box says "Ideal's//Posie//Doll//with exclusive//MAGIC KNEE ACTION//The walking doll of a hundred life-like poses," MIB, circa 1954 – 1956, $250.00. *Courtesy Iva Mae Jones.*

9" all-vinyl, Tearie Dearie, marked "© 1964//Ideal Toy Corp//B W9-4" on head, rooted saran hair, sleep eyes, lower painted lashes, drinks, wets, and cries real tears, blows bubbles with bubble pipe, in box that converts to rocking cradle, played-with condition, missing hair in front, with five outfits, circa 1964 – 1967, $35.00. *Courtesy Jodie Portias.*

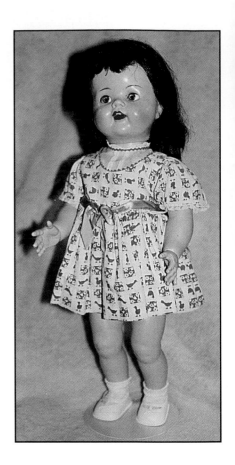

22" hard plastic, Saucy Walker, marked "Ideal Doll" on head and body, brown rooted hair with bangs, flirty blue sleep eyes, open mouth, two inset top teeth, holes in body for cry mechanism, walks and turns head from side to side when arm is held, original green and white print dress, circa 1951 – 1955, $125.00. *Courtesy Judie Conroy.*

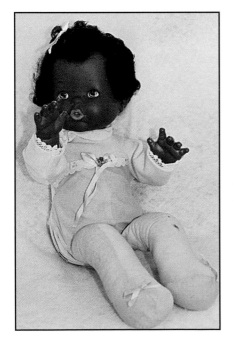

17" vinyl, black Wake-up Thumbelina, marked "1975//Ideal Toy//Corp//WB-18-H-281//Hollis, NY" on back of head, "soft skin" vinyl head, black rooted hair, painted brown eyes, open/closed mouth, vinyl arms, plastic body, cloth stuffed legs are part of outfit, raises head, turns from side to side, raises body, turns over, and holds up arms, battery operated, circa 1976, $30.00. *Courtesy Adrienne Hagey.*

14" hard plastic, Toni with blue/green plastic sleep eyes, eyeshadow, real and painted lashes, closed mouth, synthetic wig, marked on back of head "Ideal Doll//Made in USA" and on back "P-90//Ideal Doll//Made in USA," red leatherette center-snap shoes, original white with red dot organdy dress, blue rick-rack trim, over blue cotton slip, Toni hang tag, circa 1949, $350.00. *Courtesy June Allgeier.*

19" hard plastic, Toni, with brunette synthetic wig, blue plastic sleep eyes, eyeshadow above eyes, real and painted lashes, closed mouth, marks, "ideal Doll//P-92" on body, in dress with red skirt and green plaid top, red center-snap leatherette shoes, Toni hang tag with pink vinyl curlers, circa 1949, $500.00. *Courtesy June Allgeier.*

14" hard plastic, Toni, with blue sleep eyes, real lashes, feathered brows, painted lower lashes, eyeshadow, closed mouth, original blonde nylon wig, in original set, 5-piece hard plastic body with vinyl arms, dressed in original pink/white piqué tagged dress, original panties, socks, and shoes, marked on head "Ideal Doll//Made in USA," on back "Ideal Doll//P-90," shipping box, brochures, circa 1949+, $925.00. *Courtesy McMasters Doll Auctions.*

Kenner Dolls

The "Star Wars" movie was made in 1977, and the sequel, "The Empire Strikes Back," in 1980. Kenner made large Star Wars figures in 1978 in Hong Kong, ranging in heights from 7" to 15" including Princess Leia Organa, Luke Skywalker, R2-D2, Chewbacca, Darth Vader, and C-3P0. In 1979 Boba Fett, Han Solo, Stormtrooper, Ben (Obi-Wan) Kenobi, Jawa, and IG-88 were added. They also made 3" – 4" figures starting in 1979.

What to look for:

Kenner has made a variety of modern character dolls, such as "Bob Scout" with a Boy Scout uniform and accessories, sports figures, and fashion type dolls. Look for a boxed all-original doll, clean with good color. Star War figures are more popular with toy collectors, but always collectible, as are celebrities such as the Six Million Dollar Man figures. Look for them at garage sales, flea markets, and estate sales.

5" vinyl, Strawberry Shortcake, red rooted synthetic hair, painted blue eyes, freckles, painted features, green striped legs, pink and red outfit with strawberries, matching bonnet, circa 1979, $25.00. *Courtesy Bertha Melendez.*

Klumpe Dolls

Klumpe is known for caricature figures made of felt-over-wire armature with painted mask faces, produced in Barcelona, Spain, from circa 1952 to the mid 1970s. Figures represent professionals, hobbyists, Spanish dancers, historical characters, and contemporary males and females performing a wide variety of tasks. Of the 200 or more different figures, the most common are Spanish dancers, bullfighters, and doctors. Some Klumpes were imported by Effanbee in the early 1950s. Originally the figures had two sewn-on identifying cardboard tags.

What to look for:

These amusing characters may be missing their tags, but are still very collectible. Often passed over by more sophisticated collectors, they can still be found for reasonable prices. Look for those with more accessories, tags, or labels. They should be clean, with bright colors. The more intricate the costume and accessories, the more desirable they are to collectors. Must be pristine with all labels to command highest prices. Keep on the lookout at estate sales, antique malls, flea markets, and doll shows for these.

13" cloth, Majorette, tagged "No. n-. 1313//Made in Spain," felt-over-wire armature with painted mask face, black net stockings, black top hat, circa 1952 – 1970s, $175.00. *Courtesy Sharon Kolibaba.*

Klumpe Dolls

11" felt, Vendor, with painted features, snood over mohair wig, wire armature in body, lace trimmed apron, mitt gloves, paisley skirt, gold foil Klumpe tag attached to skirt, circa 1950s, $100.00. *Courtesy Dolores Jesurin.*

12" cloth, with painted features, Fruit Seller, floss wig, all original costume white blouse, multi-striped skirt, apron, straw hat with ribbons, carries basket of fruit, gold Klumpe foil sticker "Barcelona" on skirt, circa 1958 – 1961, $115.00. *Courtesy Nancy Ritchey.*

10½" cloth, girl, felt-over-wire armature with painted mask face, holding umbrella in one hand, yellow basket in other, scarf hat, circa 1952 – 1970s, $175.00. *Courtesy Betty Strong.*

Lenci Dolls

Elena von Konig Scavini was born in Italy in 1886, and after the loss of her firstborn child started making cuddly dolls. She called the dolls Lencina or Little Lenci. Her dolls were used as decorative accessories in bedrooms and cars and were carried with designer costumes. Early dolls were characters, tagged with a small Lenci button. Some of the most intricate were made during the 1920s, and this era is noted for rooted hair, hand embroidery, and pieced felt costumes with felt flowers. The American stock market crash threw the company into bankruptcy, and the company was taken over by Pilade Garella who narrowed the product line from clothing, costumes, ceramics, furniture, and handbags to only dolls. The 1930s dolls were more simplistic with fewer styles. Mascottes (7½") and miniature (9") dolls in regional and nursery rhyme costumes and dressed as children were heavily produced and promoted. Glass flirty eyes were added in 1935. Baby dolls were introduced in the 1930s with two face models, but were not popular. Boudoir dolls with elongated arms and legs dressed as celebrities were very popular and were made throughout the company's history. By 1940, Madame Lenci had lost her husband, Enrico, sold her remaining shares, and severed all ties to the Lenci Company. In the 1940s, Lenci quality diminished as production was needed for wartime necessities. In 1942, Beppe Garella, Pilade's son, came into the business, becoming president after his father's death in 1968. In the 1950s, the Lenci dolls popularity again slowed, and the company made dolls of other materials. In 1978, the company again started making felt dolls a profitable move. Madame Lenci died in 1974; in 1993, Beppe Garella died; his daughter Bibija now runs the company.

What to look for:

Lenci dolls are made of felt, with double layer ears and scalloped cotton socks. Early dolls can have rooted mohair wigs, 1930s dolls may have frizzed played-with looking wigs, 1940s dolls may have hard cardboard type felt faces. Value depends on condition such as cleanliness, originality, wear, and costumes that are more elaborate.

8" cloth, tagged "Lenci//Made in Italy//" on dress, "Provizione Originale//Lenci" on cardboard tag on dress, pressed felt swivel head, painted brown surprise eyes, painted upper lashes, open/closed mouth, blonde mohair wig, cloth torso and legs, felt arms with fingers indicated by stitching, original white organdy dress, plaid felt belt, knit socks, white felt shoes, holding green wooden pot with pink felt rose, circa 1920s – 1930s, $400.00. *Courtesy McMasters Doll Auctions.*

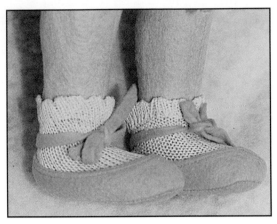

15" felt, with mohair wig, oil painted features including side-glancing brown eyes, two-tone painted lips with highlights on lower lip, accent dots at nose, in yellow organdy original dress, scalloped socks, and felt shoes, marked "Lenci" on bottom of left foot, circa 1930s. Middle photo shows gold felt shoes with ankle ties and scalloped cotton socks; right photo shows stitched middle fingers. $500.00+. *Courtesy Patrice Hunker.*

15" felt, with mohair wig, oil painted features including side-glancing brown eyes, two-tone painted lips with highlights on lower lip, accent dots at nose, in white organdy original dress with matching bonnet, trimmed with two-tone pink felt flower trim, scalloped socks, and felt shoes, marked "Lenci" on bottom of left foot, circa 1930s, $500.00+. *Courtesy Patrice Hunker.*

21" felt, Pierrot, expressive felt mask face, holding mandolin, black and white Pierrot costume with big white buttons, early beret with felt feather, circa 1920s, $1,950.00. *Courtesy Elizabeth Fielding.*

25" cloth, Fad-ette Smoker, unmarked, painted mask face, slitted eyes, thick eyebrows, thin eyelashes below eyes, red heart-shaped mouth with hole for cigarette, cloth body with felt over upper body, jointed at head, shoulders, waist, hips, elbows, and knees, individual thumb and fifth fingers, black felt pantsuit, turquoise and black striped trim, turquoise felt buttons, pearl necklace, high-heeled soft leather shoes, circa 1923, $375.00. *Courtesy McMasters Doll Auctions.*

11" cloth, ethnic boy, marked "Lenci//Made in Italy" on blue and white ribbon tag on back of vest, pressed felt swivel head, painted brown eyes to side, painted lashes, applied ears, brunette mohair wig, cloth torso and legs, felt arms with stitched fingers, original ethnic clothing with white shirt, black felt short pants, red felt vest trimmed with green, striped grosgrain ribbon around waist, black felt hat, original socks, black felt shoes, circa 1930s, $375.00. *Courtesy McMasters Doll Auctions.*

17" cloth, boy in regional costume, #300 series, felt mask face, swivel head, oil painted features, brown painted eyes, painted lashes, closed mouth, black mohair wig, cloth torso, felt arms and legs, applied ears, three fingers stitched together, holding stick, tan pants with brown fringe, tan top with darker tan felt vest trimmed in blue and orange, black hat with flowers, circa 1925 – 1930s, $2,200.00. *Courtesy Betty Warder.*

17" cloth boy, #300 Series, "Lenci//Made in Italy" on cloth tag, "Lenci//Turin (Italy)//Di E Scavini//Made in Italy//300/10" on paper tag, painted side-glancing brown eyes, mohair wig, gray felt short pants, knit sweater and socks, circa 1930s, $800.00. *Courtesy Sandra Lizut.*

16" cloth, Boxer, marked "Lenci//Made in Italy" on shirt ribbon tag, "Lenci//Turin (Italy)//Di E. Scavini//Made in Italy//1005//Pat. Sept. 8-1921-Pat. N. 142433//Ste. S.G.D.G. X 87395-Brevetto 501-178" on paper tag, pressed felt swivel head, painted eyes, closed mouth, applied ears, mohair inserted into head, felt body, hollow torso, jointed at shoulders/hips, red felt shirt, white shorts, black cap, brown leather shoes, replaced boxing gloves, circa 1929, $775.00. *Courtesy McMasters Doll Auctions.*

18" cloth, smooth face girl, unmarked, pressed felt swivel head, oil painted features, brown eyes, molded lids, painted lashes, closed pouty mouth, applied felt ears, human hair wig, cloth torso with felt-type cloth arms and legs, original red felt dress trimmed with felt flowers, red and green bow in hair, cotton underwear combination with felt rickrack trim, dark blue cotton socks, leather shoes, circa 1930s, $325.00. *Courtesy McMasters Doll Auctions.*

14" cloth, smooth face girl, unmarked, pressed felt swivel head with oil painted features, brown side-glancing eyes, applied felt ears, mohair wig, cloth torso, felt arms and legs, stitched fingers with separate thumb, first finger and little finger, green felt dress, white net and organdy pinafore with felt flowers, straw hat, white cotton teddy, replaced socks, red felt shoes, circa 1930s, $375.00. *Courtesy McMasters Doll Auctions.*

9" felt, dubbed Becassine by collectors, but never called Becassine by the Lenci Company, blonde hair, surprise eyes, surprise O-shaped mouth, molded/pressed face, French Provincial costume, wooden shoes, circa 1930s, $400.00. *Courtesy Nancy Lazenby.*

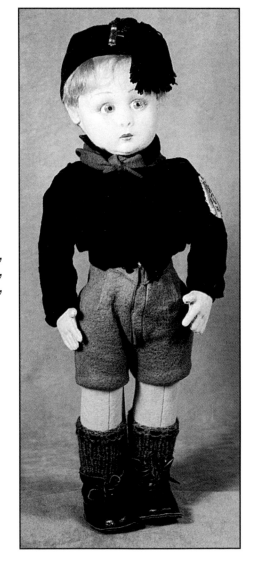

14" felt, rare Fascist Boy, blonde hair, brown side-glancing eyes, painted lashes, closed mouth, black jacket, matching hat with tassel, brown short pants, knitted socks, black leather shoes, circa 1930s, $1,600.00. *Courtesy Nancy Lazenby.*

16" felt, Dutch Boy & Girl, boy has blue side-glancing eyes, cigarette in mouth, blonde frizzy hair, girl has long blonde braided hair, brown side-glancing eyes, closed mouth, both in Dutch costume, wooden shoes, circa 1930s, $1,600.00 for pair. *Courtesy Nancy Lazenby.*

16" felt, 110 Series girl, long hair in sausage roll curls, green dress with darker green felt top, matching dark green on layered ruffles of skirt, green felt shoes, knit socks, circa 1930s, $1,200.00. *Courtesy Nancy Lazenby.*

Mattel, Inc. Dolls

Mattel has been a dominant force in the doll industry with their Barbie doll, Chatty Cathy, and others. The company began in 1945 when Ruth and Elliott Handler and their friend Harold Matson founded the Mattel Company in Los Angeles. The name came from "Matt" for Matson and "el" for Elliot. They began making picture frames, evolving into toy furniture. Matson left the company because of ill health, and Ruth Handler began to handle marketing. She advertised in 1955 on children's TV show, "The Mickey Mouse Club." In 1959, they marketed a fashion doll Barbie named after their daughter, and the company prospered. Barbie doll (see separate section) has become the number one collectible doll in the world. Mattel also has manufactured quite a list of celebrity dolls as well as characters from TV shows. The Handlers are no longer associated with the company.

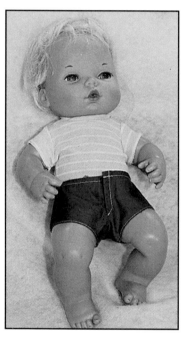

18" vinyl, Baby First Step, battery-operated walker, blue sleep eyes, rooted blond hair with side part, rigid vinyl body, original dress, box reads, "I really walk all by myself – New//She Skates" with red skates on white shoes., circa 1965 – 1967, $30.00. *Courtesy McMasters Doll Auctions.*

13" vinyl, Baby Brother Tender Love, marked "©1972//Mattel, Inc.," blonde hair, anatomically correct, realistic skin, can be bathed, blue and white striped shirt, dark blue short pants, with box, circa 1972, $40.00. *Courtesy Adrienne Hagey.*

19" vinyl, Cynthia, blonde rooted wig, blue decal eyes, open/closed smiling mouth with painted teeth, pink dress with turquoise trim, white plastic shoes, circa 1972, $60.00. *Courtesy Maria Traver.*

10¾" vinyl, Talking Buffy and Mrs. Beasley, with painted eyes, blonde wig in ponytails, in original red and white dress, with Mrs. Beasley in aqua and white dotted dress, yellow rickrack trim, and glasses, in box that reads "TV's Talking Buffy and Mrs. Beasley, A Small Talk Doll by Mattel," circa 1967 – 1974, $185.00. *Courtesy McMasters Doll Auctions.*

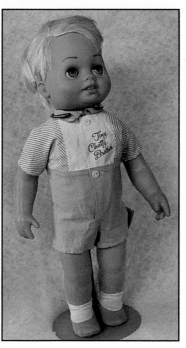

20" vinyl, Chatty Cathy, with rigid plastic body containing a pull-string talker mechanism, with sleep eyes, blonde rooted hair, open mouth with two teeth, freckles. wears original yellow dress with red and turquoise trim, white collar, circa 1960 – 1965, $400.00. *Courtesy McMasters Doll Auctions.*

15½" vinyl, Tiny Chatty Brother, marked "Tiny Chatty Baby™//Tiny Chatty Brother™//©1962 Mattel//Hawthorn, Calif., USA//US Pat #3-017-187//Other U.S. and Foreign Patents Pending//Patented in Canada 1962" on middle of lower back, large blue sleep eyes, open/closed mouth with two teeth, rooted blonde hair parted on the side, original blue and white outfit, circa 1963, $25.00. *Courtesy Betty Strong.*

9½" x 17½" plastic Kiddle-Mobile, marked "#5169//©
1968 Mattel Inc.//USA Printed in U.S.A.," with two Liddle
Kiddles, circa 1968, $30.00. *Courtesy Adrienne Hagey.*

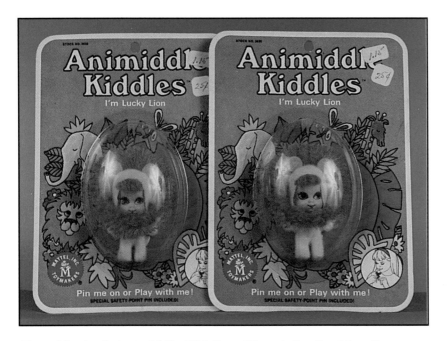

Two 2" vinyl Animiddle Kiddles, "I'm A Lucky Lion," orange
felt ears, orange yarn bangs, mane, and tail, blue eyes, wears a
yellow two-piece brushed nylon lion suit, special safety point
pin on back so they can be worn as a corsage, NRFP, circa 1969
– 1970, $180.00. *Courtesy McMasters Doll Auctions.*

18" vinyl, Hot Water Bottle Splash Happy Sal, flat vinyl doll
with painted features, side-glancing blue eyes, hot water
bottle cap in back of head, head marked "Mexico," body
marked "Mattel//1972," companion for bed and bath, circa
1972, $15.00. *Courtesy Beverly Kimmel.*

9" all-vinyl, Mork from the planet
Ork, portrayed by Robin Williams
on the TV series "Mork and
Mindy," marked "© 1979 PPC TAI-
WAN," painted hair and features,
fully jointed, space pack has talking mechanism that says eight
phrases, MIB, circa 1979, $25.00.
Courtesy Betty Strong.

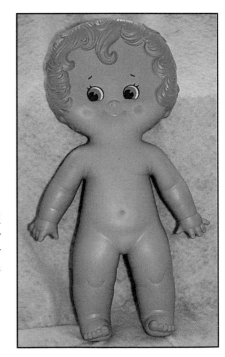

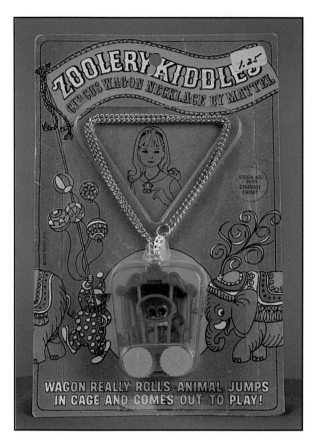

¾" vinyl Zoolery Kiddles, "Chummy Chimp," pink vinyl body, lighter pink painted face and ears, blue eyes, orange removable bow-tie, circus wagon cage is blue plastic and has green wheels, goldtone neck chain attached to a loop on top of the cage, NRFP, circa 1969 – 1970, $330.00. *Courtesy McMasters Doll Auctions.*

14" rigid vinyl Shoppin' Sheryl, marked "1970//Mattel//Hong Kong," blonde hair, one magnetized hand and one hand with flexible thumb for holding miniature supermarket products, pushes shopping cart, walks with help, circa 1971 – 1972, $25.00. *Courtesy Betty Strong.*

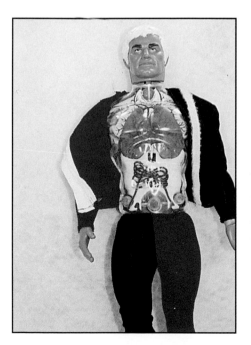

14" vinyl, Pulsar Man, marked "©Mattel, Inc.//1976 USA//3," molded painted white hair, painted blue eyes with heavy brown eyebrows, closed mouth, in red and black outfit, box reads "Pulsar, The Ultimate Man of Adventure, you activate his vital system, push his back, heart beats, lungs breath, blood flows, insert mission disks in brain, he almost comes alive", circa 1976, $10.00. *Courtesy Adrienne Hagey.*

Monica Dolls

Monica was the creation of Mrs. Hansi Share, owner of the Monica Doll Studios of Hollywood, California, who first advertised her dolls in 1941. Early dolls were 20" and 24" sizes.

In 1947, *Toys and Novelties,* a toy trade publication, advertised 15", 17", and 20" sizes. Individual dolls had names like Veronica, Jean, and Rosalind and later in hard plastic, Elizabeth, Marion, or Linda were offered by high-end stores such as F.A.O. Schwarz and Neiman Marcus. In October 1949 Monica Doll Studios announced the arrival of an all-plastic Marion with rooted hair and sleep eyes.

18" composition, Bride, painted blue eyes, closed mouth, brown rooted human hair, in white wedding gown tagged "MONICA//DOLL//HOLLYWOOD," long white veil, pearl necklace, bouquet tied to wrist, circa 1940s, $525.00. *Courtesy Elizabeth Fielding.*

What was remarkable about this doll from the beginning is the ingenious idea of rooting human hair first in the composition head and then later in the hard plastic one. If any of you endured the 1960s and 1970s era indulging in the tortuous beauty shop treatment of "frosting" your own hair, this is a similar process in reverse. In the beauty shop treatment, a plastic hood was placed over the patron's hair, and the hairdresser pulled the strands of hair through the plastic cap, and applied bleach to lighten the hair which gave a "frosted" appearance. Beauty hurt in those days, as the hair was pulled through the tiny holes; fortunately Monica did not have to feel the painful experience of having hair poked into her composition head.

Mrs. Share managed to come up with a process to place small portions of fragile human hair in the composition and plastic heads during the manufacturing process to give the appearance of "real rooted" hair. Other companies such as American Character fashioned a rooted hair skullcap on Sweet Sue and their 8" Betsy McCall as they tried to adapt this unique patented feature. Hair rooted into the head became an accepted practice with the use of vinyl for making dolls in the 1960s. The Monica Doll Company made dolls until 1952.

The Monica line of dolls is also interesting, because it typifies the re-entry of fashion dolls into the world of dolls. A Patsy-type doll of the 1930s such as Patsy and Shirley Temple had an early child-like all-composition body with a pudgy body. In 1935, Effanbee introduced the Patricia line and advertised them as an older sister of about 12 years of age with just the hint of breasts. In 1940, Effanbee showed "Little Lady" dolls still with an older child body, but wearing sophisticated negligees over panties and bras.

Monica dolls in 1941 had all-composition unmarked bodies with flat feet, and the arms and hands seem somewhat heavy and awkward in contrast to the sophistication of the hair, makeup, and facial features. Monica dolls had painted eyes, eyeshadow, a closed mouth, rosy cheeks, and most important, the unique rooted human hair feature. All of this makes the composition dolls dramatic and appealing. In the hard plastic medium, Monica is not as striking because the features become softened. The dramatic look given by the painted eyes diminishes with sleep eyes. These dolls had sophisticated wardrobes and came dressed in fancy short dresses, suits, long evening dresses, or bridal gowns. Additional costumes were available separately. Neiman Marcus's 1945 Christmas catalog featured Monica with a white peasant blouse, red peasant skirt and bolero, fruit-trimmed hat, and black ballerina slippers. Montgomery Ward's 1947 catalog pictures an all-composition Monica in net dress with ruffles, rayon underskirt, rayon panties, and long stockings and her rooted human hair wig beside an Effanbee doll costumed in transparent black rayon marquisette negligee with matching bra and panties.

Monica, appearing first in composition and making the transition to hard plastic, is an example of a doll that spans the gap from the 1930 child dolls to the more glamorous dolls of the 1950s. She has the same mystique as today's Gene dolls with her sophisticated Hollywood glamour makeup. Her short life, unique features, and Hollywood presence make her an interesting and desirable collectible.

What to look for:

Two identification tips are the rooted hair and painted eyes, although she was later made with sleep eyes. Try to find Monica with great hair and costumes; hard to find is the 11½" size.

20" composition doll with rooted human hair, painted eyes, eyebrows worn off, brown check suit, circa 1949 – 1951, $350.00. *Private collection.*

20" composition doll, painted blue eyes, eyeshadow, closed mouth, rooted human hair with widow's peak, 5-piece composition body, original ecru brocade and tulle dress trimmed with flowers and lace, original underclothing, socks and shoes, flower decorations in hair, wrist hang tag booklet reads "Monica Doll//Hollywood," circa 1941 – 1949, $275.00. *Courtesy McMasters Doll Auctions.*

21" composition, painted eyes, closed mouth, auburn rooted human hair, original costume with white blouse, bolero and red skirt all trimmed in rickrack, featured in the 1945 Neiman Marcus catalog, $650.00. *Courtesy June Allgeier.*

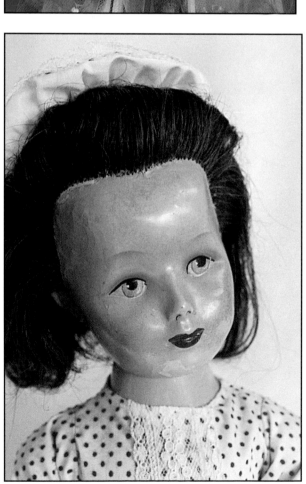

18" composition doll, marked "Monica," painted eyes and mouth, rooted brown hair, molded fingers, composition jointed body, fair condition, new white dress with red polka dots, circa 1930s – 1940s, $385.00. *Courtesy Nelda Shelton.*

Nancy Ann Storybook Dolls

Nancy Ann Storybook Dolls was started in 1936 in San Francisco, California, by Rowena Haskin (Nancy Ann Abbott). The dolls were painted bisque with mohair wigs, painted eyes, head molded to torso, jointed limbs, either with a sticker on the outfit or a hang tag. Later they made an 8" hard plastic Muffie and hard plastic Miss Nancy Ann Style Show, 18", then made 11" Debbie with vinyl head and hard plastic body, and Lori Ann at 7½" with vinyl head and hard plastic body. The company also made vinyl high heel fashion type dolls in the late 1950s and 1960s, Miss Nancy Ann, 10½", and Little Miss Nancy Ann.

What to look for:

The newer the doll, the more complete and mint it should be. That is what collectors are looking for. In competition, the older, rarer, more mint, original, beautiful doll is the one that catches the judge's eyes. That leaves a lot of played-with, soiled, with faded clothing or missing accessories dolls that are still collectible, and perhaps you can salvage some great dolls that others have skipped over. You can certainly find enough to collect, but always look for the one with more intricate costume, prettier coloring, and original clothing, tags or labels, or those in boxes.

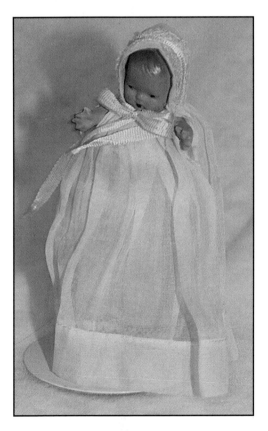

5½" painted bisque, Pretty as a Picture, red mohair wig, painted eyes, closed mouth, dress with apron, ribbon in hair, painted black shoes, circa 1943 – 1947, $35.00. *Courtesy Shari Freitas.*

3½" painted bisque baby, molded painted hair, painted eyes, closed mouth, open star-shaped hands, long white organdy gown and bonnet, circa 1938+, $250.00+. *Courtesy Shari Freitas.*

4½" bisque bride, marked "STORY//BOOK//DOLL//USA," blonde mohair wig, painted eyes, closed mouth, one-piece bisque body and head with jointed arms, white dress with lace net skirt overlay, cap with net veil, circa 1943 – 1947, $35.00. *Courtesy Barbara Hull.*

5½" bisque, A Dillar A Dollar on original gold foil bracelet, marked "Nancy Ann Storybook Doll," painted features, auburn mohair wig, red and white taffeta dress, large white felt hat/brim turned up, MIB, circa 1944, $50.00. *Courtesy Diane Graves.*

5½" painted bisque, 93 Winter, blonde mohair wig, painted eyes, closed mouth, red dress, green hat and jacket, gold tag reads "93 Winter," in white box with red polka dots, circa 1941 – 1947, $75.00. *Courtesy Patricia Christlieb.*

5½" hard plastic, Curly Locks, black sleep eyes, brown mohair wig, box marked Fairyland Series, "Curly Locks," pink felt hat, pink dotted Swiss dress and matching long pants, white box with polka dots, circa 1949, $55.00. *Courtesy Susana Auza-Smith.*

5" hard plastic child, black sleep eyes, closed mouth, auburn mohair wig, yellow print dress, circa 1949 – 1953, $25.00. *Courtesy Peggy Millhouse.*

4" hard plastic child, sleep eyes, closed mouth, blonde mohair wig, blue dress with white lace trim, white box with large pink dots, circa 1949 – 1953, $35.00. *Courtesy Peggy Millhouse.*

5" hard plastic, Little Miss Muffet, sleep eyes, closed mouth, auburn mohair wig, red striped dress with aqua apron, circa 1949 – 1953, $40.00. *Courtesy Peggy Millhouse.*

5½" hard plastic, Nun, marked "Storybook Doll USA//™," blue sleep eyes, black habit with cross attached to cord, circa 1952 – 1955, $35.00. *Courtesy Diane Graves.*

5½" hard plastic, Bridesmaid, marked "STORYBOOK//DOLLS//U.S.A.//TRADEMARK//REG.," blue sleep eyes, auburn hair, in pink dress with net covering, pink box #9133, MIB, circa 1953, $35.00. *Courtesy Betty Strong.*

5½" hard plastic, Bride, marked "STORYBOOK//DOLLS//U.S.A.//TRADEMARK//REG.," blue sleep eyes, blonde hair, in white wedding dress with lace overlay, matching lace hat, white satin sash with flowers at waist, MIB, circa 1953, $35.00. *Courtesy Betty Strong.*

8" hard plastic, Muffie, marked "Storybook Dolls//California//MUFFIE," sleep eyes, painted upper lashes, rooted auburn saran wig, hard plastic body, walker, blue organdy dress with lace trim and red flower, straw hat/red flower, circa 1955 – 1956, $250.00. *Courtesy Peggy Millhouse.*

4½" hard plastic, Little Sister, black sleep eyes, brown mohair wig, red net dress, white box with polka dots, circa 1949, $40.00. *Courtesy Susana Auza-Smith.*

8" hard plastic, Muffie, marked "Storybook Dolls//California," ballerina, blue sleep eyes, painted lashes, reddish-blonde synthetic wig, strung, pink and white tutu, circa 1953, $200.00. *Courtesy Peggy Millhouse.*

8" hard plastic, Muffie, marked "Storybook Dolls//California," sleep eyes, painted lashes, auburn synthetic wig, strung, pink rosebud on white dress, straw hat, circa 1953, $175.00. *Courtesy Peggy Millhouse.*

8" hard plastic, Muffie, marked "Storybook Dolls//California//MUFFIE," brunette synthetic wig, sleep eyes, blue dress with red rickrack, red straw hat, circa 1953 – 1956, $150.00. *Courtesy Peggy Millhouse.*

Nurse Dolls

Some sources believe that as long ago as 4000 BC, temples were used as hospitals and as training schools for doctors. Primarily, the care of the sick fell to religious groups. Usually there was no formal training; apprentices learned from experienced nurses and in turn, passed on their training to others. There was little or no classroom work. Nurses provided low-cost service to institutions and then worked in private homes or agencies. By 1836, some schools for training nurses were founded in Germany and in Kaiserswerth one of their pupils was Florence Nightingale. Nightingale was appalled at the lack of sanitation and poorly trained and supervised nurses. When the Crimean War broke out in 1954, she volunteered and organized nurses and provided skilled care during this crisis, significantly dropping the mortality rate among the sick and wounded. At the close of the war in 1860, she founded a nursing school in London, marking the beginning of professional education in nursing.

About this time, a Swiss philanthropist, Jean Henri Dunant, organized world leaders to found societies to care for the wounded in wartime. At a conference in 1864, officials of 12 nations signed the first Geneva Convention specifying rules of treatment for wounded and protection of medical personnel. A symbol of this movement was adopted at this time — a white flag with a red cross. The organization became known as the Red Cross, an international humanitarian agency that alleviates suffering during wars and major disasters and performs other public service. Clara Barton

founded the American Red Cross in 1881. Barton was called the "Angel of the Battle" for setting up a supply service during the Civil War, nursing the wounded and searching for the missing. Congress chartered the Red Cross in 1900.

Little has been documented about nurse dolls as a specific category, but does rate two pages in *Coleman's Collectors Encyclopedia of Dolls, Vol. II*. Coleman's cites specific nurse dolls as early as 1885. Certainly world events played a role in the popularity of nurse dolls. Before 1900, a nurse was most often portrayed as a nanny who took care of a baby or child. With the advent of World War I, however, dolls with the familiar Red Cross emblem on their costume were seen. In 1934, the birth of the Dionne Quintuplets revived the image of the nurse helping Dr. Dafoe with the quintuplets. Alexander was granted the license to produce the official Dionne Quintuplets. Freundlich and others jumped on the bandwagon with unlicensed

14" composition, French Nurse, "1" stamped in red on head, socket head, blue glass eyes, feathered brows, painted upper and lower lashes, open mouth with six upper teeth, original mohair wig, jointed wood and composition French body, dressed in well-detailed original World War I nurse uniform with blue wool cape and white hat, circa 1913 – 1918, $575.00. *Courtesy McMasters Doll Auctions.*

quintuplets and nurse sets. World War II again brought dolls dressed in the image of a nurse in a white uniform, blue cape lined with red, and a white cap. They were produced by a variety of manufacturers.

Mattel promoted a television character, Julia, as a nurse, a Barbie-type, circa 1969 – 1971. Still later, Hasbro's military G.I. Joe also had a plastic 10½" GI Action Girl in 1967, authentically outfitted in a white hospital uniform and Red Cross hat with an accessories pack with crutches, bandages, stethoscope, plasma bottle, and more. Nurses as a collectible provide an interesting avenue to pursue and can be a niche category that may be overlooked. The scope and range of this can be as broad or as narrow as you make it.

What to look for:

Both antique and modern dolls can be found. An average day on eBay will find over 100 collectibles listed in the "Nurse" category. The more modern the doll, the more complete it has to be, including all accessories to be more valuable. Look for costuming that has added details and for dolls that are always clean, bright, tagged, boxed or labeled.

16" composition, Halco Nurse, blue plastic sleep eyes, eyeshadow, real lashes, painted lashes below eye, open mouth, four upper teeth, blonde mohair wig, all original in white nurse uniform, blue short cape, white hat with red cross, tagged with silver and blue round tag, "Quality//Halco//Doll//Made in U.S.A.," no marks on body, circa 1940s, $450.00. *Courtesy Harlene Soucy.*

Old Cottage Toys

This firm was founded around 1948 by Mrs. Margaret E. Fleischmann who fled her native Czechoslovakia to England during the war years. Mrs. Fleischmann first made dolls for her daughter Suzanne and later for sale. The heads are made of a hard composition/hard plastic type material, with bodies of felt-over-padded-wire armature. The features are molded and painted, with mohair wigs. Fleischmann registered her trademark in 1948, and the dolls have an oval paper hang tag with a cottage pictured on one side and marked "Old Cottage Doll Made in England" on the other. They made historical figures, literary figures, English policemen, guards, and pearly figures. In 1968 she made Tweedledee and Tweedledum for a B.B.C. production of Lewis Carroll's "Through the Looking-Glass."

What to look for:

This category of dolls is currently sought-after, very collectible, and rising in value. Most desired are the literary characters, pearly dolls, and dolls with added detail. Lucky you to find Tweedledee or Tweedledum in a box at a sale or shop. Dolls should be clean, tagged, and original to command highest prices.

9" composition, "Elizabethan Lady," royalty, painted features, cloth body, molded hands, bell-shaped brocade gown, white ruffle around neck, red hair up in curls and trimmed with jewels, hang tag reads "OLD COTTAGE DOLL//MADE IN ENGLAND," circa 1950+, $175.00. *Courtesy Dorothy Bohlin.*

9½" composition, royal doll with composition hands, red mohair wig, blue eyes, closed mouth, dressed in gold dress with gold threads, ruby at throat, three rubies down front of dress, pearl necklace, and circlet in hair, circa 1950s, $200.00. *Courtesy Dorothy Bohlin.*

9" composition, royalty, painted features, cloth body, molded hands, maroon velvet Victorian-style outfit, fur-trimmed sleeves, matching hat, hang tag reads "OLD COTTAGE DOLL//MADE IN ENGLAND," circa 1950+, $175.00. *Courtesy Dorothy Bohlin.*

9" composition, Catherine of Aragon, royalty, painted features, molded hands, cloth body, brown hair, lavender and green brocade gown, matching hat, white ruffle around neck, circa 1950+, $175.00. *Courtesy Dorothy Bohlin.*

9" composition, painted eyes, closed mouth, auburn wig with green ribbon decoration, stuffed felt body, mitt hands, original green and gold long dress, has Old Cottage Doll oval tag with house logo, circa 1960s, $175.00. *Courtesy Dorothy Bohlin.*

9" composition, royalty, painted features, molded hands, cloth body, green velvet over gold and white brocade gown, headpiece, fur cuffs, hang tag reads "Old Cottage Toys//HAND MADE IN GREAT BRITAIN," circa 1950+, $175.00. *Courtesy Dorothy Bohlin.*

9½" composition, Pearlies, so-called because of the pearl buttons on black hats and clothes, cloth bodies, mitt hands, hang tags read "Old Cottage Toys//HAND MADE IN GREAT BRITAIN," circa 1950+, $175.00 each. *Courtesy Dorothy Bohlin.*

9" composition, Grandmother, painted features, cloth body, mitt hands, white hair, rust overcoat with black buttons and fur collar, black hat, carrying cane and purse, circa 1950+, $175.00. *Courtesy Dorothy Bohlin.*

Quintuplets Dolls

Alexander Doll Co. won the license to produce the official Dionne Quintuplets after their birth in 1934 to a Canadian farm family. Designed by Bernard Lipfert, they were all-composition, with painted eyes, molded hair, and jointed baby bodies. They were also made as toddlers in different sizes. Not to be outdone, other companies came out with their own sets of five babies to try to hitch on to the selling frenzy that followed the Dionnes' fame. Quint collectors have their own newsletter and collect all sorts of related memorabilia as well as the dolls. See Collectors' Network for information on the *Quint News*.

What to look for:

Dolls should be clean, bright, with good color and original clothing. Look for dolls other than Alexanders, as other companies made dolls to compete with the licensee, and other quints should not be priced as high as Alexanders.

7½" composition Madame Alexander, marked "Dionne//Alexander" on heads and backs, molded painted hair, painted brown side-glancing eyes, compo baby bodies, white outfits, in crib and high chairs, circa 1935 – 1939, $1,750.00. Dr. Dafoe, painted blue eyes, gray wig, white uniform, circa 1937 – 1939, $1,200.00. Nurse, blonde wig, brown sleep eyes, white uniform, circa 1936 – 1937, $700.00. *Courtesy Donna Hadley.*

7½" composition Madame Alexander , marked "Dionne//Alexander" on heads and backs, molded painted black hair, painted brown side-glancing eyes, closed mouths, composition baby bodies, all original in tagged clothes and original swing, circa 1935 – 1939, $1,200.00+. *Courtesy Donna Hadley.*

7½" composition Madame Alexander, marked "Dionne//Alexander" on heads and backs, molded painted hair, painted brown side-glancing eyes, compo baby bodies, in rompers and matching bonnets, sitting in wooden swan with a decal of each name on swan, circa 1935 – 1939, $1,200.00. *Courtesy Donna Hadley.*

Quintuplets Dolls

7½" composition Madame Alexander, marked "Alexander" on heads, painted brown eyes, closed mouths, molded/painted hair, 5-piece compo toddler bodies, organdy dresses, bonnets, panties, and bibs embroidered "Quintot," each outfit trimmed in different color ribbon and embroidery according to the Quint wearing it, each with name pins, original wooden bed, name decals, tagged rompers, circa 1935 – 1939, $2,500.00. *Courtesy McMasters Doll Auctions.*

11" composition Madame Alexander, Cecile, molded painted hair, brown sleep eyes, white baby dress, bootees, green trim/name embroidered on bib, MIB, circa 1936, $750.00 each. Dionne Quintuplets set with Dr. and Nurse, both redressed, $4,250.00. *Courtesy Sharon Kolibaba.*

19" composition Madame Alexander, Marie, molded painted dark brown hair, brown sleep eyes, lashes, painted lashes below, closed mouth, all original tagged dress, hat, shoes, socks, slip, panties, circa 1936 – 1938, $700.00. *Courtesy Donna Hadley.*

11" composition Madame Alexander, Annette, molded painted hair, brown sleep eyes, white baby dress, bootees, yellow trim/name embroidered on bib, MIB, circa 1936, $750.00 each. Dionne Quintuplets set with Dr. and Nurse, both re-dressed. $4,250.00. *Courtesy Sharon Kolibaba.*

Quintuplets Dolls

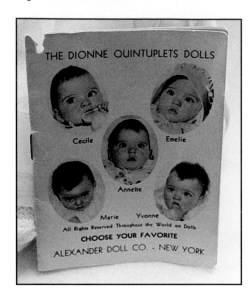

11" composition Madame Alexander, Yvonne, molded painted hair, brown sleep eyes, white baby dress, bootees, pink trim/name embroidered on bib, MIB, circa 1936, $750.00 each. Dionne Quintuplets set with Dr. and Nurse, both re-dressed. $4,250.00. *Courtesy Sharon Kolibaba.*

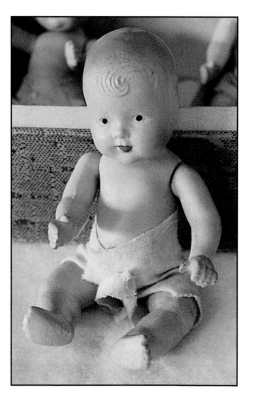

7" composition Freundlich, Five Baby Dolls and a Nurse, unmarked dolls; 9½" Nurse, molded painted hair, painted eyes, closed mouths, 5-piece composition bodies, extra pink dresses, diapers, bottles; advertised in *Playthings*, November 1935, in original case, circa 1935, $650.00. *Courtesy Donna Hadley.*

7" composition, Superior, molded painted hair, painted brown side-glancing eyes, closed mouths, 5-piece composition bodies, in original pink robes and diapers, original pink case with bibs, circa 1934+, $375.00+. *Courtesy Donna Hadley.*

7" hard plastic, Madame Alexander "Fischer Quints," one boy, four girls (Little Genius), molded painted hair, blue sleep eyes, open mouth for bottles, vinyl bodies, tagged shirts, diapers, pink blanket, bottles, all original in box, circa 1964, $550.00 set. *Courtesy Donna Hadley.*

Raggedy Ann & Andy Dolls

Designed by Johnny Gruelle in 1915, the dolls have been made by various companies. Ann wears a dress with apron, and Andy, a shirt and pants with matching hat.

P.J. Volland, 1918 – 1919
Unmarked all cloth, shoe button eyes, skinny brown wool hair, crude hands and feet, no elbow or knee joints, cardboard heart in stuffed body.

P.J. Volland, 1920 – 1934, torso stamped "Patented Sept. 7, 1915"
All cloth, thick brown yarn hair, shoe button eyes, printed features with outlined nose, six eyelashes, crooked thin line smiling mouth, turned-out feet, oversize hands, cardboard heart inside body, striped legs go only to knee.

P.J. Volland, 1920 – 1930
Had only one eyelash, smile had red center, bold triangular eyebrows, no patent stamp. **After 1931**, has arched eyebrows, four eyelashes.

Exposition Doll & Toy Mfg. Co., 1935
Made Raggedy Ann only, produced less than one year, no marks on doll, dress tagged, printed features with pie-cut eyes, red wool hair, no eyebrows or lashes, smile has no red center, toes point forward, stripes to hip, rump designated by darts, oversize hands. This is the rarest of Raggedy Anns.

Molly-'es Doll Outfitters, Mollye Goldman, 1934 – 1937
Marked on chest, "Raggedy Ann and Andy Dolls//Manufactured by Molly'es Doll Outfitters," red yarn wig, printed side-glancing eyes, long outlined nose, red center in smile, three eyelashes, jointed elbows, jointed knees, multi-colored striped legs to hips, blue shoes point forward, red printed heart.

Mollye Goldman, 1935 – 1938
Marked on chest: "Raggedy Ann and Andy Dolls Manufactured by Mollye's Doll Outfitters." Nose outlined in black, red heart on ches, reddish orange hair, multi-colored legs, blue feet, some have oilcloth faces.

Georgene Novelties, 1938 – 1962
Ann has orange hair and a topknot, sic different mough styles, early dolls had tin eyes, later plastic, six different noses, seams in middle of legs and arms to represent knees and elbows. Feet tirn ofrward, red and white striped legs. All have hearts that read: "I love you" printed on chest. Tag sewn to left side seam, several varitations, all say "Gerogene Novelties, Inc."

Knickerbocker, 1962 – 1982
Printed features, hair color change from orange to red; there were five mouth and five eyelash variations, tags were located on clothing back or pant seam.

16" cloth, Volland "Raggedy Ann," brown yarn hair, printed face, cardboard heart, legs need repair, family doll, circa 1920 – 1925, $1,000.00. *Courtesy M. Pamela Penn.*

18" cloth, Georgene Averill "Beloved Belindy," marked "Johnny Gruelle's Own//" "Beloved Belindy//Trade Mark Reg.//U.S. Pat Office//Copyright 1928 by Johnny Gruelle//Georgene Novelties Inc.//NYC," white button eyes, outlined red nose, outlined smiling mouth, turned-out red feet, red/white striped legs, white bloomers, red outfit/matching turban on head, yellow flowered skirt, all original, circa 1940 – 1944, $500.00. *Courtesy Judi Domm.*

Bernard & Frances Ravca

Bernard Ravca was born in Paris in 1904. He was touring the United States when Germany invaded his country. Ravca, who had already won prizes for his life-size dolls in the 1930s, remained in the U.S., where he met Frances Diecks. Later, they married and he became a citizen of the U.S. Members of NIADA, called sculptors in cotton. Ravca and his wife work primarily in cloth, initally making French ethnic type characters and later expanding their lines. They traveled the world, lecturing and displaying their dolls and at one time had a museum.

9" cloth, woman seated at wooden spinning wheel, "Original Ravca//Fabrication Francaise" on label, needle-sculpture painted features, wooden shoes, tagged, purchased directly from Ravca in 1981, $175.00 to $200.00 with two personal letters and postcards. *Courtesy Richard Allen.*

9" cloth, man standing with cane, holding newspaper and flowers, needle sculpture, painted features, wooden shoes, tagged, purchased directly from Ravca in 1981, $175.00 to $200.00 with two personal letters and postcards. *Courtesy Richard Allen.*

Remco Dolls

Remco Industries Inc., was founded by Sol Robbins, in the 1960s. They made television promotional dolls and advertised heavily on television. The company was bought by Roth American, but closed in January 1974. Playcraft Toys Inc. of Canada made some dolls under a license agreement with Remco. Some of their better known dolls include the Littlechap Family, Heidi, and the Beatles.

6" vinyl, Heidi, marked "©1964//Remco Industries Inc.//#K280//"Heidi," painted side-glancing eyes, long blonde rooted hair, press magic button and right hand waves, green dress, circa 1964, $30.00. *Courtesy Nelda Shelton.*

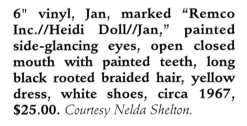

6" vinyl, Jan, marked "Remco Inc.//Heidi Doll//Jan," painted side-glancing eyes, open closed mouth with painted teeth, long black rooted braided hair, yellow dress, white shoes, circa 1967, $25.00. *Courtesy Nelda Shelton.*

6" vinyl, Pip, marked "Remco Inc.//Pip," painted side-glancing eyes, closed mouth, blonde rooted hair, blue and white dress with matching bonnet, circa 1967, $20.00. *Courtesy Nelda Shelton.*

6" vinyl, Spunky, marked "#A211//Remco Inc.//Spunky," blue painted side-glancing eyes, glasses, open closed mouth with painted teeth, rooted red hair, white leather vest, red canvas pants, white shoes, circa 1968, $25.00. *Courtesy Nelda Shelton.*

Richwood Dolls

Richwood Toys, Inc., Annapolis, Maryland, produced Sandra Sue from the late 1940s through the 1950s. Sandra Sue is a hard plastic walker, head does not turn, with slim body, saran wig, and sleep eyes. Some had high-heel feet, and their only marks are numbers under an arm or a leg. Sandra Sue was a higher quality hard plastic doll, similar to others produced at this time, but this doll had more attributes than most.

Sandra Sue has sleep eyes with molded lashes, closed mouth, jointed arms and legs, was made as both a walker and non-walker, and had an extensive wardrobe as well as a line of furniture. She had saran wigs, and the suggestion of a fashion body with gently molded breasts and a slimmer waist. She was modeled with both flat and high-heel feet. One tip for identification is dark orange painted eyebrows and painted lashes below eyes. The hands are formed with fingers together, separate thumbs, and facing toward the body.

Sandra Sue's head does not turn when she walks. Her wardrobe could be the envy of many of the contemporary dolls, with a large selection of pieces that could be purchased separately. These included evening and bridal gowns, sportswear, such as ski apparel, skating costumes, skirts and blouses, dresses and hats, coat and dress ensembles with accessories, daytime dresses, and more.

What to look for:

Often dismissed as one of the smaller hard plastic "gas station" dolls, Sandra Sue can be found at garage sales with a collectible assortment of clothes. Dolls should be clean, with original clothing and good facial coloring. Sandra Sue's original box is easily recognizable with a silhouette in an oval and her name marked on top.

8" hard plastic, Ballerina, unmarked, sleep eyes, taupe painted lower lashes, closed mouth, saran wig, strung, slim body, flat foot, non-walker, pink tutu with silver trim, pink flowers in hair, circa 1952, $250.00. *Courtesy Peggy Millhouse.*

8" hard plastic, blue sleep eyes, auburn saran wig, flat feet, Scotch suit, red jacket, green plaid skirt, red Glengary cap, circa 1952 – 1958, $200.00. *Courtesy Peggy Millhouse.*

8" hard plastic, G – 12, D.A.R. Special Edition outfit on basic doll, sleep eyes, auburn saran wig, flat feet, circa 1953, $200.00. *Courtesy Peggy Millhouse.*

8" hard plastic, sleep eyes, auburn saran wig, red and white dress with hat, circa 1952 – 1958, $200.00. *Courtesy Peggy Millhouse.*

Robert Tonner Doll Company

The Robert Tonner Doll Company began in the early 1990s with multi-jointed porcelain fashion dolls but hit the jackpot when it first licensed Betsy McCall as a 14" vinyl doll. Betsy is reminiscent of the McCall paper doll from the 1950s and is available dressed or with additional outfits.

In 1999 Tonner also produced a vinyl 10" Ann Estelle from the charming character created by Mary Englebreit. Ann Estelle has a blonde Dutch bob and blue eyes and comes dressed in her undies or a special costume. Additional wardrobe is available, Tonner also introduced an 8" vinyl Kripplebush Kid with rooted hair, jointed arms and legs, a great travel doll.

Eagerly anticipated before its late 1999 introduction, Tonner's new 16" vinyl fashion doll is Tyler Wentworth. Tonner created a history for Tyler, stating that from an early age she was destined to be a high flyer in the world of high fashion.

"During the 1950s, Tyler's great-aunt, Regina Wentworth established the House of Wentworth in New York City and created innovative collections that set the standard for the 7th Avenue fashion design. Years later, Tyler, who had always loved the glamor and excitement of her great-aunt's business, joined the prestigious house's design staff. She proved to be exceptionally talented, and it was not long until she was promoted to Regina's first assistant.

"With the House of Wentworth's reputation firmly established, Regina began to consider passing the reins to a new talent. Spurring her on was her relationship with Carlos, a young artist who had instantly fallen in love with the chic, elegant, older designer. Soon Regina made her decision to move with Carlos to the south of France, and she turned the company over to Tyler.

"Although young for the job, Tyler quickly showed that she was equal to her new responsibilities. With only a few short seasons of fashion experience, she confidently assumed leadership of the House of Wentworth and received rave reviews over her first collection."

What to look for:

Check eBay, Internet doll shops, doll magazines, and your local doll or gift shop for the latest releases. Special costumed dolls produced in limited editions produced for functions like the Roy Rogers Betsy McCall from the first Betsy McCall convention and Ann Estelle from the UFDC luncheon in limited edition costume are available on the secondary market and are increasing in price. Tonner dolls are fun to costume and play with, fun to collect!

10" vinyl, Ann Estelle, style #20610, "Ride 'em Cowgirl," blue eyes, closed mouth, blonde wig, gold rimmed eyeglasses, rigid vinyl body, blue and white checked shirt, red print bandana, red skirt with tan leather fringe, matching leather gloves, lariat, black belt, brown cowboy hat, red/white/black/yellow cowboy boots, circa 2000, $99.99. *Photo courtesy Robert Tonner Doll Company.*

10" vinyl, Ann Estelle, style #20605, "Happy Birthday," blue eyes, closed mouth, blonde wig, gold rimmed eyeglasses, rigid vinyl body, pink satin dress with ruffles, pink net overlay, large pink plaid ribbon sash in front with pink roses, pink polka dot bow in hair, pink shoes, white socks trimmed with pink, gift, circa 2000, $89.99. *Photo courtesy Robert Tonner Doll Company.*

10" vinyl, Ann Estelle, style #20607, "Star Spangled Sailor," blue eyes, closed mouth, blonde wig, gold rimmed eyeglasses, rigid vinyl body, white dress with blue trim and red stars, matching hat with red pompon on top, red shoes, white socks, white slip trimmed with lace, carrying American flag, circa 2000, $89.99. *Photo courtesy Robert Tonner Doll Company.*

10" vinyl, Ann Estelle, style #20603, "Gardening with Grandpa," blue eyes, closed mouth, blonde wig, gold rimmed eyeglasses, rigid vinyl body, green overalls, pink and white plaid shirt with matching hairbow, pink and white tennis shoes with white ribbon ties, carrying a basket of vegetables, circa 2000, $89.99. *Photo courtesy Robert Tonner Doll Company.*

10" vinyl, Ann Estelle, style #20602, "Barefoot in the Sand," blue eyes, closed mouth, blonde wig, gold rimmed eyeglasses, rigid vinyl body, red, yellow, blue and white print one-piece outfit, white hat with blue ribbon trim and yellow flower, red and white striped sandals, beach ball, circa 2000, $79.99. *Photo courtesy Robert Tonner Doll Company.*

10" vinyl, Ann Estelle, style #20601, "Blue Bird," blue eyes, closed mouth, blonde wig, gold rimmed eyeglasses, rigid vinyl body, blue print dress with red trim, red buttons, white collar with red trim, blue polka dot ribbon in hair, purple slip on shoes, white stockings, carrying bird cage, circa 2000, $79.99 dressed doll, $39.99 outfit only. *Photo courtesy Robert Tonner Doll Company.*

10" vinyl, Ann Estelle, blue eyes, closed mouth, blonde wig, gold rimmed eyeglasses, rigid vinyl body, style #20643, "Warm & Fuzzy," brown jacket with sheepskin type trim on bottom, cuffs, collar, matching boots and hat, red gloves, black stockings, snowman, circa 2000, $39.99 outfit only. *Photo courtesy Robert Tonner Doll Company.*

10" vinyl, Ann Estelle, style #20608, "Gift Giver," blue eyes, closed mouth, blonde wig, gold rimmed eyeglasses, rigid vinyl body, tan and white print dress with pink lace flower trim, white eyelet slip, straw bonnet with loose weave, tan one-strap shoes, white stockings, carrying gift, circa 2000, $89.99. *Photo courtesy Robert Tonner Doll Company.*

10" vinyl, Ann Estelle, style #20609, "Trick or Treat", blue eyes, closed mouth, blonde wig, gold rimmed eyeglasses, rigid vinyl body, orange and black print pointed witch hat, black and orange cape, yellow, orange and white print dress with orange, rickrack trim, white apron, orange striped stockings, black shoes with orange pompons, circa 2000, $99.99 dressed doll, $44.99 outfit only. *Photo courtesy Robert Tonner Doll Company.*

10" vinyl, black Georgia, friend to Ann Estelle, style #20632, "Calendar Girl," brown eyes, closed mouth, black wig, rigid vinyl body, red dress trimmed with black ribbon and buttons, black stockings, black bow in hair, red one-strap shoes, white eyelet slip, carrying brown teddy bear with red ribbon around neck, circa 2000, $89.99 dressed doll, $39.99 outfit only. *Photo courtesy Robert Tonner Doll Company.*

10" vinyl, black Georgia, friend to Ann Estelle, style #20630, brown eyes, closed mouth, black wig, rigid vinyl body, white top with pink ribbon, matching ribbon in hair, pink and white bottoms, black shoes, white socks, circa 2000, $69.99. *Photo courtesy Robert Tonner Doll Company.*

10" vinyl, Sophie, friend to Ann Estelle, style #20621, "Scotty Girl," brown eyes, closed mouth, strawberry blonde wig, rigid vinyl body, black dress, black/white polka dot sleeves, multicolored cuffs/collar trimmed in white lace, black Scotty on bib of dress, red felt Scotty purse stitched on black skirt attached with red strap around neck, red shoes, white socks, black polka dot bow in hair, circa 2000, $79.99. *Photo courtesy Robert Tonner Doll Company.*

16" vinyl, Tyler Wentworth, long dark brown rooted hair in a high ponytail, plastic eyes, closed mouth, hard plastic body, bendable knees, dressed in "Beverly Hills Chic," style #20832, classic white linen jacket, matching white linen trouser skirt and a fitted man-tailored shirt, brown belt, carrying a matching purse, black sandal high-heels, open edition, circa 2000, $59.99 outfit only. *Photo courtesy Robert Tonner Doll Company.*

16" vinyl, Tyler Wentworth, long brown rooted hair pinned up, plastic eyes, closed mouth, hard plastic body, bendable knees, dressed in "Manhattan Music Awards," style #20823, gown of black cut velvet with stripe insets of cobalt blue silk charmeuse, matching cobalt blue stole, bag and shoes, drop black jet earrings, limited edition of 3,000, circa 2000, costume only $59.99. *Photo courtesy Robert Tonner Doll Company.*

16" vinyl, Tyler Wentworth, long brown rooted hair pinned up, plastic eyes, closed mouth, hard plastic body, bendable knees, dressed in "Opera Gala," style #20866, red and black jacquard gown with matching cropped jacket, black fur trim, glittering jet buttons, black jet jewelry, black elbow length gloves, opera glasses in a matching silk pouch, red shoes, limited edition of 3,000, circa 2000, $169.99. *Photo courtesy Robert Tonner Doll Company.*

16" vinyl, Tyler Wentworth, long black rooted hair, plastic eyes, closed mouth, hard plastic body, bendable knees, dressed in "Russian Renaissance," style #20809, two-piece suit of brown and gold brocade, jacket is three-quarter length with black velvet stand-up collar and cuffs, short slim skirt, black velvet hat with gold leaf pin, matching bag, black shear stockings, black pumps, limited edition of 3,000, circa 2000, costume only $69.99. *Photo courtesy Robert Tonner Doll Company.*

16" vinyl, Tyler Wentworth, long blonde rooted hair in a high ponytail pinned up, plastic eyes, closed mouth, hard plastic body, bendable knees, dressed in "Shakespeare in the Park," style #20822, silver silk lamé gown with tiered skirt of pleated organza, bouquet of red roses, silver high heel sandals, necklace, limited edition of 3,000, circa 2000, $89.99 outfit only. *Photo courtesy Robert Tonner Doll Company.*

16" vinyl, black Tyler Wentworth, long black rooted hair, plastic eyes, closed mouth, hard plastic body, bendable knees, dressed in "Weekend Retreat," style #20833, Tyler's signature jeans, lush cotton cable knit sweater, double-breasted coat of red wool double banded in black, white wool check duffle bag and black boots, limited edition of 3,000, circa 2000, costume only $59.99. *Photo courtesy Robert Tonner Doll Company.*

16" vinyl, Esme Cover Girl, long black rooted hair pinned up, plastic eyes, closed mouth, hard plastic body, bendable knees, dressed in a Tyler Wentworth original gown style #20808, peach and gold lace dress with jewel neckline, lined in a sheer sparkle net and peach silk chiffon, sash on the dress ties in back to make a luxurious train of the chiffon, earrings, limited edition of 3,000, circa 2000, $149.99. *Photo courtesy Robert Tonner Doll Company.*

Roldan Dolls

Roldan Characters in many respects are similar to Klumpe figures. They were made in Barcelona, Spain from the early 1960s until the mid 1970s, of felt-over-wire armature with painted mask faces. Like Klumpe, Roldan figures represent professionals, hobbyists, dancers, historical characters, and contemporary males and females performing a wide variety of tasks. Some Roldans, were imported by Rosenfeld Imports and Leora Dolores of Hollywood. Figures originally came with two sewn-on, identifying cardboard tags. Roldan characters most commonly found are doctors, Spanish dancers, and bullfighters. These characters tend to have somewhat smaller heads, longer necks, and more defined facial features than the Klumpe characters.

What to look for:
Look for bright and clean doll tags; the more accessories, the more collectible these whimsical characters.

10" felt, Flamenco Dancer, felt-over-wire armature, painted features, red ruffled dress, holding marimbas, circa 1960s – 1970s, $100.00. *Courtesy Sharon Kolibaba.*

Shirley Temple Dolls

In 1934, after Shirley Temple stole the show with her performance in "Stand Up and Cheer." Ideal gained the license to produce Shirley Temple dolls, hired Bernard Lipfert to sculpt a prototype, cast her in composition, and soon had a Shirley Temple doll in red and white polka dotted dresses on the market. The costumes were designed by Mollye Goldman during 1934 – 1936 and show the NRA markings on their labels. The costumes were sold separately as well as with the doll.

The composition dolls had sleep eyes, or flirty eyes, open mouth with six upper teeth, multi-stroke eyebrows, a 5-piece jointed body, mohair wig, and came in a range of sizes from 11" to 27". The first dolls were packaged with a pinback button and signed photograph. Dolls were marked on the head and/or torso with "SHIRLEY TEMPLE//IDEAL NOV. & TOY CO." and "SHIRLEY TEMPLE" on the body. In late 1935, a Shirley Temple Baby was introduced followed by baby carriages, and accessories. Shirley Temple dolls were popular through the early 1940s, declining when real-life Shirley reached adolescence.

In 1957, Ideal reissued a vinyl 12" Shirley to coincide with the release of her movies to television and Temple's own television series. These dolls have plastic script pins and paper hang tags. In the 1960s, 15", 17", and 19" vinyl dolls were issued. In 1972, to celebrate its 100th anniversary Montgomery Ward issued a 15" vinyl Shirley Temple. In 1982, Ideal made 8" and 12" Shirley Temple dolls costumed as Heidi, Stowaway, Stand Up and Cheer, The Little Colonel, Captain January, and The Littlest Rebel. Danbury Mint has made more recent Shirley Temple, including porcelain 20" dolls costumed from movies, designed by Elke Hutchens. See Collectors' Network for information on several Shirley Temple publications and groups.

What to look for:

Composition Shirley Temples are difficult to find in excellent condition because the painted finish crazes and those in very good condition have risen drastically in prices. Collectors may wish to search for the vinyl and newer dolls as they too will eventually become collectible. Check composition dolls for crazing, vinyl should have good color, and clothing should be clean and bright. Shirley collectors like all Shirley Temple related items, such as marked products, paper, and advertising.

Composition

20" composition, Ideal, marked "20 (backwards)//Shirley Temple//Cop. Ideal N&T Co." on back of head, "Shirley Temple" on back, hazel sleep eyes, real lashes, painted lower lashes, open mouth with six upper teeth, molded tongue, mohair wig, 5-piece composition child body, original pleated organdy dress with ribbons, underwear combination, socks, center-snap shoes, replaced ribbon in hair, circa 1934+, $775.00. *Courtesy McMasters Doll Auctions.*

13" composition, Ideal, marked "Shirley Temple" on head and "Shirley Temple//13" on back, flirty eyes with real lashes, open mouth with six upper teeth, original mohair wig, 5-piece composition child body, "Genuine Shirley Temple Doll" tag on flowered organdy dress, original underclothing, socks and shoes, circa 1934+, $675.00. *Courtesy McMasters Doll Auctions.*

20" composition, Ideal, marked "20(backwards)//Shirley Temple//Cop Ideal N & T Co." on back of head, "Shirley Temple//20™" on back, hazel sleep eyes, open mouth, six upper teeth, mohair wig, 5-piece composition child body, tagged pleated organdy dress with Shirley Temple button, old replaced socks, shoes, all original except socks, circa 1934+, $700.00. *Courtesy McMasters Doll Auctions.*

20" composition, Ideal, marked "SHIRLEY TEMPLE//Cop. Ideal N & T Co." on head, sleep eyes, open mouth with teeth, rosy cheeks, mohair wig, re-dressed as a bride, circa 1934+, $800.00. *Courtesy Rachel Quigley.*

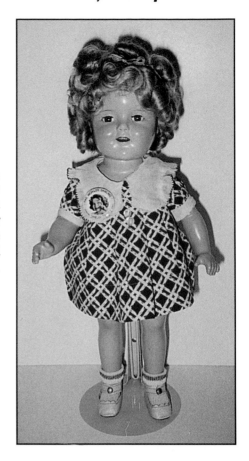

16" composition, Ideal, Sixth Birthday Doll, sleep eyes, open mouth with teeth, dimple, curly mohair wig, original red and white dress with white collar and cuffs, circa 1935, $850.00. *Courtesy Rachel Quigley.*

22" composition, Ideal, marked "SHIRLEY TEMPLE//COP. IDEAL N & T CO." on head, and "SHIRLEY TEMPLE//22" on body, sleep eyes, open mouth with teeth, curly mohair wig, vintage tagged dress, circa 1934+, $1,350.00. *Courtesy Rachel Quigley.*

20" composition, Ideal, Captain January outfit, marked "SHIRLEY TEMPLE//Cop//Ideal//N&T Co." on head, "SHIRLEY TEMPLE//20" on body, mohair wig, hazel sleep eyes, open mouth, six upper teeth, dimples, 5-piece compo body, designed by Bernard Lipfert, circa 1934+, $2,250.00. *Courtesy Iva Mae Jones.*

18" composition, Ideal, from "The Little Princess," marked "SHIRLEY TEMPLE//Cop. Ideal N & T Co." on head, flirty sleep eyes, open mouth with teeth, curly mohair wig, dressed in pink taffeta with a lace overskirt and dainty underthings in the same color, Shirley Temple pin, circa 1934+, $4,000.00+. *Courtesy Rachel Quigley.*

18" composition, Ideal, MIB, green sleep eyes, open mouth, teeth, dimples, mohair wig, uncommon red dress, original pin, circa 1934+, $950.00. *Courtesy Iva Mae Jones.*

18" composition, Ideal, marked "Shirley Temple//Cop. Ideal N & T Co." head, "Shirley Temple" on back, hazel sleep eyes, open mouth, six upper teeth, mohair wig, 5-piece composition child body, dressed in red/white dress from "Merrily Yours," all original, circa 1934+, $475.00. *Courtesy McMasters Doll Auctions.*

22" composition, Ideal marked "Shirley Temple" on head, "Shirley Temple//22" on back, designed by Bernard Lipfert, hazel sleep eyes with real lashes, painted lower lashes, open mouth, six upper teeth, dimples, mohair wig in original loose curls, 5-piece composition body, "Littlest Rebel" costume, center-snap shoes, dress and slip tagged "22" on back inside seam, all original, circa 1934+, $625.00. *Courtesy McMasters Doll Auctions.*

18" composition, Ideal, marked "18//Shirley Temple//Cop Ideal N & T Co." on back of head and "Shirley Temple" on back, hazel sleep eyes, open mouth, six upper teeth, mohair wig, 5-piece composition body, original red Scottie dress, replaced one-piece underwear, old replaced socks and shoes, circa 1934+, $650.00. *Courtesy McMasters Doll Auctions.*

18" composition, Ideal, flirty eyes, open mouth with teeth, dimples, curly hair, wearing a long pink dress with puff sleeves and blue ribbons on skirt, tiara in hair, circa 1934+, $1,000.00. *Courtesy Rachel Quigley.*

18" composition, Ideal, all original, sleep eyes, open mouth, teeth, dimples, mohair wig, blue dress with white polka dots, tagged, rayon dress tag, original pin, circa 1934+, $850.00. *Courtesy Iva Mae Jones.*

11" composition, Ideal, in original Rangerette costume, with hat marked "Texas Centennial," original pin-back button shirt, with original box, circa 1936, $1,750.00. *Courtesy Jennifer Scott.*

13" brown composition, Ideal, Marama, painted side-glancing eyes, painted teeth, black yarn wig, uses Shirley Temple mold, marked on back of head, "13//Shirley Temple" and "U.S.A.//13" on body, meant to portray Marama character from "Hurricane" movie, circa 1940, $500.00. *Courtesy Ashlyn Johnson.*

11" composition, Ideal, Texas Ranger, marked "SHIRLEY TEMPLE 11" on head and body, designed by Bernard Lipfert, hazel sleep eyes, real lashes, open mouth, six upper teeth, dimples, mohair wig, 5-piece compo body, outfit designed for the 1936 Texas Centennial celebration, plaid shirt, leather vest, chaps, holster, metal gun, original pin, missing hat, all original with trunk, blue "Stand Up and Cheer" dress, and coin dotted organdy dress, circa 1936, $3,000.00. *Courtesy Iva Mae Jones.*

Vinyl

12", sleep eyes, open/closed mouth, teeth, synthetic rooted wig, blue dress with lace trim, gold plastic script pin reading "Shirley Temple," marked "Ideal Doll//ST//12" on head, "Ideal Doll" on body, nice color, all original boxed, circa 1957, $200.00. *Courtesy McMasters Doll Auctions.*

15", marked "Ideal Doll//ST-15-N" on head, hazel sleep eyes, real lashes, painted lower lashes, open/closed mouth with six upper teeth, rooted hair in original set, 5-piece vinyl body, blue cotton dress with matador-type sleeves, attached slip, socks and shoes, Shirley Temple script pin, near mint with box, circa 1962, $275.00. *Courtesy McMasters Doll Auctions.*

Left, 15", Cinderella, marked "Ideal Doll//ST-15-N" on head, sleep eyes, open/closed mouth, six teeth, dimples, rooted hair, pearl crown, white taffeta skirt/red velvet bodice, all original, circa 1961, $325.00; right, "Shirley Temple", marked "Ideal Doll//ST-19" on head, flirty sleep eyes, open/closed mouth, six teeth, dimples, rooted hair, tagged pink/blue nylon dress, wrist tag w/curlers, mint-with-box, circa 1957, $650.00. *Courtesy McMasters Doll Auctions.*

15", Ideal, Heidi marked "Ideal Doll//ST-15-N" on back of head, sleep eyes, curly rooted hair, MIB, circa 1961, $375.00. *Courtesy Rachel Quigley.*

12", Ideal, from store counter display, dress tagged "Petite Fashions by Debutante," and "ST-12," traditional tagged pink Shirley Temple slip, circa late 1950s, $325.00. *Courtesy Rachel Quigley.*

36", Ideal, sleep eyes, open/closed mouth with painted teeth, dimples, high cheek color, rooted curled saran hair, hard plastic walker, name pin, cardboard hang tag, gold wristwatch, does not have jointed wrists, yellow nylon dress, MIB, circa 1960, $1,950.00. *Courtesy Leslie Tannenbaum.*

12", marked "Ideal Doll//ST-12" on head, sleep eyes, synthetic rooted wig, open/closed mouth, teeth, dimples, rosy cheeks, green pants, matching hat, gray button-up jacket with fur lining, white socks, black shoes, circa 1957, $395.00. *Courtesy Iva Mae Jones.*

Shirley Temple Accessories

Two 8" bisque unlicensed Shirley Temple dolls, marked "Made in Japan," left marked "S1224," right marked "S1225," painted side-glancing eyes, heavily molded and painted hair, molded painted shoes and socks, circa 1930s, left, $250.00; right, $225.00. *Courtesy Martha Sweeney.*

Terri Lee Dolls

Terri Lee dolls were made from 1946 until 1962, in Lincoln, Nebraska, and Apple Valley, California. The first dolls were composition, then hard plastic and vinyl dolls were added. Marked on torso, "TERRI LEE," and early dolls, "PAT. PENDING," Terri Lee dolls have closed pouty mouths, painted eyes, wigs, and jointed bodies.

Recently the Terri Lee molds were acquired to remake Terri Lee dolls, but the new mold owners were barred from doing so by legal action from heirs of the company's founder. See Collectors' Network for more information on collector groups and the bibliography for additional resource material.

What to look for:

Composition dolls are hard to find in good condition, as most have crazing in moderate to severe stages. Hard plastic dolls should be clean with rosy face color and with original clothing when possible. Hair can be restyled and pattern clothes made for nude dolls. Again a stable environment and cleanliness help slow down deterioration of the plastic materials.

16" hard plastic, painted brown eyes, closed mouth, blond wig, original peach formal, circa 1951 – 1962, $350.00. *Courtesy Cornelia Ford*.

16" hard plastic, with platinum synthetic wig, brown painted eyes, painted upper lashes, one-stroke brown eyebrows, red dots at nose, bright red lips, in Brownie dress and hat, circa 1951 – 1962, $350.00. *Courtesy June Allgeier*.

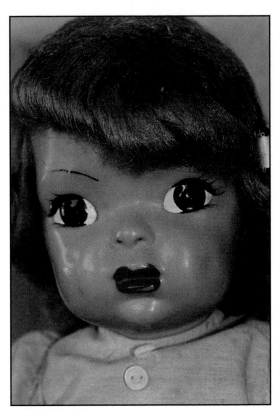

16" hard plastic, painted brown eyes, blonde wig, yellow dress, circa 1950 – 1951, **$150.00.** *Courtesy Betty Strong.*

16" hard plastic, black Patty Jo, marked "Terri Lee//Pat. Pending" on back, painted brown eyes, black hair, green checked dress, circa 1950 – 1951, **$150.00.** *Courtesy Betty Strong.*

16" hard plastic with walker, marked "Terri Lee" on head, on back, and on walker, painted brown eyes, closed mouth, original wig, 5-piece hard plastic body, tagged dark blue print dress with white piqué collar and sleeves, ruffled panties, socks, brown/white saddle shoes, standing on labeled red metal Terri Lee walker, when pushed, feet will take steps, circa 1950s, **$950.00.** *Courtesy McMasters Doll Auctions.*

16" hard plastic, Jerri Lee, marked "Terri Lee" on back, large painted brown eyes, painted lashes, closed mouth, original skin wig, 5-piece hard plastic body, tagged polka dot shirt, denim pants, leather belt, rayon socks, leatherette brown and white saddle shoes, contained in Connie Lynn box marked "Creators of a new Era in Dolls//Apple Valley, California//Connie Lynn//Sleepy Baby," circa 1950s, $275.00. *Courtesy McMasters Doll Auctions.*

16" hard plastic, Jerri Lee, painted brown eyes, caracul wig, cowboy clothing, circa 1950 – 1951, $200.00. *Courtesy Betty Strong.*

10½" vinyl, Tiny Terri Lee, with © on neck, sleep eyes, caracul wig, plaid shirt, blue jeans marked "Terri Lee," circa 1955 – 1958, $65.00. *Courtesy Betty Strong.*

Vinyl Dolls

By the mid-fifties, vinyl (polyvinylchloride) was being used for doll bodies. This material is soft to the touch, and hair could be rooted, both attractive features in dolls. Vinyl has become a desirable material, and the market has been deluged with vinyl dolls. Many dolls of this period are from little-known manufacturers, unmarked or marked only with a number. With little history behind them, these dolls need to be mint in box and complete to warrant top prices. An important factor to remember when purchasing vinyl dolls is that all aspects of originality, labeled costume, hang tag, and box, are more critical when these dolls are entered into competition.

What to look for:

Clean dolls, all original with good color, with the vinyl not sticky. There can be some real bargains in this area for the collector with a limited budget. Often overlooked character and celebrity dolls in vinyl can still be found at garage sales, flea markets, discount outlets, and antique malls.

18", Daisy Kingdom Dolls Daisy Dolly, blue eyes, closed mouth, molded painted blonde hair, dress made from Daisy Kingdom Doll Dress Panels, wearing original underwear, look for patterns by Simplicity®, circa 1991, $14.95 at JoAnne's Fabrics or Michael's. *Courtesy Millie Busch.*

14½", Jolly Toys Small Stuff, with synthetic tuff of hair and painted hair, blue plastic sleep eyes, real lashes, closed mouth, original red print dress with black rickrack trim, hang tag reads "JOLLY'S//Small Stuff*//®TRADE MARK//A PRODUCT OF JOLLY TOYS INC.//NEW YORK, N.Y.," circa 1960s, $35.00. *Courtesy Connie Bedenkop.*

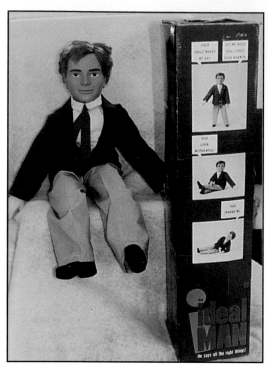

25" rigid vinyl, Italian boy, blonde wig, blue sleep eyes, closed mouth, gray felt pants, green cap, Tyrolean outfit, circa 1960 – 1970s, $150.00+. *Courtesy Richard Ybarra.*

24" Gemmy Industries, "The Ideal Man," box marked "Gemmy Industries, © 1989," dark blonde hair, painted blue eyes, closed mouth, vinyl hands and feet, cloth body, dressed in white shirt, tan pants, blue suit jacket, red tie with black polka dots, squeeze body and he says eight phrases, circa 1989, $25.00. *Courtesy Adrienne Hagey.*

17½" Royal Doll Co. Jackie, tagged "A Royal Doll//Playmate for a Princess," blue sleep eyes, open/closed mouth, blonde rooted saran wig, hard plastic body, lavender nylon dress, circa 1960s, $35.00. *Courtesy Betty Strong.*

20" Valentine Bride, marked "20 BAL HH," brown sleep eyes, closed mouth, rooted auburn hair, all original, circa 1960s, $75.00. *Courtesy Janet Horst.*

Vogue Dolls

Jennie Graves started her Vogue Doll Shop business in Somerville, Massachusetts, in 1922, dressing German dolls for department stores. She used cottage industry home sewers as her business expanded. Just before the war, she established a storefront, but depended on home sewers again during the war years, as all able-bodied workers were needed in the defense plants. In 1945, she incorporated Vogue Dolls, Inc. and opened a factory in Medford, Massachusetts. By 1949, she contracted Commonwealth Plastics Company to make an 8" hard plastic doll. At no time did she manufacture dolls, but she did open a 15,000 square-foot factory where the dolls were dressed and packed for shipment.

Graves designed the costumes for over 20 years. She dressed German Armand Marseille bisque Just Me dolls in Vogue's early years, and these are highly prized today for the costumes. She also used imported German Kammer & Reinhardt (K*R) doll as well as composition dolls made by Arranbee and Ideal. In 1937, Graves had doll designer Bernard Lipfert design an 8" composition doll Toddles which she produced until 1948 when she had the doll made in hard plastic and named her Ginny. In the 1950s, Graves promoted a doll with wardrobe to increase year-around sales. Vogue advertising promoted Ginny as a leader in the doll fashion society and noted she had 50 outfits available. This brought such a spurt of growth that Graves had to borrow money to open another factory in 1953. Her success gave rise to competition such as Ginger by the Cosmopolitan Doll Company.

In 1957, Vogue became the largest doll manufacturer in the U.S. In 1958, Vogue purchased Arranbee Doll Company and reported gross sales of over $6 million. Graves retired in 1960 and turned the control of the company over to her daughter Virginia Graves Carlson and son-in-law, Ted Carlson, in 1966 when Virginia retired. In 1972, Vogue was sold to Tonka Corp. who began manufacturing the dolls in Asia, and in 1977, the company was purchased by Lesney Products. During the Lesney era, Ginny was redesigned with a much slimmer body. After several changes of ownership, Meritus in 1984 and R. Dakin in 1986, the rights to all Vogue dolls and molds, including Ginny, were purchased by Vogue Doll Company, Inc. founded in 1995, by Linda and Jim Smith, Wendy and Keith Lawton (of the Lawton Company), and others. Today, president Linda Smith handles marketing while talented Wendy Lawton oversees designs, making Ginny again a great collectible doll.

What to look for:

Early composition dolls should have minimal crazing and good color. Hard plastic dolls should have good color and original clothing. Clean dolls that have no mold or odor are important considerations. Hair can be restyled with patience. Vogue's Ginny dolls were a big favorite of the Baby Boomers during the 1950s and remain an appealing collectible with new dolls of today, attracting new as well as older collectors.

Composition

7½" Toddles Draf-Tee, painted blue side-glancing eyes, painted upper lashes, closed mouth, original mohair wig, 5-piece compo toddler body, original brown military uniform, brown leather belt with small metal gun attached, cap, brown side-snap shoes, marked "Vogue" on head, "Doll Co." on back, round gold "Vogue" tag on right front uniform, NM, circa 1937 – 1948, $350.00. *Courtesy McMasters Doll Auctions.*

Hard Plastic

8" Ginny, April, #24 from the Kindergarten Afternoon series, sleep eyes, painted lashes, blonde Dynel wig, strung, white organdy dress with dotted organdy and lace trim with pink bows, circa 1953, $325.00. *Courtesy Peggy Millhouse.*

8" Ginny, Glad, #42 from the Tiny Miss series, strung, blue sleep eyes, red Dynel wig, wearing red pinafore dress with white band trim, red and green berries trim dress and green straw hat, green shoes, white socks, all-original, circa 1953, $325.00. *Courtesy Lee Ann Beaumont.*

8" Ginny, brown sleep eyes, auburn Nutex wig, transitional, strung, wearing white outfit with pink trim and straw hat from her trunk set, circa 1951, $325.00. *Courtesy Peggy Millhouse.*

8" Ginny, Skater, from the Sports Fashion group, painted side-glancing eyes, auburn braided mohair wig, strung, original red and white costume, circa 1950, $400.00. *Courtesy Peggy Millhouse.*

8" Ginny, marked "Vogue" on head, blonde mohair wig, painted blue side-glancing eyes, closed mouth, original pink multicolored dress, pink shoes, ink spot tag, circa 1948 – 1950, $375.00. *Courtesy Lessa Whiteman.*

8" Country Fair Ginny, from the Town & Country Collection, marked "Ginny's Signature TM//1988//The Vogue Doll Company//Made in China, red rooted hair, plastic sleep eyes, jointed hard plastic body, yellow and white checked dress with blue and white checked pinafore, straw hat, white leatherette shoes with a real snap on the strap, circa 1996, $40.00. *Courtesy Vogue Doll Company.*

8" School Days, African American Ginny from the School Days Collection, marked "Ginny's Signature TM//1988//The Vogue Doll Company//Made in China," black rooted hair, plastic sleep eyes, jointed hard plastic body, navy pleated skirt, white blouse, navy hat, red sweater, white stockings, black leatherette shoes with a real snap on the strap, circa 1996, $40.00. *Courtesy Vogue Doll Company.*

8" School Days Ginny, from the School Days Collection, marked "Ginny's Signature TM//1988//The Vogue Doll Company//Made in China," blonde rooted hair, plastic sleep eyes, jointed hard plastic body, navy pleated skirt, white top, navy sweater, matching tam, white stockings, black leatherette shoes with a real snap on the strap, circa 1996, $40.00. *Courtesy Vogue Doll Company.*

8" Concert Pianist Ginny, from the On Stage Collection, marked "Ginny's Signature TM//1988//The Vogue Doll Company//Made in China," brown rooted hair, plastic sleep eyes, jointed hard plastic body, dark dress with piano key trim around bottom of skirt, ribbon in hair, black leatherette shoes with a real snap on the strap, circa 1996, $40.00. *Courtesy Vogue Doll Company.*

8" Caramel Apples Ginny, from the Ginny Cooks Collection, marked "Ginny's Signature TM//1988//The Vogue Doll Company//Made in China," red rooted hair, plastic sleep eyes, jointed hard plastic body, brown and white checked dress, brown ribbon in hair, black leatherette shoes with a real snap on the strap, holding cookie sheet with caramel apples, circa 1996, $40.00. *Courtesy Vogue Doll Company.*

8" Gingerbread Cookies Ginny, from the Ginny Cooks Collection, marked "Ginny's Signature TM//1988//The Vogue Doll Company//Made in China," brown rooted hair, plastic sleep eyes, jointed hard plastic body, red and white checked dress with white apron, white chef's hat, black leatherette shoes with a real snap on the strap, holding cookie sheet with gingerbread cookies, circa 1996, $40.00. *Courtesy Vogue Doll Company.*

8" Hot Cocoa Ginny, from the Ginny Cooks Collection, marked "Ginny's Signature TM//1988//The Vogue Doll Company//Made in China," blonde rooted hair with pigtails tied with pink ribbons, plastic sleep eyes, jointed hard plastic body, pink/white striped gown, white housecoat, black leatherette shoes with a real snap on the strap, with one hand holding a plate with a cupcake and a cup of hot cocoa in the other hand, circa 1996, $40.00. *Courtesy Vogue Doll Company.*

8" Black Stepping Out Ginny, from the Town & Country Collection, marked "Ginny's Signature TM//1988//The Vogue Doll Company//Made in China," black rooted hair, plastic sleep eyes, jointed hard plastic body, blue dress with white lace lace trim, white ribbon in hair, white leatherette shoes with a real snap on the strap, circa 1996, $40.00. *Courtesy Vogue Doll Company.*

8" Travel Doll Ginny, from the Ginny Travels Collection, marked "Ginny's Signature TM//1988//The Vogue Doll Company//Made in China," blonde rooted hair, plastic sleep eyes, jointed hard plastic body, navy coat with matching hat, blue and white dress with large white collar trimmed in lace, black leatherette shoes with a real snap on the strap, circa 1997, $40.00. *Courtesy Vogue Doll Company.*

8" Farmer's Market Ginny, from the Town & Country Collection, marked "Ginny's Signature TM//1988//The Vogue Doll Company//Made in China," blonde rooted hair, plastic sleep eyes, jointed hard plastic body, red and white watermelon print dress with green and white trim, matching red straw hat, black leatherette shoes with real snap on the strap, circa 1997, $40.00. *Courtesy Vogue Doll Company.*

8" Barbecues Ginny, from the Ginny Cooks Collection, marked "Ginny's Signature TM//1988//The Vogue Doll Company//Made in China," blonde rooted hair, plastic sleep eyes, jointed hard plastic body, wearing a blue print dress with white print cooking apron, mitten, and matching chef's hat, holding a hamburger in one hand, black leatherette shoes with real snap on the strap, circa 1997, $40.00. *Courtesy Vogue Doll Company.*

8" Bakes Bread Ginny, from the Ginny Cooks Collection, marked "Ginny's Signature TM//1988//The Vogue Doll Company//Made in China," auburn rooted hair, plastic sleep eyes, jointed hard plastic body, blue checked dress, white apron, white ribbon in hair, blue leatherette shoes with real snap on the strap, holding cookie sheet with two loaves of bread, circa 1997, $40.00. *Courtesy Vogue Doll Company.*

8" **Pansies Ginny**, from the Ginny Gardens Collection, marked "Ginny's Signature TM//1988//The Vogue Doll Company//Made in China," blonde rooted hair in braids, plastic sleep eyes, jointed hard plastic body, flower print jumper with matching cap, white blouse, white leatherette shoes with real snap on the strap, with garden tools and flower seeds, circa 1997, $40.00. *Courtesy Vogue Doll Company.*

8" **Bobby Soxer Ginny**, from the Fabulous Fifties Collection, marked "Ginny's Signature TM//1988//The Vogue Doll Company//Made in China," blonde rooted ponytail tied with red ribbon, plastic sleep eyes, jointed hard plastic body, red letter sweater, white shirt, rolled-up blue jeans, black and white oxford shoes, circa 1998, $40.00. *Courtesy Vogue Doll Company.*

8" **Car Hop Ginny**, from the Fabulous Fifties Collection, marked "Ginny's Signature TM//1988//The Vogue Doll Company//Made in China," dark blonde rooted hair, plastic sleep eyes, jointed hard plastic body, pink uniform with white cuffs, collar and apron, matching hat, white leather shoes on skates, circa 1998, $40.00. *Courtesy Vogue Doll Company.*

8" **Pajama Party Ginny**, from the Fabulous Fifties Collection, marked "Ginny's Signature TM//1988//The Vogue Doll Company//Made in China," blonde rooted hair, plastic sleep eyes, jointed hard plastic body, blue and white babydoll pajamas, matching head scarf, pink rollers in hair, holding pink telephone, blue scuffs, circa 1998, $40.00. *Courtesy Vogue Doll Company.*

8" Ice Skates Ginny, from the Fabulous Fifties Collection, marked "Ginny's Signature TM//1988//The Vogue Doll Company//Made in China," brown rooted hair, plastic sleep eyes, jointed hard plastic body, red skating costume with white fur trim, matching hat with white ear muffs, white tights, white leather shoes on skates, circa 1998, $40.00. *Courtesy Vogue Doll Company.*

8" Miss 1900s Ginny, from the Ginny's Century Collection, marked "Ginny's Signature TM//1988//The Vogue Doll Company//Made in China," red rooted hair, plastic sleep eyes, jointed hard plastic body, white lace dress, white ribbon in hair, black leather boots, Miss 1900s ribbon, circa 1999, $40.00. *Courtesy Vogue Doll Company.*

8" Miss Millennium Ginny, from the Ginny's Century Collection, marked "Ginny's Signature TM//1988//The Vogue Doll Company//Made in China," brown rooted hair, plastic sleep eyes, gold earrings, jointed hard plastic body, long gold evening gown, matching gloves, necklace, holding Miss Millennium ribbon, circa 1999, $40.00. *Courtesy Vogue Doll Company.*

8" Miss 2000 Revisited Ginny, from the Ginny's Century Collection, marked "Ginny's Signature TM//1988//The Vogue Doll Company//Made in China," blonde rooted hair, plastic sleep eyes, jointed hard plastic body, red and gray outfit, red leather boots, white Miss 2000 Ribbon, red hat with three metal coils on top, circa 1999, $40.00. *Courtesy Vogue Doll Company.*

8" Ginny's Stuffie Frog, from the Ginny & Her Stuffies Collection, marked "Ginny's Signature TM//1988//The Vogue Doll Company//Made in China," red rooted hair, plastic sleep eyes, jointed hard plastic body, green and white plaid outfit, green hat, red leatherette shoes with real snap on strap, holding yellow and green frog, circa 1999, $40.00. *Courtesy Vogue Doll Company.*

8" Bandstand Ginny, from the Fabulous Fifties Collection, marked "Ginny's Signature TM//1988//The Vogue Doll Company//Made in China," blonde rooted ponytail tied with pink ribbon, plastic sleep eyes, jointed hard plastic body, navy and white polka dot skirt, pink sweater, white blouse, pearl necklace, pink net can-can slip, black and white oxford shoes, circa 1999, $50.00. *Courtesy Vogue Doll Company.*

8" The Land I Love Ginny, limited to the 2000 Ginny Doll Club, marked "Ginny's Signature TM//1988//The Vogue Doll Company//Made in China," blonde curly rooted hair, plastic sleep eyes, jointed hard plastic body, red, white and blue patriotic outfit, blue ribbon with white polka dots in hair, with gold pin on dress that says "Ginny for President," white leatherette shoes with real snap on strap, circa 2000, $40.00. *Courtesy Vogue Doll Company.*

8" Ginny for President, from the Ginny for President Collection, marked "Ginny's Signature TM//1988//The Vogue Doll Company//Made in China," auburn rooted hair, plastic sleep eyes, jointed hard plastic body, blue skirt, red/white/blue suspenders, red top with white stars, red straw hat, white socks with red striped tops, white shoes with red and white ties, gold button says "Ginny for President," circa 2000, $45.00. *Courtesy Vogue Doll Company.*

8" Ginny Jive, from the Rock 'N Roll Collection, marked "Ginny's Signature TM//1988//The Vogue Doll Company//Made in China," blonde rooted ponytail tied with red bandana, plastic sleep eyes, jointed hard plastic body, navy pedal pushers, black jacket, white shirt, black and white oxford shoes, circa 2000, $40.00. *Courtesy Vogue Doll Company.*

8" Peppermint Ginny, from the Rock 'N Roll Collection, marked "Ginny's Signature TM//1988//The Vogue Doll Company//Made in China," brown rooted hair, plastic sleep eyes, jointed hard plastic body, pink and white checked dress with white trim and matching hat, pink leatherette shoes with real snap on strap, circa 2000, $40.00. *Courtesy Vogue Doll Company.*

8" Strollin' Ginny, from the Rock 'N Roll Collection, marked "Ginny's Signature TM//1988//The Vogue Doll Company//Made in China," blonde rooted hair, plastic sleep eyes, jointed hard plastic body, gray poodle skirt, pink sweater and matching tam, white blouse, black and white oxford shoes, circa 2000, $40.00. *Courtesy Vogue Doll Company.*

8" Rag Dolly Ginny, from the Rock 'N Roll Collection, marked "Ginny's Signature TM//1988//The Vogue Doll Company//Made in China," red yarn wig, plastic sleep eyes, jointed hard plastic body, red dress with white polka dots, multicolored plaid pinafore, white petticoat, black leatherette shoes with real snap on strap, circa 2000, $40.00. *Courtesy Vogue Doll Company.*

References

No one person can know everything despite such claims by certain enthusiastic collectors. It is necessary to input data from many sources to bring you this book because of the tremendous scope of this collecting field. With an amazing number of new dolls coming on the market each year and the entire mass of dolls that already exists, more and more collectors are grouping together to share their knowledge and interests. There are clubs, organizations, Internet chat groups, and other gatherings which specialize in one category or type of doll and are willing to network with others. If you specialize in one of the categories listed in this book and want to share your knowledge with other collectors, please send us your specialty and references; also, please let us know the dolls you would like to see featured from your collecting area.

Collectors' Network

It is strongly recommended when contacting these references and requesting information that you enclose a SASE (self-addressed stamped envelope) if you wish to receive a reply. Do not ask those who have volunteered to network to assume the postage burden; not only you but 100 other collectors may be wanting an answer. These networking collectors may already have many obligations on their time and resources, but they might more likely to answer if they received an envelope ready for return.

ACCESSORIES
Best Dressed Doll
PO Box 12689
Salem, OR 97309
Phone: 1-800-255-2313
Catalog, $3.00
E-mail: Tonilady@aol.com

AMERICAN CHARACTER - TRESSY
Debby Davis, Collector/Dealer
3905 N. 15th St.
Milwaukee, WI 53206

ANTIQUE
Can research your wants

Matrix
PO Box 1410
New York, NY 10002

ANTIQUE & MODERN
Rosalie Whyel Museum of Doll Art
1116 108th Avenue N.E.
Bellevue, WA 98004
Phone: 206-455-1116
Fax: 206-455-4793

AUCTION HOUSES
Call or write for a list of upcoming auctions or if you need information about selling a collection.

McMasters Doll Auctions
James and Shari McMasters
PO Box 1755
Cambridge, OH 43725
Phone: 1-800-842-3526
Phone: 614-432-4419
Fax: 614-432-3191

Dream Dolls Gallery & More
5700 Okeechobee Blvd. #20
West Palm Beach, FL 33417
Phone: 1-888-839-3655
E-mail: dollnmore@aol.com

Jaci Jueden, Collector/Dealer
575 Galice Rd.
Merlin, OR, 97532
E-mail: fudd@cdsnet.net

Steven Pim, Collector/Dealer
3535 17th St.
San Francisco, CA 94110

BETSY MCCALL
Betsy's Fan Club
PO Box 946
Quincy, CA 95971
Marci Van Ausdall, Editor
Quarterly, $15.50 per year

CELEBRITY
Celebrity Doll Journal
Loraine Burdick, Editor
413 10th Ave. Ct. NE
Puyallup, WA 98372
Quarterly, $10.00 per year

CHATTY CATHY, MATTEL
Chatty Cathy Collector's Club
Lisa Eisenstein, Editor
PO Box 140
Readington, NJ 08870-0140
Quarterly newsletter, $28.00
E-mail: Chatty@eclipse.net

COMPOSITION
Effanbee's Patsy Family
Patsy & Friends Newsletter
PO Box 311
Deming, NM 88031
Bi-monthly, $20.00 per year
Send address for sample copy
E-mail: patsyandfriends@zianet.com

COSTUMING
Doll Costumer's Guild of America, Inc.
341 S. McCadden Pl.
Los Angeles, CA 90020
Bimonthly, $18.00 per year

French Fashion Gazette
Adele Leurquin, Editor
1862 Sequoia SE
Port Orchard, WA 98366

DELUXE READING
Penny Brite
Dealer/Collector
Carole Fisher
RD 2, Box 301
Palmyra, PA 17078-9738
E-mail: Rcfisher@voicenet.com

DIONNE QUINTUPLETS
Quint News
Jimmy and Fay Rodolfos, Editors
PO Box 2527
Woburn, MA 01888

Connie Lee Martin, Collector/Dealer
4018 East 17th St.
Tucson, AZ, 85711

DOLL ARTISTS
Jamie G. Anderson, Doll Artist
10990 Greenlefe, P.O. Box 806
Rolla, MO 65402
Phone: 573-364-7347
E-mail: Jastudio@rollanet.org

Martha Armstrong-Hand, Doll Artist
575 Worcester Drive
Cambria, CA 93428
Phone: 805-927-3997

Betsy Baker, Doll Artist
81 Hy-Vue Terrace
Cold Spring, NY 10516

Cynthia Baron, Doll Artist
7796 W. Port Madison
Bainbridge Is., WA 98110
Phone: 206-780-9003

Charles Batte, Doll Artist
272 Divisadero St. #4
San Francisco, CA 94117
Phone: 415-252-7440

Atelier Bets van Boxel, Doll Artist
De Poppenstee
't Vaartje 14
5165 NB Waspik – Holland
Web: www.poppenstee.nl
E-mail: bets@poppenstee.nl

Cheryl Bollenbach, Doll Artist
PO Box 740922
Arvada, CO 80006-0922
Phone 303-424-8578
E-mail: cdboll@aol.com

Laura Clark
PO Box 596
Mesilla, NM 88046

Ankie Daanen Doll-Art
Anton Mauvestraat 1
2102 BA HEEMSTEDE NL
Phone: 023-5477980
Fax: 023-5477981

Jane Darin, Doll Artist
5648 Camber Drive
San Diego, CA 92117
Phone: 619-514-8145
E-mail: Jdarin@san.rr.com
Web: http://www.janedarin.com

Marleen Engeler, Doll Artist
m'laine dolls
Noordeinde 67 1141 AH Monnickendam
The Netherlands
Phone: 31-299656814
E-mail: Mlwent4.2@globalxs.nl

Judith & Lucia Friedericy, Doll Artists
Friedericy Dolls
1260 Wesley Avenue
Pasadena, CA 91104
Phone: 626-296-0065
E-mail: Friedericy@aol.com

Originals by Goldie, Doll Artist
8517 Edgeworth Drive
Capitol Heights, MD 20743
Phone: 301-350-4119

Lillian Hopkins, Doll Artist
2315 29th Street
Santa Monica, CA 90405
Phone: 310-396-3266
E-mail: LilyArt@Compuserve.com

Marylynn Huston, Doll Artist
101 Mountain View Drive
Pflugerville, TX 78660
Phone: 512-252-1192

Kathryn Williams Klushman, Doll Artist
Nellie Lamers, Doll Artist
The Enchantment Peddlers
HC 6 Box 0
Reeds Spring, MO 65737
Phone: 417-272-3768
E-mail: Theenchantmentpeddlers@yahoo.com
Web: www.inter-linc.net/TheEnchantmentPeddlers/

Joyce Patterson, Doll Artist
FabricImages
PO Box 1599
Brazoria, TX 77422
Phone: 409-798-9890
E-mail: Clothdol@tgn.net

W. Harry Perzyk
2860 Chiplay St.
Sacramento, CA 95826

Daryl Poole, Doll Artist
450 Pioneer Trail
Dripping Springs, TX 78620
Phone: 512-858-7181
E-mail: Eltummo@aol.com

Peggy Ann Ridley, Doll Artist
17 Ridlon Road
Lisbon, ME 04250
Phone: 207-353-8827

Anne Sanregret, Doll Artist
22910 Estorial Drive, #6
Diamond Bar, CA 91765
Phone: 909-860-8007

Sandy Simonds, Doll Artist
334 Woodhurst Dr.
Coppell, TX 75019

Linda Lee Sutton, Doll Artist
PO Box 3725
Central Point, OR 97502

Goldie Wilson, Doll Artist
8517 Edgeworth Drive
Capitol Heights, MD 20743

DOLL REPAIRS
Doc. Doc. Assoc.
1406 Sycamore Rd.
Montoursville, PA 17754
Phone: 717-323-9604

Fresno Doll Hospital
1512 N. College
Fresno, CA 93728
Phone: 209 266-1108

Kandyland Dolls
PO Box 146
Grande Ronde, OR 97347
Phone: 503-879-5153

Life's Little Treasures
PO Box 585
Winston, OR 97496
Phone: 541-679-3472

Oleta's Doll Hospital
1413 Seville Way
Modesto, CA 95355
Phone: 209-523-6669

GIRL SCOUTS
Girl Scout Doll Collectors Patch
Pidd Miller
PO Box 631092
Houston, TX 77263

Diane Miller/Collector
13151 Roberta Place
Garden Grove, CA 92643

Ann Sutton, Collector/Dealer
2555 Prine Rd.
Lakeland, FL 33810-5703
E-mail:Sydneys@aol.com

HASBRO – JEM
Linda E. Holton, Collector/Dealer
P.O. Box 6753
San Rafael, CA 94903

HITTY
Artists

Judy Brown
506 N. Brighton Ct.
Sterling, VA 20164

Ruth Brown
1606 SW Heather Dr.
Grants Pass, OR 97526

DeAnn R. Cote
5555 – 22nd Avenue South
Seattle, WA 98108-2912
E-mail: DRCDesign@aol.com
Web: http://members@aol.com/DRCDesign

Janci
Jill Sanders/ Nancy Elliot
2442 Hathaway Court
Muskegon, MI 49441-4435

Lotz Studio
Jean Lotz
PO Box 1308
Lacombe, LA 70445-1308
Phone: 504-882-3482

Friends of Hitty Newsletter
Virginia Ann Heyerdahl, Editor
2704 Bellview Ave
Cheverly, MD 20785
Quarterly, $12.00 per year

Collectors' Network

IDEAL
Ideal Collectors Newsletter
Judith Izen, Editor
PO Box 623
Lexington, MA 02173
Quarterly, $20.00 per year
E-mail: Jizen@aol.com

INTERNET
eBay Auction site
http://cayman.ebay

About.com Doll Collecting
Denise Van Patten
Web: http://collectdolls.about.com
E-mail: denise@dollymaker.com

AG Collector List
For American Girl, Heidi Ott and other 18" play dolls, no
selling, just talk, e-mail: ag_collector_request@lists.best.com

Barbie chat
E-mail: Fashion-l@ga.unc.edu

Dolls n' Stuff
E-mail: Dollsnstuff@home.ease.lsoft.com

Doll Chat List
Friendly collectors talk dolls, no flaming permitted, a great
group.
E-mail is forwarded to your email address from host, no
fees. To subscribe, e-mail:
DollChat-Request@nbi.com, type subscribe in body of
message.

Not Just Dollmakers
http://www.notjustdollmakers.com
Information: e-mail, carls@isrv.com

Sasha
E-mail: sasha-1-subscribe@makelist.com

Shirley Temple
E-mail: shirleycollect-subscribe@makelist.com

KLUMPE
Sondra Gast, Collector/Dealer
PO Box 252
Spring Valley, CA 91976
Fax: 619 444-4215

LAWTON, WENDY
Lawton Collectors Guild
PO Box 969
Turlock, CA 95381

Toni Winder, Collector/Dealer
1484 N. Vagedes
Fresno, CA 93728
E-mail: TTUK77B@prodigy.com

LIDDLE KIDDLES
For a signed copy of her book, *Liddle Kiddles,* $22.95 post-
pd., write:
Paris Langford
415 Dodge Ave
Jefferson, LA 70127
Phone: 504-733-0676

MANUFACTURERS
Alexander Doll Company, Inc.
Herbert Brown
Chairman & CEO
615 West 131st Street
New York, NY 10027
Phone: 212 283-5900
Fax: 212 283-6042

American Girl
8400 Fairway Place
PO Box 620190
Middleton, WI 53562-0190

Collectible Concepts
Ivonne Heather
President
945 Hickory Run Lane
Great Falls, VA 22066
Phone: 703 821-0607
Fax: 703 759-0408
E-mail: ivonnehccc@aol.com

Effanbee Doll Company
19 Lexington Ave.
East Brunswick, NJ 08816
Phone: 732-613-3852
Fax: 732-613 8366

Gene – Ashton-Drake Galleries
1-888-For Gene
9200 N. Maryland Ave.
Niles, Il 60714-9853

Susan Wakeen Doll Company, Inc.
PO Box 1321
Litchfield, CT 06759
Phone: 860 567-0007
Fax: 908 788-1955
E-mail: Pkaverud@blast.net

Robert Tonner Doll Company
Robert Tonner Doll Club
PO Box 1187
Kingston, NY 12402
Dues: $19.95
Credit Card: 914 339-9537
Fax: 914 339-1259

Vogue Doll Company
PO Box 756
Oakdale, CA 95361-0756
Phone: 209 848-0300
Fax: 209 848-4423
Web: http://www.voguedolls.com

MODERN DOLL COLLECTORS, INC.
Patsy Moyer, Registrar
12415 W. Monte Vista Rd.
Avondale, AZ 85323
E-mail: moddoll@yahoo.com

MUSEUMS
Arizona Doll & Toy Museum
602 E. Adams St.
Phoenix, AZ 85004
(Stevens House in Heritage Square)
Phone: 602 253-9337
Tues-Sun, adm. $2.50, closed Aug.

Enchanted World Doll Museum
"The castle across from the Corn Palace"
615 North Main
Mitchell, SD, 57301
Phone: 606 996-9896
Fax: 605 996-0210

Land of Enchantment Doll Museum
5201 Constitution Ave.
Albuquerque, NM 87110-5813
Phone: 505-255-8555
Fax: 505 255-1259

Margaret Woodbury Strong Museum
1 Manhattan Square
Rochester, NY 14607
Phone: 716-263-2700

Rosalie Whyel Museum of Doll Art
1116 108th Avenue N.E.
Bellevue, WA 98004
Phone: 206 455-1116
Fax: 206 455-4793
Web: www.dollart.com

NANCY ANN STORYBOOK
Elaine Pardee, Collector/Dealer
PO Box 6108
Santa Rosa, CA 95406
Phone: 707 585-3655

PRESERVATION
Twin Pines
Web: www.twinpines.com

PUBLICATIONS – MAGAZINES
Contemporary Doll Collector
Scott Publications
30595 Eight Mile
Livonia, MI 48152-1798
Subscription: 800 458-8237

Doll Reader
Cumberland Publishing, Inc.
6405 Flank Dr.
Harrisburg, PA 17112
Subcriptions: 1-800-829-3340
E-mail: dollreader@palmcoastd.com

Dolls
170 Fifth Ave, 12th Fl.
New York, NY 10010
Phone: 212 989-8700
Fax: 212 645-8976
E-mail: snowyw@lsol.net

PUBLICATIONS – NEWSLETTERS
Alexander Doll Company
The Review
Official publication of the Madame Alexander Doll Club,
Quarterly, plus 2 "Shoppers"
$20.00 per year.
PO Box 330
Mundelein, IL 60060-0330
Phone: 847-949-9200
Fax: 847-949-9201
Web: http://www.madc.org

Chere Amies de Bleuette
Barbara Hilliker
4515 Walking Stick Lane
Gainesville, GA 30506
Quarterly, $20.00 per year

Collectors United
711 S. 3rd Ave.
Chatsworth, GA 30705
Phone: 706 695-8242
Fax: 706 895-0770
E-mail: Collun@Alltel.net

Ninsyo Journal - JADE
Japanese American Dolls Enthusiasts
406 Koser Ave
Iowa City, Iowa 52246
E-mail: vickyd@jadejapandolls.com

Patsy & Friends Newsletter
PO Box 311
Deming, NM 88031
E-mail: moddoll@yahoo.com
$20.00 per year (6 issues), 36 pages

RAGGEDY ANN
Rags newsletter
Quarterly $16.00
Barbara Barth, Editor
PO Box 823
Atlanta, GA 30301

ROLDAN
Sondra Gast, Collector/Dealer
PO Box 252
Spring Valley, CA 91976
Fax: 619-444-4215

SANDRA SUE
Peggy Millhouse, Collector/Dealer
510 Green Hill Road
Conestoga, PA 17516
E-mail: peggyin717@aol.com

SASHA
Friends of Sasha
Quarterly newsletter
Dorisanne Osborn, Editor
Box 187
Keuka Park, NY 14478

SHIRLEY TEMPLE
Australian Shirley Temple Collectors News
Quarterly newsletter
Victoria Horne, Editor
39 How Ave.
North Dandenong
Victoria 3175, Australia
$25.00 U.S.

Lollipop News
Shirley Temple Collectors By the Sea
PO Box 6203
Oxnard, CA 93031
Membership dues: $14.00 year

Shirley Temple Collectors News
Rita Dubas, Editor
881 Colonial Rd
Brooklyn, NY 11209
Quarterly, $20.00 year
Web: http://www.ritadubasdesign.com/shirley/

TERRI LEE
Daisy Chain Newsletter
$20.00 per year
Editor, Terry Bukowski
3010 Sundland Dr
Alamogordo, NM 88310
E-mail: bukowski@wazoo.com

Ann Sutton, Collector/Dealer
2555 Prine Rd.
Lakeland, FL 33810-5703
E-mail: Sydneys@aol.com

Betty J. Woten, Collector/Dealer
12 Big Bend Cut Off
Cloudcroft, NM 88317-9411

UNITED FEDERATION OF DOLL CLUBS
10920 N. Ambassador Dr., Suite 130
Kansas City, MO 64153
Phone: 816 891-7040
Fax: 816 891-8360
Web: http://www.ufdc.org/

VOGUE
Ginny Doll Club
PO Box 338
Oakdale, CA 95361-0338
Phone: 1-800-554-1447

WOODS, ROBIN
Toni Winder, Collector/Dealer
1484 N. Vagedes
Fresno, CA 93728

Bibliography

Anderson, Johana Gast
—. *Twentieth Century Dolls*, Wallace Homestead, 1971.
—. *More Twentieth Century Dolls*, Wallace Homestead, 1974.
—. *Cloth Dolls*, Wallace Homestead, 1984.
Augustyniak, J. Michael
—. *Thirty Years of Mattel Fashion Dolls,* Collector Books, 1998.
Axe, John
—. *Effanbee, A Collector's Encyclopedia 1949 thru 1983*, Hobby House Press, 1983.
—. *The Encyclopedia of Celebrity Dolls*, Hobby House Press, 1983.
—. *Tammy and Her Family of Dolls*, Hobby House Press, 1995.
Blitman, Joe
—. *Francie & her Mod, Mod, Mod, Mod World of Fashion*, Hobby House Press, 1996.
Casper, Peggy Wiedman
—. *Fashionable Terri Lee Dolls*, Hobby House Press, 1988.
Crowsey, Linda
—. *Madame Alexander Collector's Dolls Price Guide #25*, Collector Books, 2000.
Clark, Debra
—. *Troll Identification & Price Guide*, Collector Books, 1993.
Coleman, Dorothy S., Elizabeth Ann and Evelyn Jane Coleman
—. *The Collector's Book of Dolls Clothes*, Crown Publishers, 1975.
—. *The Collectors Encyclopedia of Dolls, Vol. I & II*, Crown Publishers, 1968, 1986.
Cook, Carolyn
—. *Gene*, Hobby House Press, 1998.
DeWein, Sibyl and Joan Ashabraner
—. *Collector's Encyclopedia of Barbie Dolls and Collectibles*, Collector Books, 1977.
Edward, Linda
—. *Cloth Dolls From Ancient to Modern,* Schiffer Publishing, 1997.
Garrison, Susan Ann
—. *The Raggedy Ann & Andy Family Album,* Schiffer Publishing, 1989.
Hedrick, Susan & Vilma Matchette
—. *World Colors, Dolls & Dress*, Hobby House Press, 1997.

Bibliography

Hoyer, Mary
—. *Mary Hoyer and Her Dolls,* Hobby House Press, 1982.
Izen, Judith
—. *A Collector's Guide to Ideal Dolls,* Collector Books, 1994.
Izen, Judith & Carol Stover
—. *Collector's Encyclopedia of Vogue Dolls,* Collector Books, 1998.
Judd, Polly and Pam Judd
—. *African and Asian Costumed Dolls,* Hobby House Press, 1995.
—. *Cloth Dolls,* Hobby House Press, 1990.
—. *Compo Dolls, Vol. I & II,* Hobby House Press, 1991, 1994.
—. *European Costumed Dolls,* Hobby House Press, 1994.
—. *Hard Plastic Dolls, I & II*, Hobby House Press, 1987, 1989.
—. *Glamour Dolls of the 1950s & 1960s,* Hobby House Press, 1988.
—. *Santa Dolls & Figurines,* Hobby House Press, 1992.
Karl, Michele
—. *Baby Boomer Dolls,* Portfolio Press, 2000.
Langford, Paris
—. *Liddle Kiddles,* Collector Books, 1996.
Lewis, Kathy and Don Lewis
—. *Chatty Cathy Dolls,* Collector Books, 1994.
Mandeville, A. Glen
—. *Ginny, An American Toddler Doll*, Hobby House Press, 1994.
Mansell, Colette
—. *The Collector's Guide to British Dolls Since 1920*, Robert Hale, 1983.
Mertz, Ursula
—. *Collector's Encyclopedia of American Composition Dolls, 1900 – 1950,* Collector Books, 1999.
Morris, Thomas G.
—. *The Carnival Chalk Prize, I & II,* Prize Publishers, 1985, 1994.
Moyer, Patsy
—. *Doll Values,* Collector Books, 1997, 1998, 1999, 2000.
—. *Modern Collectible Dolls, Vols. I, II, III & IV,* Collector Books, 1997, 1998, 1999, 2000.
Niswonger, Jeanne D.
—. *That Doll Ginny,* Cody Publishing, 1978.
—. *The Ginny Doll Family,* 1996.
Olds, Patrick C.
—. *The Barbie Years,* Collector Books, 1996.
Outwater, Myra Yellin
—. *Advertising Dolls,* Schiffer Publishing, 1998.
Pardella, Edward R.
—. *Shirley Temple Dolls and Fashions,* Schiffer Publishing, 1992, 1999.
Perkins, Myla
—. *Black Dolls,* Collector Books, 1993.
—. *Black Dolls Book II,* Collector Books, 1995.
Robison, Joleen Ashman and Kay Sellers
—. *Advertising Dolls,* Collector Books, 1992.
Sabulis, Cindy
—. *Collector's Guide to Dolls of the 1960s and 1970s,* Collector Books, 2000.
Schoonmaker, Patricia N.
—. *Effanbee Dolls: The Formative Years, 1910 – 1929,* Hobby House Press, 1984.
—. *Patsy Doll Family Encyclopedia, Vol. I,* Hobby House Press, 1992.
—. *Patsy Doll Family Encyclopedia, Vol. II,* Hobby House Press, 1998.
Smith, Patricia R.
—. *Madame Alexander Collector Dolls,* Collector Books, 1978.
—. *Modern Collector Dolls, Series 1-8*, Collector Books.
Tabbat, Andrew
—. *Raggedy Ann and Andy,* Gold Horse Publishing, 1998.
—. *The Collector's World of Raggedy Ann and Andy,* Gold Horse Publishing, Vol I, 1996; Vol. II, 1997.
Van Ausdall, Marci
—. *Betsy McCall, A Collector's Guide,* Hobby House Press, 1999.

Index

Schroeder's
ANTIQUES
Price Guide

. . . is the #1 bestselling antiques & collectibles value guide on the market today, and here's why . . .

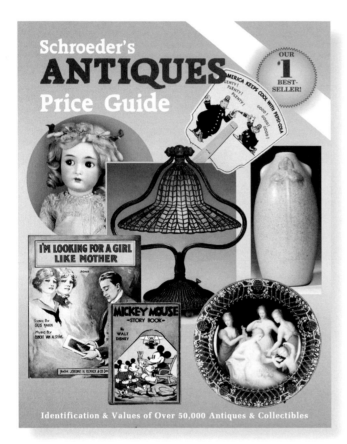

Schroeder's ANTIQUES Price Guide

OUR #1 BEST-SELLER!

I'M LOOKING FOR A GIRL LIKE MOTHER

MICKEY MOUSE STORY BOOK

Identification & Values of Over 50,000 Antiques & Collectibles

8½ x 11, 608 Pages, $14.95

• *More than 450 advisors, well-known dealers, and top-notch collectors work together with our editors to bring you accurate information regarding pricing and identification.*

• *More than 45,000 items in almost 550 categories are listed along with hundreds of sharp original photos that illustrate not only the rare and unusual, but the common, popular collectibles as well.*

• *Each large close-up shot shows important details clearly. Every subject is represented with histories and background information, a feature not found in any of our competitors' publications.*

• *Our editors keep abreast of newly developing trends, often adding several new categories a year as the need arises.*

If it merits the interest of today's collector, you'll find it in *Schroeder's*. And you can feel confident that the information we publish is up to date and accurate. Our advisors thoroughly check each category to spot inconsistencies, listings that may not be entirely reflective of market dealings, and lines too vague to be of merit. Only the best of the lot remains for publication.

Collector Books
P.O. Box 3009
Paducah, KY 42002-3009
1-800-626-5420
www.collectorbooks.com

COLLECTOR BOOKS
A Division of Schroeder Publishing Co., Inc.